OVERCROWDED WORLD?
Global Population and International Migration

6.8 billion people live on our planet today. By 2050, their number will have increased to nine billion. The bulk of this global population growth is taking place in newly industrialized and developing countries. How will the world cope with this increase? How will the balances shift? This volume looks in depth at the causes and effects of population growth and the impact of aging societies.

Rainer Münz is a demographer, and head of Research and Development at the Erste Group. He is also Senior Fellow at the Hamburg Institute of International Economics.

Albert F. Reiterer is a social scientist, who has specialized in demography, social structures, and ethnic and national relations for the past three decades.

Our addresses on the Internet:
www.the-sustainability-project.com
www.forum-fuer-verantwortung.de
[English version available]

OVERCROWDED WORLD?

Global Population and International Migration

RAINER MÜNZ AND ALBERT F. REITERER

Translated by Julia Schweizer

Klaus Wiegandt, General Editor

HAUS PUBLISHING

First published in Great Britain in 2009 by
Haus Publishing Ltd
70 Cadogan Place
London SW1X 9AH
www.hauspublishing.com

Originally published as: *Wie schnell wächst die Zahl der Menschen? Weltbevölkerung und weltweite Migration* by Rainer Münz, Albert F. Reiterer

A CIP catalogue record for this book
is available from the British Library

ISBN 978-1-906598-10-5

Typeset in Sabon by MacGuru Ltd
Printed in Dubai by Oriental Press

Mixed Sources
Product group from well-managed forests and other controlled sources
www.fsc.org Cert no. CU-COC-809367
© 1996 Forest Stewardship Council

Haus Publishing believes in the importance of a sustainable future for our planet. This book is printed on paper produced in accordance with the standards of sustainability set out and monitored by the FSC. The printer holds chain of custody.

Contents

Editor's Foreword

Sustainability Project

Sales of the German-language edition of this series have exceeded all expectations. The positive media response has been encouraging, too. Both of these positive responses demonstrate that the series addresses the right topics in a language that is easily understood by the general reader. The combination of thematic breadth and scientifically astute, yet generally accessible writing, is particularly important as I believe it to be a vital prerequisite for smoothing the way to a sustainable society by turning knowledge into action. After all, I am not a scientist myself; my background is in business.

A few months ago, shortly after the first volumes had been published, we received suggestions from neighboring countries in Europe recommending that an English-language edition would reach a far larger readership. Books dealing with global challenges, they said, require global action brought about by informed debate amongst as large an audience as possible. When delegates from India, China, and Pakistan voiced similar concerns at an international conference my mind was made up. Dedicated individuals such as Lester R. Brown and Jonathan Porritt deserve credit for bringing the concept of sustainability to the attention of the general public, I am convinced that this series can give the discourse about sustainability something new.

Two years have passed since I wrote the foreword to the initial German edition. During this time, unsustainable developments on our planet have come to our attention in ever more dramatic ways. The price of oil has nearly tripled; the value of industrial metals has risen exponentially and, quite unexpectedly, the costs of staple foods such as corn, rice, and wheat have reached all-time highs. Around the globe, people are increasingly concerned that the pressure caused by these drastic price increases will lead to serious destabilization in China, India, Indonesia, Vietnam, and Malaysia, the world's key developing regions.

The frequency and intensity of natural disasters brought on by global warming has continued to increase. Many regions of our Earth are experiencing prolonged droughts, with subsequent shortages of drinking water and the destruction of entire harvests. In other parts of the world, typhoons and hurricanes are causing massive flooding and inflicting immeasurable suffering.

The turbulence in the world's financial markets, triggered by the US sub-prime mortgage crisis, has only added to these woes. It has affected every country and made clear just how unscrupulous and sometimes irresponsible speculation has become in today's financial world. The expectation of exorbitant short-term rates of return on capital investments led to complex and obscure financial engineering. Coupled with a reckless willingness to take risks everyone involved seemingly lost track of the situation. How else can blue chip companies incur multi-billion dollar losses? If central banks had not come to the rescue with dramatic steps to back up their currencies, the world's economy would have collapsed. It was only in these circumstances that the use of public monies could be justified. It is therefore imperative to prevent a repeat of speculation with short-term capital on such a gigantic scale.

Taken together, these developments have at least significantly improved the readiness for a debate on sustainability. Many more are now aware that our wasteful use of natural resources and energy have serious consequences, and not only for future generations.

Two years ago, who would have dared to hope that WalMart, the world's largest retailer, would initiate a dialog about sustainability with its customers and promise to put the results into practice? Who would have considered it possible that CNN would start a series "Going Green?" Every day, more and more businesses worldwide announce that they are putting the topic of sustainability at the core of their strategic considerations. Let us use this momentum to try and make sure that these positive developments are not a flash in the pan, but a solid part of our necessary discourse within civic society.

However, we cannot achieve sustainable development through a multitude of individual adjustments. We are facing the challenge of critical fundamental questioning of our lifestyle and consumption and patterns of production. We must grapple with the complexity of the entire earth system in a forward-looking and precautionary manner, and not focus solely on topics such as energy and climate change.

The authors of these twelve books examine the consequences of our destructive interference in the Earth ecosystem from different perspectives. They point out that we still have plenty of opportunities to shape a sustainable future. If we want to achieve this, however, it is imperative that we use the information we have as a basis for systematic action, guided by the principles of sustainable development. If the step from knowledge to action is not only to be taken, but also to succeed, we need to offer comprehensive education to all, with the foundation in early childhood. The central issues of the future must be anchored firmly in school curricula, and no university student should be permitted to graduate without having completed a general course on sustainable development. Everyday opportunities for action must be made clear to us all – young and old. Only then can we begin to think critically about our lifestyles and make positive changes in the direction of sustainability. We need to show the business community the way to sustainable development via a responsible attitude to consumption, and become active within our sphere of influence as opinion leaders.

For this reason, my foundation *Forum für Verantwortung*, the ASKO EUROPA-FOUNDATION, and the European Academy Otzenhausen have joined forces to produce educational materials on the future of the Earth to accompany the twelve books developed at the renowned Wuppertal Institute for Climate, Environment and Energy. We are setting up an extensive program of seminars, and the initial results are very promising. The success of our initiative "Encouraging Sustainability," which has now been awarded the status of an official project of the UN Decade "Education for Sustainable Development," confirms the public's great interest in, and demand for, well-founded information.

I would like to thank the authors for their additional effort to update all their information and put the contents of their original volumes in a more global context. My special thanks goes to the translators, who submitted themselves to a strict timetable, and to Annette Maas for coordinating the Sustainability Project. I am grateful for the expert editorial advice of Amy Irvine and the Haus Publishing editorial team for not losing track of the "3600-page-work."

Taking Action – Out of Insight and Responsibility

"We were on our way to becoming gods, supreme beings who could create a second world, using the natural world only as building blocks for our new creation."

This warning by the psychoanalyst and social philosopher Erich Fromm is to be found in *To Have or to Be?* (1976). It aptly expresses the dilemma in which we find ourselves as a result of our scientific-technical orientation.

The original intention of submitting to nature in order to make use of it ("knowledge is power") evolved into subjugating nature in order to exploit it. We have left the earlier successful path with its many advances and are now on the wrong track, a path of danger with incalculable risks. The greatest danger stems from the unshakable faith of the overwhelming majority of politicians and business leaders in unlimited economic growth which, together with limitless technological innovation, is supposed to provide solutions to all the challenges of the present and the future.

For decades now, scientists have been warning of this collision course with nature. As early as 1983, the United Nations founded the World Commission on Environment and Development which published the Brundtland Report in 1987. Under the title *Our Common Future*, it presented a concept that could save mankind from catastrophe and help to find the way back to a responsible way of life, the concept of long-term environmentally sustainable use of resources. "Sustainability," as used in the Brundtland Report, means "development that meets the needs of the present without compromising the ability of future generations to meet their own needs."

Despite many efforts, this guiding principle for ecologically, economically, and socially sustainable action has unfortunately not yet become the reality it can, indeed must, become. I believe the reason for this is that civil societies have not yet been sufficiently informed and mobilized.

Forum für Verantwortung

Against this background, and in the light of ever more warnings and scientific results, I decided to take on a societal responsibility with my foundation. I would like to contribute to the expansion of public discourse about sustainable development which is absolutely essential. It is my desire to provide a large number of people with facts and contextual knowledge on the subject of sustainability, and to show alternative options for future action.

After all, the principle of "sustainable development" alone is insufficient to change current patterns of living and economic practices. It does provide some orientation, but it has to be negotiated in concrete terms within society and then implemented in patterns of behavior. A democratic society seriously seeking to reorient itself towards future viability must rely on critical, creative individuals capable of both discussion and action. For this reason, life-long learning, from childhood to old age, is a necessary precondition for realizing sustainable development. The practical implementation of the ecological, economic, and social goals of a sustainability strategy in economic policy requires people able to reflect, innovate and recognize potentials for structural change and learn to use them in the best interests of society.

It is not enough for individuals to be merely "concerned." On the contrary, it is necessary to understand the scientific background and interconnections in order to have access to them and be able to develop them in discussions that lead in the right direction. Only in this way can the ability to make appropriate judgments emerge, and this is a prerequisite for responsible action.

The essential condition for this is presentation of both the facts and the theories within whose framework possible courses of action are visible in a manner that is both appropriate to the subject matter and comprehensible. Then, people will be able to use them to guide their personal behavior.

In order to move towards this goal, I asked renowned scientists to present in a generally understandable way the state of research and the possible options on twelve important topics in the area of sustainable development in the series "*Forum für Verantwortung.*" All those involved in this project are in agreement that there is no alternative to a united path of all societies towards sustainability:

- *Our Planet: How Much More Can Earth Take?* (Jill Jäger)
- *Energy: The World's Race for Resources in the 21st Century* (Hermann-Joseph Wagner)
- *Our Threatened Oceans* (Stefan Rahmstorf and Katherine Richardson)
- *Water Resources: Efficient, Sustainable and Equitable Use* (Wolfram Mauser)
- *The Earth: Natural Resources and Human Intervention* (Friedrich Schmidt-Bleek)
- *Overcrowded World? Global Population and International Migration* (Rainer Münz and Albert F. Reiterer)
- *Feeding the Planet: Environmental Protection through Sustainable Agriculture* (Klaus Hahlbrock)
- *Costing the Earth? Perspectives on Sustainable Development* (Bernd Meyer)
- *The New Plagues: Pandemics and Poverty in a Globalized World* (Stefan Kaufmann)

– *Climate Change: The Point of No Return* (Mojib Latif)
– *The Demise of Diversity: Loss and Extinction* (Josef H Reichholf)
– *Building a New World Order: Sustainable Policies for the Future* (Harald Müller)

The public debate

What gives me the courage to carry out this project and the optimism that I will reach civil societies in this way, and possibly provide an impetus for change?

For one thing, I have observed that, because of the number and severity of natural disasters in recent years, people have become more sensitive concerning questions of how we treat the Earth. For another, there are scarcely any books on the market that cover in language comprehensible to civil society the broad spectrum of comprehensive sustainable development in an integrated manner.

When I began to structure my ideas and the prerequisites for a public discourse on sustainability in 2004, I could not foresee that by the time the first books of the series were published, the general public would have come to perceive at least climate change and energy as topics of great concern. I believe this occurred especially as a result of the following events:

First, the United States witnessed the devastation of New Orleans in August 2005 by Hurricane Katrina, and the anarchy following in the wake of this disaster.

Second, in 2006, Al Gore began his information campaign on climate change and wastage of energy, culminating in his film *An Inconvenient Truth*, which has made an impression on a wide audience of all age groups around the world.

Third, the 700-page Stern Report, commissioned by the British government, published in 2007 by the former Chief Economist of the World Bank Nicholas Stern in collaboration with other economists, was a wake-up call for politicians and business leaders alike. This report makes clear how extensive the damage to the global economy will be if we continue with "business as usual" and do not take vigorous steps to halt climate change. At the same time, the report demonstrates that we could finance countermeasures for just one-tenth of the cost of the probable damage, and could limit average global warming to $2°$ C – if we only took action.

Fourth, the most recent IPCC report, published in early 2007, was met by especially intense media interest, and therefore also received considerable public attention. It laid bare as never before how serious the situation is, and called for drastic action against climate change.

Last, but not least, the exceptional commitment of a number of billionaires such as Bill Gates, Warren Buffett, George Soros, and Richard Branson as well as Bill Clinton's work to "save the world" is impressing people around the globe and deserves mention here.

An important task for the authors of our twelve-volume series was to provide appropriate steps towards sustainable development in their particular subject area. In this context, we must always be aware that successful transition to this type of economic, ecological, and social development on our planet cannot succeed immediately, but will require many decades. Today, there are still no sure formulae for the most successful long-term path. A large number of scientists and even more innovative entrepreneurs and managers will have to use their creativity and dynamism to solve the great challenges. Nonetheless, even today, we can discern the first clear goals we must reach in order to avert a looming catastrophe. And billions of consumers around the world can use their daily purchasing decisions to help both ease and significantly accelerate the economy's transition to sustainable development – provided the political framework is there. In addition, from a global perspective, billions of citizens have the opportunity to mark out the political "guide rails" in a democratic way via their parliaments.

The most important insight currently shared by the scientific, political, and economic communities is that our resource-intensive Western model of prosperity (enjoyed today by one billion people) cannot be extended to another five billion or, by 2050, at least eight billion people. That would go far beyond the biophysical capacity of the planet. This realization is not in dispute. At issue, however, are the consequences we need to draw from it.

If we want to avoid serious conflicts between nations, the industrialized countries must reduce their consumption of resources by more than the developing and threshold countries increase theirs. In the future, all countries must achieve the same level of consumption. Only then will we be able to create the necessary ecological room for maneuver in order to ensure an appropriate level of prosperity for developing and threshold countries.

To avoid a dramatic loss of prosperity in the West during this long-term process of adaptation, the transition from high to low resource use, that is, to an ecological market economy, must be set in motion quickly.

On the other hand, the threshold and developing countries must commit themselves to getting their population growth under control within the foreseeable future. The twenty-year Programme of Action adopted by the United Nations International Conference on Population and Development in Cairo in 1994 must be implemented with stronger support from the industrialized nations.

If humankind does not succeed in drastically improving resource and energy efficiency and reducing population growth in a sustainable manner – we should remind ourselves of the United Nations forecast that population growth will come to a halt only at the end of this century, with a world population of eleven to twelve billion – then we run the real risk of developing eco-dictatorships. In the words of Ernst Ulrich von Weizsäcker: "States will be sorely tempted to ration limited resources, to micromanage economic activity, and in the interest of the environment to specify from above what citizens may or may not do. 'Quality-of-life' experts might define in an authoritarian way what kind of needs people are permitted to satisfy." (*Earth Politics*, 1989, in English translation: 1994).

It is time

It is time for us to take stock in a fundamental and critical way. We, the public, must decide what kind of future we want. Progress and quality of life is not dependent on year-by-year growth in per capita income alone, nor do we need inexorably growing amounts of goods to satisfy our needs. The short-term goals of our economy, such as maximizing profits and accumulating capital, are major obstacles to sustainable development. We should go back to a more decentralized economy and reduce world trade and the waste of energy associated with it in a targeted fashion. If resources and energy were to cost their "true" prices, the global process of rationalization and labor displacement will be reversed, because cost pressure will be shifted to the areas of materials and energy.

The path to sustainability requires enormous technological innovations. But not everything that is technologically possible has to be put into practice. We should not strive to place all areas of our lives under the dictates of the economic system. Making justice and fairness a reality for everyone is not only a moral and ethical imperative, but is also the most important means of securing world peace in the long term. For this reason, it is essential to place the political relationship between states and peoples on a new basis, a basis with which everyone can identify, not only the most powerful. Without common principles of global governance, sustainability cannot become a reality in any of the fields discussed in this series.

And finally, we must ask whether we humans have the right to reproduce to such an extent that we may reach a population of eleven to twelve billion by the end of this century, laying claim to every square centimeter of our Earth and restricting and destroying the habitats and way of life of all other species to an ever greater degree.

Our future is not predetermined. We ourselves shape it by our actions. We can continue as before, but if we do so, we will put ourselves in the biophysical straitjacket of nature, with possibly disastrous political implications, by the middle of this century. But we also have the opportunity to create a fairer and more viable future for ourselves and for future generations. This requires the commitment of everyone on our planet.

Klaus Wiegandt

Summer 2008

Authors' Foreword

The impetus for this book came from Klaus Wiegandt. He convinced us that a series of books on sustainable development would not be complete without a volume on global population and migration. At the same time, our book owes much to long-term collaboration with other researchers. This has resulted in analyses and publications that we can now draw upon. In this context, we would particularly like to name David Bloom (Harvard University), David Canning (Harvard University), Josef Ehmer (University of Vienna), Heinz Fassmann (University of Vienna), Robert Holzmann (World Bank, Washington DC), Martin Kohli (European University Institute, Florence), Bo Malmberg (University of Stockholm), Kristof Tamas (Institute for Futures Studies, Stockholm) and Ralf Ulrich (University of Bielefeld). The book builds on previous publications, including the chapter on "Population" (co-authored with Ralf Ulrich) in a sociology textbook edited by Hans Joas (http://www.campus.de/isbn/3593379201) as well as contributions to an electronic handbook on "Demography" published by the Berlin Institute for Population and Development (http://www.berlin-institut.org). This handbook was originally initiated by Hans Fleisch (Association of German Foundations).

Our analyses would not have been possible without preliminary works by researchers at the UN Population Division (New York; http://www.un.org/esa/population/unpop.htm), the

Population Reference Bureau (PRB, Washington DC; http://www.prb.org) and the World Health Organization (WHO, Geneva; http://www.who.int), who for several decades have been collecting global data on population and development in more than 200 states and territories and providing forecasts.

Heidi Kaiser-Mühlecker, Valerie Mauritz-Dulot, Laurie Richardson, and Andrea Sutter supported us in producing this book. They assisted us in the research process, in creating tables and in commenting on the emerging manuscript. Annette Maas of the ASKO Europa-Stiftung (ASKO European Foundation) managed the project.

We would like to thank everyone mentioned above!

1 Introduction: Past, Present and Future of the Global Population

This book is about the past, present and future of people on our planet – in other words, it's about our heritage and our destiny. It relies on available figures, data, and facts and portrays how a world population of almost seven billion people emerged from just 10,000 ancestors of modern humankind. The focus of our analysis is on fundamental changes in culture, economy, society, and the ecosystem that brought about this extraordinary increase in the number of people living on our planet.

At the same time, the book takes a look at our common future. The global population will continue to grow for a few more decades to come: at a slower speed, but most likely to more than nine billion people. Given existing and foreseeable global problems, the book outlines the challenges with which the people of today and tomorrow will be confronted. It also includes suggestions for change based on our belief that the Earth's already-born and future inhabitants all have the right to a life of dignity.

Population: what is it?

We all belong to the population of a municipality, a country, a continent. And each and every one of us belongs to the population of approximately 6.8 billion people who live on our planet today. The majority of us will also be members of the eight billion people who will populate our planet in the year 2025. And most of today's children and young adults will be part of a world population that will most likely have expanded to nine billion members by the year 2050.

The term "population" originally refers to an activity that early modern states engaged in, wherein attempts were made to populate certain areas with productive men and women. Systematic settlement activities resulted in the term "population" – as opposed to "people." Historically, this was linked to a number of European and American economies in which people were a scarce resource but an abundant supply of unused land existed. Populating unused or underutilized land was therefore seen as key to increasing the wealth of nations. This view was challenged at the beginning of the Industrial Revolution. Thomas Malthus (1766–1834), one of the founding fathers of modern demographic theory, was the first to assume that populations tended to grow more quickly than agricultural production (Chapter 2). It was in this context that the term "overpopulation" was coined, in order to characterize such a discrepancy.

In contrast to this, the first demographers did not bother much with abstract concepts and definitions. John Graunt (1620–1674) was surprised at the quick repletion of London's population in the 17th century after several catastrophic plagues, and searched for data to explain the dynamics he had observed. He shared this data with others interested in such questions. A century later, in a similar vein, Johann Peter Suessmilch (1707–1767), a pastor living in Berlin, became aware of the regularities of patterns and trends in population development. He, too, was eager to demonstrate them using a host of data he collected in Prussia and Berlin. In this manner, a new discipline came into being.

Today, we use the term "population" in everyday language

when talking about the inhabitants of a nation-state, a province, a local community, or a region.

As such, population cannot be interpreted as a constant. The number of people living on our planet, in a country or region changes just as the composition and spatial distribution of these inhabitants vary. The causes for this change in population *stock* are natural population *change* – births and deaths – as well as spatial mobility – i.e. migration into and out of a specific area.

Initial stock	+	Inflow	–	Outflow	=	Final Population Stock
		↓		↓		
		Births		Deaths		("natural" balance)
		Immigrants		Emigrants		(migration balance)

The differences in size, spatial and age distribution of the population have consequences for the demographic as well as the socio-economic situation of a country. Because of the slow "momentum" of demographic processes, their effects stretch far into the future: a generation of people are born and – depending on their life expectancy – remain on our planet for sixty to eighty years. In this respect, today's number of births determines the age composition of tomorrow. And, in doing so, the number of children born today also determines how many schoolchildren, how many potential parents, and how many people of working age there will be in the future.

Demographic processes have a significant influence on our lives, not only on a global scale but also at national and local levels. On the one hand, the global population continues to grow by more than 200,000 people a day, without there currently being enough food, clean drinking water, medical care, educational establishments, and jobs for all of these newcomers. On the other hand, inhabitants of most developed nation-states

– particularly in Europe and Japan – are confronted with rapidly aging and eventually shrinking domestic populations. Since we have not experienced rapid demographic aging over the past centuries, the implications and consequences of this demographic turn are less clear than we might wish.

Demography and human geography

Demographers and human geographers (as well as some economists and historians) study demographic events, structures, and processes. The analysis first focuses on the population at a particular moment or period in time. Such analysis looks at the size and structures of a given population. How many people live in the city of London, in the state of New York, in India, in the European Union (EU), or in the world? It is not the overall number but also the distribution of these inhabitants by age, sex, place of birth, nationality, number of children, etc., which is of particular interest.

Population stocks change constantly: people are born, others die, individuals immigrate to become residents of a certain territory, others leave it for an extended period or forever. The analysis therefore focuses on demographically, spatially, and socially relevant events such as births, deaths, marriages, divorces, in- and out-migrations, and naturalizations. Of interest is not just their absolute frequency during a certain time period. Usually more telling is the relative frequency of the events mentioned above. Looking at relative frequencies allows for a comparison of populations over time, as well as between countries and regions. In doing so, raw rates such as birth rate, death rate and specific indicators – e.g. the average number of births per woman (also called total fertility rate, or TFR) and other proportional figures, e.g. sex ratio, population density, can be calculated.

One important goal of the analysis is to interpret such indices, their differentiation between countries or social groups, and their evolution over time. Available indicators are used to understand trends and differences. To give an example: rising or falling numbers of births can be the result of behavioral change, leading to rising or falling numbers of children per family. Or they can be influenced by changing age structures, resulting in growing or shrinking numbers of potential parents. A comparison over time or between countries therefore leads to the question: what differences can be attributed to behavior? What is largely influenced by age structures, sex ratios, etc.? What is an effect of behavioral change? And what is genuinely linked to the dynamics of demographic processes?

Official statistics provide the most important source of information in Population Studies. Most countries organize general censuses and publish their results, as well as other data that become available in administrative processes. But official statistical offices also collect and interpret information about births, deaths, causes of illness and deaths, in- and out-migration, marriage and divorce, and a few other demographically relevant data.

Individual countries have different statistical traditions. Nonetheless, it has been possible to harmonize international classifications of births, as well as illnesses and causes of deaths, and the like. In contrast, a standardized international system for classifying migrants has yet to be agreed. In addition to these traditional sources of official statistics there are other ones such as sample surveys, in which a representative sample of the population is taken. Such sample surveys have become of paramount importance to collecting demographic and socio-economic information. They are of particular relevance in countries that do not carry out censuses on a regular basis, or which have not kept official birth statistics to date.

In highly developed countries, with well-structured administrations, conventional censuses are increasingly reduced to a pure head count. Social characteristics can be derived by amalgamating data: information from different administrative areas is summarized in a set of individual data ("population register").

From "Adam and Eve" to nine billion

One hundred and sixty thousand years ago, at most 10,000 ancestors of modern humankind lived in East Africa. We all presumably stem from these same early people. About 12,000 years ago, at the beginning of the Neolithic Age, four million people already lived on our planet. Two thousand years ago, their number had increased to about 250 million. This was about sixty times more than at the beginning of the Neolithic Age. Hunter-gatherers turned into sedentary agriculturalists and stockbreeders. Humans had not only grown in numbers, they now produced substantially more food than their nomadic ancestors. This provided the foundation for a phase of rapid population growth unprecedented in human history (Chapter 2).

Over the course of history, there were further periods of population growth as well as times of considerable population decline. Time and again diseases such as plagues, starvation, climate change, and desolation as a result of political conflict, banditry, and wars led to drastic population losses, at least at the regional level. It was only in the late 18th century that population growth accelerated significantly. Since then, humankind has experienced sustained population growth (Chapter 3).

In 1800, there were already about one billion people on our

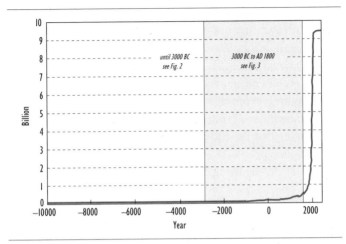

Figure I   The trajectory of world population: the very long term
Sources: McEvedy/Jones 1978; Deevey 1960

planet. One hundred and twenty-five years later, world population had already doubled to two billion (1926). The most important causes for this faster growth were the Industrial Revolution
as well as considerable increases in agricultural production, especially in Western Europe and North America (Chapter 3). Following this, it took a mere thirty-four years (1960) to reach the
three billion mark, another fourteen years for the fourth (1974),
and only thirteen years for the fifth billion (1987). In 1999, the
world population passed the six billion mark. In 2009 there were
already 6.8 billion members of the human species (Chapter 4).
Today the number of people living on our planet is twenty times
larger than during the time of the Roman emperor Augustus, and
four times larger than in 1900.

The 20th century has been the century with the most rapid
world population growth ever. Never before in the history of

humankind has there been such an increase in such a short period of time. And our planet will never again see the number of its human inhabitants quadruple. If growth were to continue at such a speed the effects would be ecologically devastating, and its socio-economic impact immense.

Medium-term forecasts for the 21st century project that world population will reach nine billion by 2050 (Chapter 4). The projected figures for the end of the 21st century are in the range of 9.5–10 billion people. During the course of the 22nd century, the number of people living on our planet will most likely start to decline. This is based on the assumption that the global trend towards fewer children will continue. As a result, women could on average give birth to fewer than two children.

Yet the fact that the global population will no longer grow "exponentially" – as was still assumed by many people 15–20 years ago – only provides modest relief. Even a world population of "only" nine billion people implies tremendous challenges. How we can offer future generations decent living conditions without disrupting the ecological balance of our environment and the social fabric of our societies? At the same time, the prospect of aging and eventually shrinking populations has also become cause for concern. Today, this is a topic mainly discussed in Europe, Russia, and Japan. Very soon it will also be an issue for China.

Currently, the world population displays an annual growth of about 79 million. This rise is due to the great imbalance between births and deaths. In 2007, 135 million children were born but only 55 million people died (Chapter 4). This translated into an increase of 218,000 per day and 9,100 per hour (Table 1).

2007 Time span	Births	Deaths	Population growth
Year	134,562,022	54,978,674	79,583,348
Month	11,213,502	4,581,556	6,631,946
Day	368,663	150,627	218,037
Hour	15,361	6276	9085
Minute	256	105	151
Second	4.3	1.7	2.5

Table I Overview of births, deaths and total growth of world
population, 2007

Source: Authors' calculations based on U.S. Census Bureau, International Division

World population growth could not be changed "overnight" even if we wanted it to, because demographics have their dynamics. The global population not only depends on current numbers of children per family, but also on an age structure influenced by the past. In past decades, global birth rates have been high: particularly in Western Asia, the Middle East, and in sub-Saharan Africa. At the same time, ever more children survive thanks to decreasing infant and child mortality (Chapter 8). Today, as a result, we have the largest generation of youths and young adults ever present on our planet. For decades to come they will be the largest parent generation of all times. This will reduce the effect of any decrease in total births, despite the fact that the number of children per family is declining significantly.

Prognosis or projections?

Demographic projections are neither prophecies nor forecasts in a strict sense. They are based on available information about today's population stock and trends, as well as on a few general assumptions: usually we assume a relatively stable social, economic, and political environment, but not the outbreak of an atomic war, the impact of an asteroid, or the emergence of fatal pandemics, although such events cannot be completely excluded. Furthermore, we assume that current trends and patterns of behavior will remain fairly consistent. For example, people remain single longer and have fewer children. There continues to be immigration from poorer to richer countries, with young adults constituting the largest bulk of migrants. As we are not able to establish these tendencies with absolute certainty, we have to try to give a possible range. In most demographic projections there is a main variant that is deemed the most probable. But usually a higher and a lower variant are published along with this main variant. A few assumptions are quite improbable, but they highlight effects that are otherwise not so clearly visible. No one presumes that there will be no future migration. Nevertheless, a demographic projection with zero migration helps to better understand the quantitative impact of migration on future population size and structure.

Problems facing the rich and poor societies of our world

Our situation is quite paradoxical: many people in the Western world are worried about their future in an aging society. Most advanced societies report the lowest number of children per family ever recorded (Chapter 4). At the same time, life expectancy is on the rise. Many people, therefore, fear the burden imposed by demographic aging and the rising number of elderly citizens (Chapter 9). Some pundits have even characterized us as a dying breed. On the other hand, the rapidly growing number of human beings is rightfully causing concern about our place on "spaceship Earth" with its limited resources.

From a demographic perspective, three major challenges determine the current debate:

- Firstly, continuous high population growth in many developing countries leads to the question of how inhabitants of the world's poorest regions will be able to secure their basic needs and live in dignity
- Secondly, the lack of sufficient numbers of children born in highly developed countries will negatively influence future labor and skills as well as social security and care giving for a growing elderly population
- Thirdly, the increasing flow of migrants from poorer countries in the south to richer countries in the north raises the question about opportunities and conflicts arising from these flows.

Finally, we are confronted with a fundamental question:

- What modes of production and which lifestyles would allow all human beings on our planet to ensure their livelihoods in a sustainable way?

The topic of migration (Chapter 5) is clearly linked to the sustainability of our own lifestyles in highly individualized societies that are based on a substantial consumption of resources. Many inhabitants of affluent nations see the influx of people from poorer countries as a threat to their own way of life. Many migrants embody patterns of behavior and aspirations that would have been familiar to inhabitants of the northern hemisphere half a century ago, but which in the meantime have become foreign to them. Thus, migrants often remind the silent majority in destination countries of a time, only one or two generations ago, in which millions of Europeans also emigrated to neighboring countries and overseas in search of a better life.

At the same time, ever more inhabitants in the highly developed world are becoming aware that aging societies with low fertility are dependent on immigration. Without importing labor and skills, our population and possibly our prosperity simply cannot be maintained. This would have dire consequences for the provision of goods and services, our financial security, and for the growing need for care in old age.

The economies of highly developed countries do not primarily produce investment and consumer goods; they are rather more service-oriented. In Europe, North America, and Japan, services constitute more than three-quarters of the gross domestic product (GDP). These include not only highly specialized, production-oriented services, but also large-scale personal services which cannot easily be outsourced or purchased on the world market. For the time being, it is precisely this that provides the most important "motor" to ensuring an additional three to four million migrants annually. They mainly come from poorer countries and migrate to richer countries (Chapter 5).

How, then, can fears of the loss of one's own way of life and identity be reconciled with the imperative to recruit new labor and skills? And how could immigrants become future citizens?

Imbalances between age groups of different sizes exist in many parts of the world (Chapter 9). Currently, the catchword "demographic aging" conjures images of graying societies with small numbers of children in the North. In contrast, a prime issue affecting the South is its abundance of youth. Poor countries, especially, are not able to provide their younger generations with enough schools, training opportunities, and jobs.

All this, however, is rapidly changing. A demographic transition (see Chapter 3) is taking place throughout the world. It has transformed, and continues to transform, societies with dominant numbers of young people into societies in which the elderly increase both in numbers and in importance. Demographic aging still lies ahead of today's emerging economies, and above all China. In the coming forty years this country will see the world's greatest increase in the elderly population. At the same time, the Chinese one-child policy (Chapter 7) reduced the number of "shoulders" on which the burden of demographic aging could be distributed. This raises the question not only for Europe and Japan, but also for China: how can the desires for retirement, sound pensions, and care in old age be reconciled with the reality of a rapidly aging society?

In the end, the following central questions can be answered at a global level: how can the completely legitimate desire for affluence and a life in dignity for all inhabitants of our planet be met while the world population grows by a further 2.5 to 3 billion people during the 21st century? This question has to be discussed in the context of Earth's limited resources and an ecosystem that is already overstretched today.

Growing global imbalances

The demographic evolution is already compounding current inequalities. A glance at the past thirty years does, however, show us that the population of all developing and mid-income countries put together is growing at a considerably slower pace today than during the 1980s and early 1990s. Fertility is dropping globally while modern family planning and birth control methods have become more widely available (Chapter 7). The number of unplanned and unwanted pregnancies, however, is still considerable. This points to an unmet need for family planning services. And it also indicates that many women are still unable to make decisions about their own lives and bodies (Chapter 10).

About 95% of the global increase in human population is taking place in developing and mid-income countries. Populations in the poorest countries continue to grow the most rapidly. This leads to the imminent issue of the life opportunities for the children born there today – and the youth of tomorrow. Many of these prospects are dire in manifold ways (Chapter 10).

Many people in Asia, Africa, and Latin America, and – to a lesser degree – in Eastern Europe presently live in poverty. Hundreds of millions have no access to clean drinking water, are underemployed or unemployed, and can neither read nor write. In this situation, rapid population growth hampers the search for solutions. It overstrains the capacity of local labor markets to absorb as well as the capacities of existing infrastructure. Despite general improvements, this leads to a rise in the number of humans who live in poverty and destitution, who cannot attend school, or who have no access to medical care when ill, pregnant, or giving birth.

In addition, economic and social advances have almost inevitably led to a considerable rise in the exploitation of natural resources. The richest 20% of the global population presently draw 85% of the extracted commodities and energy. This privileged lifestyle cannot be adopted globally. A similar level of energy and resources consumption by 6.8 and soon nine billion people is hard to imagine. At the current level of consumption and emissions, this would quickly exhaust the capacities of our ecosystem. A life of dignity for everyone is hardly possible without changes to our lifestyles and reduced exploitation of resources.

This book is about population development, its causes, and possible consequences. It is based on data describing our demographic and socio-economic past as well as projections of the likely future of world population. At the same time, this volume raises many unresolved problems and challenges. How can we cope with them? In later chapters there are some insights about specific demographic topics: family planning, reproductive health and HIV/AIDS prevention, the position of women, urbanization, international migration, and, of course, demographic aging. Other volumes in this series discuss related topics that have a significant effect on the future of humankind on our Earth – from nutrition and land use to climate change and the future of oceans, to the dangers posed by new epidemics.

2 The Global Population from Prehistoric to Early Modern Times: Between "Nature" and "Culture"

In 1735, the Swedish scholar Carolus Linnaeus (1707–1778), also known as Carl Linné, wrote one of the most influential books in scientific history. Entitled *Systema Naturae*, Linné proposed a comprehensive classification of all animals and plants. The Linnaean classification system distinguishes between phylum, class, order, family, genus, and species. The denotation follows the two-name, binomial nomenclature of genus and species. At first, he only classified plants, but with the tenth edition, published in 1758, he took in animals and introduced the term *homo sapiens* to incorporate humankind into his classification system. But he did not describe humans in the same way as other beings: instead he solely added *nosce te ipsum* – know thyself!

Today, we still use the quintessential classification of the Linnaean system. Human beings fall under the class of mammals and the order of primates (humans, apes).

In addition to the hominids, the suborder of humanlike beings includes other primate families. Biologically we are closely related to apes (*pongidae*), with comparatively small segments of our genetic makeup differing from their own. Human beings form a distinct genus (*homo*) within this family. For the past 25,000 years, modern humans (*homo sapiens*) have been the only remaining species of this genus.

Linnaeus was not a theoretician who longed to explain biological evolution: he merely intended to bring order into natural history by way of classification. Yet his classification system and his terms called for reflection on the genealogy of humankind and our biological "kinship" with other species. The first to take up this idea was the French biologist and botanist Jean-Baptiste de Lamarck (1744–1829). He believed that organisms play an active role in the evolutionary process.

Independently of one another and in clear contrast to Lamarck's ideas, the British natural scientists Charles Darwin (1809–1882) and Alfred R. Wallace (1823–1913) laid the foundation for modern evolutionary theory. This theory is based on the assumption that there is a natural principle guiding the evolution of living creatures – including plants, animals, and ultimately human beings – through gradual variation and natural selection. Based on knowledge gleaned in modern biology and genetics, evolutionary theory attempts to explain the slow separation of organisms into many different species. This is considered to be a result of coincidental genetic mutations and their effect on the process of adapting to natural habitats. Better adaptation is clearly an evolutionary advantage that improves the chances of survival and procreation.

The separation of the hominid family from other primates took place in several steps. About fifteen million years ago, an early great ape separated from the group of common ancestors. The orangutan is the only other representative of this great ape still to exist. Many millions of years later, another separation occurred: our ancestors parted from those of the gorillas. And finally, a further bifurcation took place about seven million years ago, when the ancestors of chimpanzees and humans went their separate ways – even if "walking" in the rain forest habitat was yet to become a reality at that time.

About 4.5 million years ago, the so-called *Australopithecines* – or "southern apes" – evolved in Africa. The first sample of an Australopithecus was found in Taung, South Africa, in 1924. The well-preserved skull of this hominid, who died at about 3 years of age, is known as the "Taung Child." In 1974, excavations in Hadar yielded an almost complete skeleton of this species. It was the well-preserved skeletal remains of a woman who lived 3.2 million years ago in present-day eastern Ethiopia near the Djibouti border. The archaeologist, Don Johanson, named her "Lucy," it is said, because the Beatles song "Lucy in the Sky with Diamonds" just happened to be playing on the camp's transistor radio. Lucy had been able to walk on two legs. Other than this, though, distinctions from today's great apes were minor. The volume of Lucy's brain was only slightly larger than that of a chimpanzee (390 cm^3 on average). Today's humans have an average brain volume of 1400 cm^3. Further *Australopithecine* footprints found in the Olduvai Gorge in the Tanzanian part of the Rift Valley can be seen as proof that this genus was able to walk upright.

The first beings belonging to the genus *homo* most likely evolved more than two million years ago and stemmed from the *Australopithecines*. Findings bear witness to the habitat of hominids on Lake Turkana in present-day Kenya as well as in the bordering areas of Ethiopia and Tanzania. One characteristic of these human ancestors is that some groups already used simple tools, stones in particular. Some anthropologists have therefore referred to the creatures of these groups as "skilled humans" (*homo habilis*). Almost two million years ago, the genus of the first group of hominids known in biology as "humans" (*homo ergaster* and *homo erectus*) finally separated from other hominids. Groups of *homo erectus* rapidly dispersed throughout Africa, and advanced through the Middle East into parts of Asia and Europe. A few years ago, anthropologists found remains of this type in Dmanisi near Tbilisi (Georgia). These early humans lived there 1.8 million years ago.

Originally, all hominids were Africans. Today, anthropologists are convinced that the cradle of present-day humankind lay in East Africa. Modifications of our genetic makeup took place via occasional mutations. Re-combination of genetic information during procreation and natural processes of selection resulted in our chimpanzee-like ancestors developing in multiple stages into partially new branches of a genus from which *homo sapiens* eventually resulted.

This new type of human also first emerged in Africa. About 160,000 years ago, not more than 10,000 representatives of the *homo sapiens* species lived in the savannas of Eastern Africa. These first humans constituted a reproductive community. Although they roamed around in small groups they did have children with one another, forming a jointly procreating group that we refer to as a "population." These African hunter-gatherers became the ancestors of all people living today. "Primordeal" progenitors of humankind, a kind of Adam and Eve as it were, did not exist. Beyond the biblical image this is a metaphoric way of speaking about this very small group of early humans. The term "Mitochondrial Eve" – used by molecular biologists – also refers to a group of beings that shaped our entire genetic makeup. In other words, we all stem from a comparatively small number of first humans.

The Molecular Clock

Molecular analysis of the origins of humankind looks into the human genetic makeup (DNA in the cell nucleus and in the mitochondria). One branch of these studies is concerned with decoding the so-called molecular clock. Our evolutionary trajectory is calculated in a kind of back-dating exercise. This retrospective analysis is based on information about genetic mutations that regularly play back the genetic makeup in special "key sequences." This enables a fairly precise system of dating and determining the development in different directions of so-called "anatomically modern humans" (AMH) and other humans.

On our way to becoming human beings, different groups of ancestors seem to have come together time and again over the course of a few thousand years. This resulted in mixed populations that consisted of individuals with ancestors from different genetic pools. In this respect, a complicated and long-lasting process of intermixing and separation took place among diverging groups.

A technique that can determine the geographic space within which the evolution of primates to humans took place is the examination of DNA in the mitochondria of cells. As this DNA is inherited from the mother only, fewer differences arise than in the genetic makeup of the nuclear DNA. The mitochondrial DNA can also mutate, but it does not recombine during procreation because only the cell nuclei of the maternal egg and the paternal sperm fuse together.

The results of such explorations provide additional

evidence that the first people whom we can identify as our common ancestors lived in small groups in East Africa. Some of these groups later migrated to Asia, Europe, and finally to the Americas. The genetic pool of contemporary descendants of these early emigrants from Eastern African is smaller than the genetic pool of descendants of those who remained in Africa. This clearly indicates that Asians, Europeans, and native Americans stem from geographically more isolated groups in which diversifying mutation enthroned itself later. As a result, the accumulated diversity in the genetic makeup among African peoples is larger because they had more time than those in Asia and Europe. As present-day Africans exhibit the strongest diversity in mitochondrial DNA, the origins of humankind cannot only be verified by analyzing fossils but can also be genetically substantiated. Until now, though, the extent to which early representatives of *homo sapiens* mixed with other hominids – for example Neanderthals – has not yet been completely clarified.

Evolution and proliferation of humanity: the past 130,000 years

Human beings are a part of nature. Yet at the same time their behavior is not exclusively steered by inherited patterns, but to a considerable degree also by culture. Humans can learn, they can speak to one another and, for the past few thousand years, they have also been able to use letters or icons for writing. This mix of inherited and culturally transmitted patterns also applies to our reproductive behavior. Because of this, we are able to analyze our individual reproductive and demographic development in total, and also to intervene in it. How and where did this natural and cultural being come to be?

Starting in East Africa, the hunter-gatherers gradually expanded their habitat to other parts of Africa. They seemingly first occupied the southern part and later parts of western Africa. Eventually, some of these early people expanded their habitat into northern Africa. During the last ice age, this area was not characterized by deserts but periodically enjoyed a Mediterranean climate. Our ancestors also reached the Nile Valley in present-day Sudan and Egypt. About 110,000 years ago, people began to emigrate from Africa. Their path either took them via the "Horn of Africa" in the northeast of present-day Somalia and the straights between Djibouti and Aden (Bab el Mandeb), or via Sinai to Asia Minor. Outside Africa the oldest existing skeletal remains of anatomically modern humans – our immediate ancestors – were found in Palestine. They are about 100,000 years old. The Middle East became the hub for the later settlement of anatomically modern people in the neighboring regions of Asia and southern Europe. Here, they met other human populations – such as the Neanderthals, who were named after their place of discovery in Germany. Their ancestors had already left Africa at an earlier time for Europe and Asia. The different human species did not vary at all in the tools they used. In other words, there was no identifiable difference in cultural material. Fossil bones found at archaeological sites are the only existing indicators of which humans – Neanderthals or anatomically modern humans – were living in a certain area.

Eighty thousand years ago, it is likely fewer than 40,000 members of the species *homo sapiens* existed. About 74,000 years ago, their number apparently dwindled to approximately 15,000. Anthropologists and molecular biologists describe this as the emergence of a "genetic bottleneck." Some researchers trace this to the Toba volcanic explosion on the Indonesian island of Sumatra. Tremendous quantities of particles were ejected into the higher atmosphere. This partly blocked the sunlight for an extended period of time, bringing on a dramatically cold climate. Many of Earth's inhabitants probably fell victim to this so-called volcanic winter, which most likely lasted for many years. Other scientists disagree or cast some doubt on the ultimate long-term effects of the so-called "younger Toba event." As a result, there is a lively debate about the actual impact and importance of this volcanic eruption on the humans and other living creatures of that time, and on human evolution in general. In any event, it is clear that a larger population of anatomically modern humans survived in Africa. Elsewhere, only smaller groups seem to have survived during this period. In the aftermath, ancestors of the remaining peoples of Africa once again expanded their habitats into the rest of Asia and Europe. Here, these new migrants genetically mixed with those populations that had migrated from Africa 40,000 years earlier and had then survived the cold period. DNA analysis across the globe clearly indicates that the genetic differences between all present-day humans are very minor. At the same time, greater variations exist between the peoples of Africa, Europe, the Middle East, and South and East Asia; these include, for example, skin, eye, and hair color as well as characteristic facial features. The period of the past 70,000 years would have been too short for their evolution on the basis of a stable gene. Scientists therefore assume that some of these differences had already emerged among the groups that had left Africa during the first exodus.

Despite the catastrophic event that apparently took place 74,000 years ago, *homo sapiens* dispersed throughout large parts of Asia and Europe during the following tens of thousands of years. Humans also settled in the Pacific region as well as in North and South America. This expansion throughout all of the continents afforded human beings a considerably larger nutritional basis, and laid the foundation for the first substantial population growth in human history – a development that began about 60,000 years ago. About 40,000 to 35,000 years ago, the human population on our planet may have already totaled half a million people. It is unclear whether the different human groups existing at the time went to war, evicting one another from their habitats, or whether anatomically modern people mixed with other archaic people. In any event, present-day humans – referred to by some as *homo sapiens sapiens* – are the only surviving human species for the past 25,000 years.

Humankind spread from Africa via the Middle East to Europe and Asia. From Southeast Asia, human beings continued settling throughout the islands of present-day Indonesia to Australia, New Guinea, and the western Pacific islands. Settlement took place on the sea route crossing the so-called "Wallace Line" – a boundary separating different worlds of flora and fauna that runs between the islands of Indonesia – Sumatra, Java, and Bali on one side, and Timor on the other. Archaeological evidence (Lake Mungo, Devil's Lair) suggests that the aborigines of Australia and New Guinea had possibly already settled in their present territory 60,000 to 50,000 years ago. Polynesia and Melanesia were settled about 30,000 years ago. Whether the first settlers of Polynesia came from present-day Indonesia or directly from East Asia – present-day South China and Taiwan – is disputed. On the other hand, settlers from Polynesia only reached New Zealand some 2000 years ago.

The origins of America's first inhabitants are also clear. They came from northeastern Asia via a land bridge between Siberia and Alaska ("Beringia") that existed during the last ice age. The exact period of the migration to North and South America, however, is unclear. Archaeological sites in South America have revealed at least one settlement (Monte Verde in present-day Chile) that is estimated to be 30,000 years old. It is uncertain whether the human beings who lived there were ancestors of today's indigenous populations of the Americas. A recognizable continuity of culture and settlement – beginning with the so-called Clovis-style in the southwest of present-day USA – can only be established for the last 12,000 to 11,000 years. It seems that there have been multiple waves of settlement into the Americas via the land bridge between Asia and Alaska. It was only during the warmer spells following the last ice age that this land bridge was flooded by the rising sea level. Migration from Asia was largely, but not completely, discontinued: the ancestors of the present-day Inuit most likely came to North America and Greenland not much earlier than 2000 years ago.

Some parts of the world were as yet uninhabitable for humans. In West and South Asia as well as in Europe, settlement only occurred from the southern shores of these continents up to about 50° northern latitude. Lichtenberg, for example, an archaeological site in Germany with more than 30,000-year-old traces of human settlement, lies at 53° northern latitude. North of this, vast parts of Europe and Asia lay under perennial ice or were barely inhabitable because of the frozen soil (permafrost).

Today it is clear that population growth starting during the Paleolithic period some 40,000 years ago was only the beginning of a swift expansion. For the people of the time, the growth was hardly noticeable. Yet towards the end of the Paleolithic period, about 14,000 years ago, a midrange estimate puts the global population at already four to five million people.

The inhabitants of this prehistoric period lived in small local kin groups of twenty to fifty people. The spatial distance to neighboring groups was relatively large. Members of different such groups did, however, meet on a regular basis – most likely at common places of worship. Caves discovered during the 19th and 20th century reveal astonishingly elaborate mural paintings: these include Altamira, Cap Blanc, Lascaux, and Niaux among others. They could have been meeting points for kinship networks as well as for supraregional communities. Excavations led by German archeologist Klaus Schmidt at Göbekli Tepe in eastern Anatolia have unearthed vast temple grounds made of stone. They appear to have been constructed by people who had not yet become sedentary. "First came the temple, then the town," is Klaus Schmidt's theory. Contact with members of other groups was essential for survival. To a certain degree, the people of that period were dependent on partners who did not come from their own group for purposes of procreation. Groups that are too small cannot establish a stable reproductive community. At least a few hundred or even a thousand people are needed. Since the Upper Paleolithic period and possibly earlier, therefore, kinship networks have existed that have stretched beyond local boundaries. This entailed rivalries as well as notions of loyalty, shared identity, and of a common origin.

Estimates of the size of the prehistoric global population are based on calculations taken from the genetic variability of present-day humankind. Estimates for later periods are based on empirical values and calculations of how many people might have been able to feed themselves as hunter-gatherers. Population density and the availability of natural resources both play a central role in these calculations.

Assumptions about the land requirements of hunter-gatherers in prehistoric times help us to estimate the ecologically feasible population of a region. Anthropological studies have shown that, depending on environmental conditions, hunter-gatherers require a surface area of between one and 10 km^2 for every adult member of a group of hunter-gatherers. For comparison, the present-day Netherlands has a population density of 394, while the UK has a density of 253 inhabitants per km^2. Population density in the USA is only 33 inhabitants per km^2. In Canada, where a substantial part of the country lies within the subarctic climate zone, there are only about three inhabitants per km^2. Present-day population densities are, in other words, up to 4000 times higher than those prevalent during the Stone Age. Yet human beings still do not completely live independent from the realities of nature. Disciplines like anthropology, agricultural and ecological studies refer to the Earth's so-called carrying capacity.

During the Paleolithic, the life expectancy of our ancestors was not particularly high. Fertility was also comparatively low. We know from anthropological studies that hunter-gatherers were already prone to conducting farsighted family planning. A series of behavioral norms and taboos reduced the likelihood of pregnancies. Long nursing periods reduced the chances of conceiving a further child because they tended to delay ovulation. At least as effective was post-birth family planning. The San people, some of whom live as hunter-gatherers in the Kalahari desert, give us an idea how this might have worked during prehistoric

The Earth's Carrying Capacity

Carrying capacity is a term embedded in the Malthusian tradition. This line of thought refers to demographic development determined by the raw forces of nature and, in this sense, by external factors that are largely independent of human behavior.

- The *agricultural carrying capacity* indicates whether and, if so, how well a population can sustain itself with its own agrarian production at a constant level of development.
- The *potential carrying capacity* presumes that a population has the best possible tools and methods at its disposal in order to produce food and other goods.
- The *maximum carrying capacity* is concerned with the sole fulfillment of a population's subsistence level.

The reliance of population size on the carrying capacity of a certain area is neither a natural given nor mindless automatism out of reach for the humans concerned. Specific socio-economic circumstances do, of course, entail an upper limit for food production. This would determine the maximum possible population. But where this limit lies is less clear. Some eat well whereas others survive on less. Humans were able to influence their own reproduction very early on, and most certainly did so. Hunter-gatherers synchronized their reproductive behavior – and with this the number of their offspring to a certain extent – with their own living conditions. Observations among Australian indigenous peoples – the Aborigines – show that they had fewer children than the carrying capacity of their land would have allowed. They aimed for what they viewed as optimal solutions.

Population constraints and growth supported by the

environment is sometimes referred to as a Malthusian situation. However, human beings consciously modify their behavior according to their ecological conditions and the technical options available to them. This is the opposite of what the founder of modern demographic thinking, Thomas Malthus (1766 to 1834), assumed: he originally hypothesized that population growth takes place exponentially (Malthus used the term "geometrically"), outpacing food supply, which he saw as merely growing at a constant marginal rate (in his words, "arithmetically"). The number of people and available food would find an equilibrium only through famine, unanticipated crises and catastrophes (*positive checks*). He imagined restrictions on the number of children, with that leading to a reduction in population growth (*preventive checks*) through external force – or, in other words, through social control and political coercion.

In fact, and throughout a large part of human history, fecundity and the maximum number of births possible during a woman's lifetime are biologically rooted in sexuality and the ability to reproduce. The number of children actually born, however, is determined by cultural, social, and religious norms influencing collective human behavior. Individuals are not always conscious of the cultural and moral rules they follow and which regulate their number of children. While humans are able to influence their fertility according to individual preferences and social norms, mortality is, to a larger degree, structurally determined by the level of material development. In other words, it is less open to influence through individual behavior and compliance with "culturally inherited" norms. In this way, life expectancy is strongly dependent on levels of well-being.

times. Traditionally San women did not permit men to be present during delivery. If newborns were weak or otherwise undesired, they were killed. The men were later told that a stillbirth had occurred. This sort of post-birth family planning was also practiced in ancient Greece and Rome.

The practices kept the number of children in nomadic hunter-gatherer societies low. Despite this, some long-term population growth did occur during this period in human history. Between the Paleolithic minimum 74,000 years ago of perhaps 15,000 people and the beginning of the Neolithic period 12,000 to 10,000 years ago, the number of human beings on our planet increased about 250 times. The primary precondition for this was the constant geographic expansion of human settlement areas from Africa and the Middle East to all continents. Settlement was extremely sparse, but it already stretched across most of the Earth's surface.

The Neolithic Revolution

One of the most far-reaching cultural and societal changes in the history of humankind occurred during the Neolithic era. Some nomadic groups became sedentary in villages, where they were lucky enough to control the means to meet their needs in favorable climatic conditions. As they began growing fruit, and cultivating gardens and fields the climate changed, and they had to look for other means of subsistence. Some groups – "pastoralists" – had already started breeding livestock while living as nomads. Historians and anthropologists refer to this as the "Neolithic Revolution." This transformation started in the area of the so-called Fertile Crescent, a region of the Middle East stretching from the lower Nile valley through the Levant, the Jordan Valley and the southern and eastern parts of Anatolia to Mesopotamia, and into the Euphrates and Tigris estuaries. The first farmers and shepherds in human history settled in this region. Genetic studies show that the cereals we are familiar with today – emmer, wheat and barley, even rye, but not maize and sorghum – were most likely first grown as domesticated and cultivated crops in southeastern Anatolia. The first fortified temples in human history are even older than the first human settlements. They had already been erected by nomadic peoples. One of the most important cradles of our civilization was located in the center of the fertile crescent. Jerf al-Ahmar, an archeological site in the middle reaches of the Euphrates in present-day Syria, apparently holds the ruins of one of humanity's oldest known settlements. They are only marginally younger than the temple grounds at Göbekli Tepe.

Some of these larger villages later developed into the first advanced urban civilizations. Some 8000 years ago a settlement excavated near Çatal Hüyük in southern Anatolia already had thousands of inhabitants. The oldest large town that has been discovered to date is Hamoukar in present-day northeastern Syria. Obsidian was processed there during the 6th and 5th millennia BC. This volcanic stone was used by people before the beginning of the Metal Age as a raw material to make weapons and other blades. Already then, the town of Hamoukar had a surface area of 32 hectares.

The passage from nomadic hunter-gathering to agriculture and animal husbandry enabled a much more reliable food supply. The quality of the food did not necessarily increase, though, and it most likely even decreased at first. Furthermore, sedentary people cohabited in much closer quarters, and this as well as the proximity to domesticated animals increased the danger of infections and their rapid transmission.

Life expectancy during the Paleolithic era was not particularly high. But it apparently sank again following the end of the Mesolithic. Some researchers have even spoken of a "Neolithic mortality crisis." Studies of burial grounds in Mergahr (Pakistan) and other locations have shown that life expectancy among hunter-gatherers shortly before the passage to the Neolithic was significantly higher than that of farmers 2000 years later. Mortality, especially child mortality among Neolithic farmers and livestock breeders, increased considerably compared to earlier times. And not only that: adult farmers and livestock breeders displayed a higher mortality during the Neolithic era than their nomadic ancestors during the outgoing Mesolithic. Despite this, the population began to grow. How could this occur?

During the Neolithic era, fertility seemed to increase more rapidly than mortality. Farmers had to worry much less about their future food base than did hunter-gatherers, as they were continuously producing future supplies. Small children posed fewer "logistical problems" because they did not have to be constantly carried once their parents had settled in a particular place. In contrast, children could contribute to their families' livelihoods quite early on, for instance, by taking on the role of shepherds and the like. This was presumably why the numbers of children per family among farmers and livestock breeders were substantially higher than among nomadic hunter-gatherers.

It was not a higher life expectancy or a general improvement of living standards but increased fertility that led to population growth towards the end of the Neolithic period. During the late Neolithic, which gave way to the Metal Age about 4000 BC – or about 6000 years ago – some seven million people lived on our planet. By 3000 BC, the world population had doubled to about fourteen million following the foundation of early advanced civilizations in Mesopotamia and the Nile Valley. Around the year 2000 BC the Earth may have had twenty-seven million inhabitants,

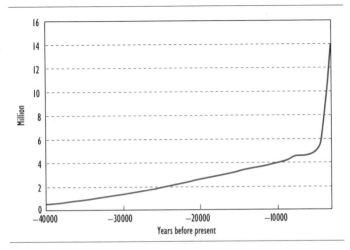

Figure 2   The trajectory of world population: the long term – Stone Age
Sources: MacEvedy/Jones 1978; Deevey 1960

and 1000 years later – at the time of Moses in the Judeo-Christian and Islamic tradition – this number had increased to fifty million.

Growth accelerated even more during the next millennium. At the time of Jesus Christ, shortly before the peak of Roman Antiquity, the world population already had become three to six times larger than a thousand years earlier. Estimates stretch from 170 to 400 million. A medium value of around 250 million is probably most realistic. In contrast to the beginning of the Neolithic, this spells a seventy-fold rise in the world population within a timeframe of only 10,000 years.

The first civilizations

With the start of the 4th millennium BC, Mesopotamia became a center for monumental progress in agriculture and technology. The wheel and the potter's wheel had been invented and now, for the first time, land cultivation and animal breeding were carried out at a larger scale. Urban centers evolved: first Eridu and Uruk in Mesopotamia, or present-day Iraq, with Uruk becoming the world's first metropolis during the following centuries. No less than 40,000 people lived in this city during its heyday. A sophisticated society emerged that was comprised of merchants, public officials, soldiers, priests, construction workers, and craftsmen. Uruk became a center of considerable influence, establishing itself as the world's first great power.

This had substantial cultural ramifications. Archaic cults were replaced by a pantheon of gods boasting a personal profile: Marduk was Uruk's main god; Adad the weather god; Sin the moon god; Ishtar the goddess of love and war. The first multiple-storey temple complex – a Ziggurat dedicated to the sky god Anu – was built shortly after the invention of writing. The new culture spread throughout Mesopotamia and its neighboring regions in the Levant by the 4th millennium BC.

The small class of dominating bureaucratic, military, and religious elites was united by one common interest: to increase productivity. On the one hand, technological innovations improved agricultural productivity: these included plows aided by draft animals, as well as the systematic irrigation of fertile soil. Irrigation systems in areas with seasonally varying rainfall instigated complex sets of social regulations and bureaucratic organization. These were essential in order to guarantee that water was actually collected during the wet season and that a fair amount of water was available to all during the dry season.

The challenge of taming nature and ensuring the use of periodically recurring floods led to the emergence of a new society.
Professional groups of administrators and irrigation specialists
became important alongside peasants and warriors.

The great Mesopotamian rivers, the Euphrates, Tigris, and
Karun, and also smaller ones further to the north not only irrigated the fields of Uruk; they also served as fishing grounds and
trade channels. Craftsmen and technicians were needed and a
public administration evolved. Uruk and Eridu became centers
of the first advanced civilization. The administrative system
began to take on such complex forms that it no longer became
manageable without documentation. Writing was most likely
invented in Uruk.

In addition to the political and administrative centers, towns
emerged around production locations and trade routes. Reference has already been made to Hamoukar and its obsidian production. A further example was unearthed at the edge of the Red
Sea town of Akaba. Archeologists found one of the oldest industrial towns there displaying signs of early metallurgy. Copper was
already melted and cast in the workshops more than 5500 years
ago. The archeologists also discovered multiple-storied ware-
houses as well as textile production tools.

Early advanced agrarian cultures produced far higher quantities of food than their predecessors. The ruling elite did not
always siphon off the entire surplus, permitting the peasants to
feed and raise more of their own children. This led to a certain
population increase, and a cumulative demographic process.

If we analyze this from an economic point of view, the factor
limiting the production of food was by no means the land. Soils
of inferior quality were virtually boundlessly available to the
relatively small population of the time. The availability of top
quality soils already freed of stones or brush, cultivated and

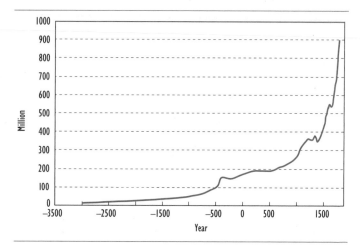

Figure 3   The trajectory of world population: from the emergence
of states until 1800
Sources: MacEvedy/Jones 1978; Deevey 1960

potentially irrigated by humans continued to be scarce, however.
Agronomists use the term ameliorations to describe this labor.
Ameliorated land was still very rare, but the actual inhibiting
factor at that time and well into a comparatively recent past was
humankind itself. There were often not enough children and
adults to fully exploit land that was theoretically available and
improvable.

First censuses

A main aim of the – often competing – ruling elites in early agrarian civilizations was territorial expansion. Their main goal was

to conquer land as well as to produce a surplus. Such motives drew attention to the available resources, which included individuals willing and able to labor, cattle herds, and especially fertile land. The first population censuses and tax assessments were carried out. The Latin term census itself refers to tax assessment.

The forerunners of such censuses were already carried out in Ancient Egypt. Reports of early censuses were passed down from the Old Kingdom. The validity of early censuses in calculating population size is disputed, however. This also applies to later periods. Numbers sometimes only took on a metaphorical meaning: "600,000" could simply mean "a lot," no matter whether it was actually 25,000 or 800,000.

Regulations and control mechanisms to develop complex irrigation systems for rice cultivation also played an important role in the emergence of bureaucratically organized advanced civilizations in China. Chinese historians have attempted to portray the history of China as a coherent and purposeful state expansion that was disrupted by scant periods of decay. In doing so, they shifted all innovations important to the advancement of civilization into a nebulous prehistory and attributed them to various "primordial emperors" – cultural heroes, as anthropologists call such partly historic but partly imagined personalities. For this reason China looks back on a long tradition of censuses that stretches into mythical times. According to these accounts, the first census was conducted by the Great Yu, a legendary emperor in the 3rd millennium BC.

Other regions have given rise to similar recounts. The Bible speaks of an Israelite census conducted by Moses (Numbers 1, 1–46). We know that during the Roman Empire a series of censuses actually took place from early on. The best known to date is the census conducted under Emperor Augustus, which is mentioned in the Christmas Vespers.

The first censuses in China for which we have historical evidence took place during the Chou Period in the 7th century BC. Still, the results are difficult to interpret. "Gates" (households) and "mouths" (persons) were counted. The same figure of almost twelve million in the year 680 BC was at one point listed for the "gates" and then also for the "mouths" at another point. It was probably not until the Chinese census from the year AD 2 that the first realistic figures were produced. The results of this census were 12.2 million households with a total of 60 million people. This population size seems to have remained constant – with major or minor fluctuations – for an entire millennium.

The population of South Asia – present-day India, Pakistan, Bangladesh, and Sri Lanka – is less well documented. An advanced civilization emerged in the Indus Valley in the northwest of the Indian subcontinent far earlier than was the case in China. Yet "India" remained a cultural-geographic term and only became more of a political category under the British Raj, or British colonial rule, from the mid-19th century onwards. Prior to this, the subcontinent never formed a political entity, with the exception of some rather short periods.

Clear instructions on what a prince needed to know can be found, however, in a classic Indian political literature work, the *Artaşastra*, which was written in the 3rd century BC. Yet the author, referred to as Kautilya in the work and apparently a minister in the first great Indian empire of Chandragupta Maurya, considered livestock and goods to be more important than people. Chandragupta Maurya ruled from about 320 to 293 BC, and is referred to in Greek sources as Sandrakottos following the invasion of Alexander. The *Artaşastra* mainly seems to have remained theoretical, never becoming a practical handbook for administrations. Pre-modern censuses most likely did not exist in India.

Global population in the ancient world

We are no longer dependent on rough estimates when it comes to informing ourselves about demographic developments during the last 2000 years of history. For this period we also have access to historical information concerning the number of people residing in certain towns, regions, or countries. Even if no census was carried out we might have information about, for example, the amount of cereals imported and consumed, or the number of soldiers they were able to recruit. Thus, we can give a more systematic overview for the last 2,000 years.

At the beginning of the first millennium, following the birth of Christ, about 250 million people lived on our planet. Two-thirds of the population lived in Asia, with a large proportion residing in India and China. Over sixty million people probably lived in the Indian sub-continent and about the same number in China.

At around the same time in the West, the Roman emperor Augustus – who lived from 63 BC to AD 14 – sought to produce a heroic portrayal of his era: the *Monumentum Ancyranum*. Most likely published in AD 13 at the end of his rule, it contains an abundance of information which historians used to estimate the population of the Roman empire. In 1886 for example, Julius Beloch placed the figure at fifty-four million people.

Another quarter of the almost 250 million people were spread around the rest of the populated world. These possibly seventy million people mainly lived in present-day Southeast Asia and Indonesia, as well as in Western Asia, in particular in the Parthian empire. Comparatively few people lived in non-Roman northern Europe. The same can be said of the Americas, as well as of sub-Saharan Africa. Africa's more populated north was already included in the demographic calculation for the Roman

Empire. The Middle East, including part of present-day Iraq, Israel, Palestine, and Syria, as well as most parts of Asia Minor, or present-day Turkey, were also administrated by the Romans.

In Africa, beyond the Roman Empire, there were wide regions almost devoid of human life at the beginning of the first millennium. On the one hand, these consisted of the deserts in the continent's north (Sahara) and south (Kalahari). On the other hand, the tropical rainforests in the Congo basin were very thinly settled. Agricultural societies did exist in western, eastern and southern Africa. Many of these cultures already used metal tools. The number of people who lived in sub-Saharan Africa in total, however, is difficult to estimate. There were most likely only a few million.

In the Americas, ancient high civilizations were already present 2000 years ago in the Andes in present-day Peru and Ecuador as well as on the shores of the Gulf of Mexico. The Olmecs in Mexico possibly already used pictographic script. A short time later, the Mayas founded a number of city-states on the Gulf of Mexico and further south. They also had their own writing system. Better-developed agrarian societies also existed in the southwest of present-day USA, in the Mississippi Valley and in the southeast, in present-day Florida, Georgia, and Alabama. On the other hand, the rainforests along the Amazon and the Orinoco were only sparsely settled.

In Australia, hunter-gatherers continued to live in the "Paleolithic" until early modern times. They were nomads, were not familiar with metal, and only numbered a few thousand inhabitants.

Behind demographic numbers are processes that are just as important, if not more so, to our understanding of their evolution. Individuals worked, migrated, and reproduced together. Yet this has always taken place in ways that are particular to a given

Territorial Units

We need territorial units in order to estimate the historical development of populations. But which regions make sense? Some authors fall back on present-day states and – in some cases – on states that existed earlier. In academic literature, one therefore often encounters terms like "former Soviet Union." Yet during the late Middle Ages this region included comparatively highly developed *khanates* in Central Asia as well as completely backward regions and huge areas like Siberia with almost no population.

Continents would provide another frame of reference. But where does "Europe" end, and what belongs to "North Africa"? Was 11th-century Spain part of "Europe" or did it rather belong to "North Africa?" Small regions, such as cities and their surrounding areas, can be more easily demarcated. Yet historic continuity does not always prevail: from a demographic point of view, present-day Istanbul, the largest city of modern Turkey, has very little to do with its urban predecessor, Constantinople, the capital of the Byzantine Empire that had been conquered by the Ottoman Turks in 1453.

Populations are social systems established by a continuous process of reproduction. A political entity can encompass one or several such systems. By the same token, populations as reproductive systems can transgress political, ethnic and cultural boundaries.

society. In this sense, even "antiquity" does not refer to a con-
solidated society but to a longer historical period with multiple
formative cultures and power centers.

Societal problems in ancient Greece with its small city-states,
or *polis*, were very different from those of the Roman Empire.
Beginning in the 1st century BC, the latter comprised the entire
Mediterranean and had a central administration, a common cur-
rency, and a common legal system. Yet both formations, the con-
glomeration of historically and culturally linked city-states and
the great empire were dependent on agriculture and their very
low productivity at the time. This continued to be the case for a
long time afterwards.

Depending on the area and cultivation method, the labor of
ten to twenty farmers was required in order to maintain one
single non-peasant member of society – such as an urban crafts-
man, a civil servant, or a soldier. Both ancient Greece and the
Roman Empire were historical eras that – similar to China and
India later on – were not particularly innovative in economic and
technical matters. To be sure, there were technological inventions, not the least in the military field. In the 1st century AD,
Heron of Alexandria even experimented with steam engines –
the famous "Heron's balls." However, most of these inventions
did not turn into practical innovations which explains why agricultural productivity did not improve considerably.

The population grew, but the land did not expand, and productivity could barely keep pace with population growth. In
antiquity's early stages, the more successful city-states in the
Mediterranean "solved" the problem of growing populations
that could not longer be fed at the local level. They not only
imported cereals from the northern coast of the Black Sea, for
example, but also founded colonies in sparsely settled coastal
regions or littoral zones where indigenous inhabitants could

not defend themselves against the occupation of their land. By employing this method, the Phoenicians founded Carthage as well as Gades, the present-day Cádiz. The Greek city-states, especially, made use of this technique, which became a classic form of expansion. As a result, cities like Syracuse in Sicily, Barcelona, now the capital of Catalonia (Spain), and Lisbon, now the capital of Portugal, all started as Greek settlements. As Plato stated in his dialogue Phaedo, the Greeks eventually sat around the Mediterranean like frogs surrounding a pond.

The extensive growth of the Greek city-states and their colonial diaspora ended once the Romans had established their dominant role throughout the entire Mediterranean region. The Mediterranean population apparently stagnated from the beginning of the 1st millennium AD onwards. During the final period of the Western Roman Empire, it may even have declined. But how did people live and die in those days?

Mortality was high during the Roman Empire. Life expectancy at birth might have been twenty-five years or even lower. Those who survived the first year of life could expect a life span of approximately thirty-three years. Fertility was low in the few existing cities – especially in Rome. This applied above all to the aristocracy and the Roman upper class. We know that Emperor Augustus was concerned about this, since he instituted pro-natalist policies to encourage Roman citizens to have more children. Similar views on population and fertility instigated by cultural pessimism can also be found earlier on. Polybius was a Greek historian in the service of the Scipio family, and very prone to subscribing to Roman supremacy. He tells us that in Greece "men had fallen into such a state of pretentiousness, avarice, and indolence that they did not wish to marry, or if they married, to rear the children born to them, or at most as a rule but one or two of them" (Book 36, Chapter 17, sentence 7). The

text refers to the 2nd century BC. Beyond old-fashioned conserva-
tism in these lines is a hint that urban society even in those times
had begun to look upon children not as an undisputed value, but
as an onerous liability.

In contrast, like most agrarian populations, the majority of
peasants had more offspring, but a significant number did not
survive the first year of life. Infant and child mortality is thought
to have cost the lives of almost one-third of all newborns.

The Middle Ages: population starts to grow

During the European Middle Ages, around the year AD 1000,
about 250 to 350 million people lived on the planet. The global
population was thus the same or only slightly larger than at
the beginning of the first millennium AD. China and India had
the same populations as 1000 years before. Europe most likely
gained somewhat in population. In America, a highly developed
Toltec polity emerged in the area of present-day Mexico City.
And an advanced civilization had also emerged on America's
Pacific Coast – that of the Zapotecs. Meanwhile, the Maya societies on the Gulf of Mexico had, to a large extent, disappeared
because of rapid short-term population growth that became
unstable during unfavourable circumstances, or due to a quick
climate change for the worse. On the other hand, demographic
development in the Andes gained in dynamism. Numerous early
polities were precursors of the Inca civilization. Population estimates for North and South America reached thirteen million
inhabitants, or more than twice as many as at the beginning of
the 1st millennium AD. During the following five centuries, this
dynamic growth continued on both continents of the Americas.

Africa also experienced a clear population rise. The north

– present-day Egypt, Libya, Tunisia, Algeria, and Morocco – flourished culturally and economically following the spread of Islam before the turn of the millennium. Culturally and politically speaking, the majority of the Iberian peninsula was also part of this region. It can be characterized as the Arabic and Islamic world of the southern and western Mediterranean. Islamic civilization had its first heyday in this region of the world. How strongly this affected population development is disputed. Some historians assume that, compared to the Roman era, a population decrease occurred in the southern and western Mediterranean. Figures of up to 60,000 inhabitants are listed for Cairo and Cordoba – more than the populations of European cities at the same time. Yet the Byzantine capital Constantinople, or present-day Istanbul, was much larger. The Byzantine Empire enjoyed its final period of glory at the turn of the millennium and most likely provided the citizens of its capital with the same economic living standard as Augustus' Rome. Of the twelve to eighteen million people who lived in the Byzantine Empire, about half a million settled in the capital city and its immediate surroundings. In total, however, less than 10% of the Byzantine population lived in cities. There is no doubt that Western Europe, or present-day Britain, France, and Germany lagged behind economically with a standard of living lower than in Spain, North Africa, and the eastern Mediterranean. Nevertheless, it was at this time that Western Europe gradually began its socio-economic ascent.

A thousand years ago, West Africa experienced the rise of ancient civilizations in the Niger area. Of particular mention are Songhai, and Gana, after which Kwame Nkrumah named his newly independent state Ghana in 1957, and Mali, which only fully blossomed during the following centuries. Similar developments unfolded in southern Africa, mainly in present-day Zimbabwe where the so-called "empire of Monomotapa" developed the size of fifty to sixty million it had already reached in 1500. During the following decades, native Americans had their first contact with Europeans. The enormous decline in population can be explained by a variety of infectious diseases that were introduced by European adventurers, soldiers, and merchants. But there was also a sizeable deterioration in living conditions among native Americans under European colonial rule. In those days, European immigration did not compensate for the decline of the local population. First of all, the ships only had a limited capacity. Second, most Europeans did not want to emigrate permanently but hoped to return once they had made their fortunes.

The European colonial powers soon began to import slaves from Africa as a reaction to the decimation of a maltreated indigenous labor force. As a consequence, the transatlantic slave trade of the 17th and 18th centuries decimated the population in West Africa in particular. In this way, demographic decline in America had immediate consequences for Africa's demographic development – regional demographic events started to become interlinked. It was only from 1750 onwards that migration from Europe to the Americas began to increase. This was largely a consequence of strong population growth in Europe.

In the 18th century, global population began to grow by more than 0.5% annually on a permanent basis. In 1800, the Earth's total population reached one billion inhabitants. Of these, about 200 million lived in Europe, about 650 million in Asia, and somewhat over 100 million in Africa. China stood at the threshold of a considerable demographic growth spurt. In 1800, North America, South America, and the Caribbean probably had just over thirty million inhabitants.

Europe

Europe as a socio-political sphere began to take on its present-day shape following the end of Western Roman domination in the Mediterranean region. The basic patterns of a long-lasting political order began to emerge north of the Alps from the year AD 500 onwards. Europe's population at that time has been estimated at around twenty-eight million people. About half of these individuals – about fourteen million – lived in the south, including present-day Italy, Spain, the Balkans, Greece, and the European part of present-day Turkey. Western and Central Europe had about nine million inhabitants and Eastern Europe around five million.

Europe seems to have experienced a decisive population decline in the ensuing period. This was the direct consequence of a number of pandemics, beginning with the so-called "Plague of Justinian" that afflicted Constantinople in 542. We read of plagues in the years 551, 567, 590, 619, 672, 689, and 743 – these are the characteristic mortality cycles of traditional times. Above all, population losses caused by these epidemics became a main obstacle to the Eastern Roman Emperor Justinian's aspirations for a "restoration of the empire" (*renovatio imperii*). This was an ambitious project was not founded on any lasting demographic, economic, or military strength.

The European population decline was also a consequence of the Germanic migration between the 4th and the 6th century. Raids and conquests by Huns and Avars also played a role. In the end, these Barbarian invasions triggered the collapse of the historical order in the Western Roman Empire, and provoked a drastic political and social upheaval in this part of the world (Chapter 5). This period of transition lasted for more than three centuries.

are decisive factors. It is, of course, problematic to interpret the gross domestic product (GDP) per capita as a direct way of measuring the strain on resources. Industrial growth – described by many as "intelligent growth" – cannot be interpreted as an additional burden on the ecosystem as a whole, the environment, and available resources. Yet it is not possible to completely disassociate affluence and environmental impact, for example in the form of pollution or global warming. As long as we measure affluence in terms of gross domestic product (GDP) per capita, we only account for market transactions but not for household outputs or unpaid services such as nursing, raising children, and taking care of elderly family members. As a consequence a decoupling of improved welfare from material input is unlikely. The reason is that material affluence always requires material input, presupposing the use of our planet's finite resources.

In order to gain a clear understanding of the actual increase in resource exploitation during the past 200 years, we must link the rise in population size and population density with a GDP per capita that is growing almost everywhere in the world. Then, we have to attribute this growth to specific regions. With regard to localization of growth and its impact, we have to consider that exploitation of resources and pollution do not stop at national borders. The key role of imported crude oil and natural gas for Western economies and our lifestyles demonstrates this on a daily basis. And environmental pollution also crosses borders: the best known example is global warming created by rising levels of CO_2 emissions.

An historical analysis of material well-being per capita shows the following: prosperity levels and resource consumption only started to differentiate 300 years ago. Reliable studies and data collected in different regions (for example by Robert C. Allen) show that, in the late 16th century, living standards in cities of southern China and West Bengal (present-day India) did not differ much from living standards in England or in Northern Italy. It was only in the 1700s – first slowly, and then at an accelerating speed since the Industrial Revolution – that the world began to separate into regions with drastically different levels of material well-being.

African populations and societies had not yet recovered from the great slave hunts of the 17th and 18th centuries, in which Arabs, Berbers, and European colonial powers had participated, in complicity with indigenous rulers and chiefs. In the northeast of the continent, especially in present-day Sudan, slave hunts continued well into the 19th century. It was not until the 20th century that accelerated growth in Africa started. By the first half of the 20th century, the African growth rate had accelerated to 1% annually.

Social modernization and a shift in mortality

Since the 18th century, changes in life expectancy and mortality have differed between world regions. In Europe, especially, a process of sweeping modernization started to have a major impact on life expectancy. With some delay, this also had consequences for societies and populations in other parts of the world. World population growth first started in Europe. Research by demographers and historians, however, could not fully explain what triggered this development. During the late 18th and early 19th centuries, living conditions for the majority of people barely improved. In parts of Europe, they even deteriorated. Nonetheless, mortality began to drop in most parts of Western and Central Europe. In some regions, this long-term decline in mortality already started in 1770, initiating a gradual phasing out of the demographic "*Ancien Régime*" with its periodic mortality crises. France very clearly took the lead in this transformation process.

Smaller fluctuations in death rates proved to be the first outcome of this transformation. The previously effective cycle -- high mortality followed by increased birth rates and migration to replenish habitats -- began to level off. Until the end of the 18th century, crop failures as well as looting and pillaging by enemy soldiers or domestic forces were regularly followed by a regional crisis, because there were no transportation routes to bring in supplies from areas with corresponding surpluses.

With the Industrial Revolution, improved European transport routes, and more competent state apparatuses came less dramatic hunger crises. Such crises particularly appeared during hard winters, resulting in the deaths of people who were weak from illness and malnutrition.

From the 1830s onwards, steamboats and trains increased modern transport capacities. Poor harvests at the local level no longer automatically spelt a "death sentence" for people in the affected regions. The last pan-European famine occurred in 1816–1817. It was followed by a typhoid epidemic and subsequently by a cholera epidemic – the first ever recorded in Europe.

Investments in hygiene helped to further improve life expectancy. The separation of drinking water and sewage pipes introduced by public sanitation systems, as well as communal waste collection were of utmost importance. This led to a significant disruption of infectious cycles. Mass vaccination schemes and improved living standards contributed to a reduction in mortality.

The gradual transformation from higher to lower death rates was not a linear process. It was not just the technical infrastructure that counted. Mortality had already begun to fall at a time when modern transport routes and modes of production had hardly evolved. As historical evidence shows, food supply between 1750 and 1850 had not substantially improved for the lower classes. We must therefore ask ourselves: what were the causes and triggers for this transformation? The issues at stake were apparently a self-enforcing process of civilization that altered the way in which children were treated, and changing individual attitudes towards the environment.

The mortality crises on the decline

After 1770, European mortality began to decline. This, however, was not a linear process. Between 1820 and 1870, general mortality levels, and particularly infant and child mortality, increased again. The main reason for this rise was the rapid growth of Europe's major cities (see also Chapter 8). This urbanization, in turn, had social consequences. Europe's largest cities mainly grew as a result of immigration. The inflow largely consisted of people belonging to the rural underclasses, even if those migrating to urban centers tended to be somewhat better off before leaving the agrarian peripheries than those who remained. Nonetheless, mortality among immigrants with peasant backgrounds was – at times – twice as high as among the middle classes.

In Europe, declining mortality goes hand in hand with crises becoming much rarer than before. Life expectancy at birth reflects this change: some countries – for example Denmark, Sweden, and England – have demographic data covering the past 250 years. In these countries, an initial rise in life expectancy can be seen from the mid-18th century onwards. Indeed, according to information provided by early Swedish mortality tables, child mortality in Sweden during the period 1816–1840 was already much lower in the first year of life than half a century later in Bismarck's Germany.

During the first half of the 19th century, average life expectancy among Germans was about forty years. This was low compared to England and Scandinavia. Half a century later, it had declined to thirty-six years, as can be seen from mortality tables for 1870–1881. Thereafter, however, life expectancy among Germans began to rise rapidly. Yet these differences cannot be ascribed to economic performance or general prosperity – which were not higher in Sweden than in Germany at that time.

Significant regional differences also existed within states and regions. Infant mortality was higher in southern Germany than in the north. In 1850, in the first year of life there were 348 deaths per 1000 in Wurttemberg, 311 in Bavaria, 255 in Saxony and 211 in Prussia. In Schleswig-Holstein, infant mortality was already low for that that period, with only 124 newborns per 1000 dying in the first year. In Germany there were marked differences in infant mortality between the south and the north, and between western and eastern parts of the country.

Life expectancy in Europe changed dramatically within a short period of time over the course of the 19th and the early 20th centuries. Changes of similar magnitude had taken place during the transition from nomadic hunter-gatherer communities to sedentary farming societies (see Chapter 2). After 1800, life expectancy temporarily declined, even though the resources available to European societies increased rapidly.

Economists speak of a so-called Kuznets curve to describe the following phenomenon: prosperity increases, and yet a significant parameter of that prosperity worsens during the first phase of the process, before it increases for almost all members of society, regardless of their regional or social class background.

Until World War I, the Industrial Revolution's structural transformation and the accompanying socio-economic shifts in Western and Central Europe did not at first lead to improved living conditions for a majority of the people. At times it even resulted in declining living standards. Income inequality was high and on the rise. Gains resulting from the industrial and political revolutions of the 19th century first benefited the upper classes. It was only later that economic and social inequalities started to decrease with the spread of material prosperity, better living conditions, and higher survival rates. This was the result of social policies and the establishment of the welfare state, which can be seen as Europe's answer to high levels of inequality. Since the 1980s, however, inequality in Europe is again on the rise. In the USA this has been the case since the late 1960s.

In a similar way today, we can observe an environmental Kuznets curve related to the exploitation of natural resources. First, the undesired effects of development dramatically increase and only in a later phase can improvements be enforced politically and socially.

Between 1870 and 1930, mortality generally decreased quite significantly – of course, with the exception of the period of World War I. In Germany, for example, infant mortality among boys fell by one fifth during the final three decades of the 19th century: from 25% in 1871 to 20% in 1901. Yet the mortality of those surviving their first year also decreased significantly. This can be seen when analyzing life expectancy at the age of one and five. For German boys, it rose from forty-six (1871) to fifty-five years (1901) at age one while at age five it increased from forty-nine (1871) to fifty-five years (1901). For women, the average life span increased at a similar or even higher pace: for girls at age one from forty-eight (1871) to fifty-seven years (1901) and for girls at age five from fifty-one (1871) to fifty-seven years (1901).

Historical analysis shows that life expectancy above the age of five years increased, but not nearly to the same extent as among infants. During the 19th and early 20th centuries, decreasing infant and child mortality were the main driving forces accounting for an increasing life span. Regional differences became smaller during this process, as did differences between social groups. The analysis of longer periods shows that the maximum mortality values during crisis periods decreased significantly. Even more important, however, was the fact that differences between years with higher mortality and years with lower mortality became much smaller.

Fertility differences in Europe level off

Reduced infant and child mortality did not have an immediate effect on attitudes and behavior. Parents could count on considerably more children surviving infancy. This must have motivated a growing proportion of potential parents to reduce the number of pregnancies and births: people who knew that almost all of their children would survive no longer had to produce six in order to ensure that at least three of them would reach adulthood.

However, it took some time before fertility levels began to fall into line with decreasing infant mortality. People first had to acknowledge that this was a lasting situation, not only a temporary effect as had been the case in former times. This delayed adjustment in the numbers of children to decreasing infant mortality caused a period of population growth as demographic transition set in (see below).

Fertility declined much earlier in France than in other European countries. A falling number of children was already apparent in the final decades of the 18th century. At the beginning of the 19th century, fertility was already quite low compared to other European countries. France's modernization process was apparently more advanced than that of other parts of Europe. Between the end of the Napoleonic period (1815) and the bourgeois revolution of 1848 – a period referred to as the "*Juste Milieu*" – women in France had 3.4 children on average.

Women in other economically advanced countries of the time were still having far more children: estimates for England and Wales assume 5.5 children per woman in 1800. During the following decades, however, family size in England also dropped significantly. In 1850, the average number of children was 4.6, and by 1875 it had dropped to only 3.4 children per woman.

In France, birth rates and family sizes further declined during

the first half of the 19th century and the early 20th century. Before
World War I, fertility reached 2.1 children per woman – a level at
which population size, in the absence of immigration, no longer
grows. Demographers therefore call it replacement level. Several
politicians held the decline in birth rates and the low number
of children responsible for France's defeat against Germany in
the war of 1870–1871, as well as for France's initially inferior
position during World War I. Terms conjuring political, military,
and demographic competition became popular in contemporary
debates about population issues. Even after Germany's defeat
in 1918, which led to the annexation of territory and inhabitants to neighboring countries including France (Peace Treaty of
Versailles), the leading French politician Georges Clemenceau
stated: "Still 20 million too many Germans…"

Indeed, the average number of children in Germany was far
higher than in France until the 1860s. After that decade, the
decline of fertility also started in Germany, where the average
number of children also had reached 2.0 by 1913. Fertility was
even lower in parts of Scandinavia. Sweden then probably had
the lowest number of children per woman in Europe at 1.9. In
England, too, fertility had probably also dropped below the
replacement level before World War I.

In southern Europe during this period, the average numbers of
children were almost twice as high in Western Europe. Fertility
was also much higher then in the alpine countries of the Habsburg
monarchy, which is the territory of present-day Austria.

In non-European immigration countries with populations of
largely European origin – especially the USA, Canada and Australia – the average number of children during the 19th century
lay notably above Western European levels. Yet by 1910 fertility had sunk considerably there, too, with Australian women
on average having 2.4 children and American women having 2.5

children. This was still above European levels and – along with immigration – it contributed to the population growth of these countries.

During the decades before the outbreak of World War I, Europe and other world regions mainly inhabited by descendents of European immigrants experienced a period of rapid demographic modernization. During World War I, many countries involved in the war saw a sharp decline in their birth rates. Yet it was not only war-related absence of young men that could be held responsible for this decline, but also a general mood of pessimism during the Great War.

Conversely, there was a clear tendency to "catch up" with postponed births in the years immediately after World War I. This was more pronounced among populations of victorious powers than in Germany and Austria. In southern Europe, the transformation had not in any way come to an end during this period. The continuing decline in fertility thereby counterbalanced the cyclical upturn after World War I. In Italy, the average number of children during this period dropped from 3.1 (1900) to 2.3 (1925); in Spain from 3.4 (1900) to 2.3 (1925).

Asia and Africa

Outside Europe and North America, the situation was more complex. Available data provide a fragmented picture that needs to be pieced together. During the interwar period, the League of Nations – a precursor to the United Nations established in 1920 – tried to systematically collect international demographic data. However, the League of Nations did not represent all world regions. Many developing countries were still colonies or dominions of West European powers and the US (which had initiated the League, but had not become a member); and these powers only contributed data for some of their colonies. Of the least developed countries, only Ethiopia was member of the League. Even the Ethiopian government knew little about its population size.

In India, the population doubled during the 18th century. During the first half of the 19th century, it increased even further. Yet, after 1850, a substantial decline took place. British colonial rule was partly responsible for this. This rule became particularly brutal following the Sepoy Mutiny of the 1850s. During the first half of the 20th century, Indian mortality began to decline again. Fertility, however, remained at higher levels than in earlier periods. This constellation caused substantial birth surpluses leading to significant population growth.

In China, population growth already set in during the early 18th century under the Qing dynasty. Growth continued through to the mid-19th century. Here, too, demographic development was interrupted. Frequent wars and peasant rebellions during the second half of the 19th century impeded any significant population growth. The Opium Wars, the enormous loss of lives – amounting to many millions of people – during the Taiping Rebellion, when peasants for one and a half decades succeeded in creating a parallel state in southern China, and finally the suppression of the Boxer Rebellion by European powers inflicted a tremendous death toll. It is therefore all the more striking that the first half of the 20th century saw considerable growth despite anarchy, civil war and, later on, a brutal occupational regime imposed by the Japanese.

Until the mid 20th century, typical pre-modern crises determined demographic developments in the two most populous countries, India and China, and in other parts of Asia. Mortality fluctuated, yet a transition from slow to rapid population growth occurred. In China, the number of inhabitants doubled between 1800 and 1950. In India, this figure increased by about 40%.

In Latin America, fertility was high at the beginning of the 20th century. It started to decline in the richer countries with a large population of European descent, namely in Argentina, Chile, and Venezuela. Mortality also decreased during the same period of time.

We know little about demographic developments in Africa during the 19th and early 20th centuries. The data is comparatively good for Egypt, as the country was under British influence at the time. Fertility was – as in most parts of the continent – high. Mortality was high as well, though from the beginning of the 20th century onwards, it was lower than fertility levels. This led to considerable birth surpluses and a high population growth.

Data also exists for the white population of South Africa. Their mortality was similar to Western Europe's low level but fertility was almost as high as in present-day developing countries. This led to substantial growth among the white population. Moreover, migration triggered an increase in the number of inhabitants of European origin. We can only speculate about the other sparsely populated countries of sub-Saharan Africa for this period.

Demographic transition: European innovation and global diffusion

The second phase of the demographic transition in the highly developed societies of Western Europe and North America began during the early period of the Industrial Revolution. Historically speaking, this transition first began in France during the final quarter of the 18th century. In Sweden, it started at

Demographic Transition: Concept and Reality

In different regions of the world and even within individual countries,
changes in mortality and fertility do not take place simultaneously. While
searching for commonalities and trends in demographic diversity, Kingsley Davis and Frank Notestein of the Office for Population Research at
Princeton University framed the concept of "demographic transition" in
1945. This concept describes similarities in the sequence of demographic
shifts. Such commonalities have been observed in almost all countries in
the world, including Europe and North America starting in the 18th and
19th century, as well as former colonial territories and developing countries starting in the mid-20th century.

   The transition to modern demographic patterns began with a considerable decline in mortality. Before that point of no return to a non-
traditional world, there were strong variations due to plagues, war, and
natural disasters. Yet from a particular point in time onwards, the number
of deaths per 1000 inhabitants (crude death rate) declined. At first this
was mainly due to decreasing infant and child mortality. As a reaction
to this, the number of children born (fertility) declined, too, resulting
in a reduction in the number of births per 1000 inhabitants (crude birth
rate). The time lag between declining mortality and an adaptive decline
in the number of children per family led to considerable population
growth. The dynamics are clear: as long as mortality sinks while birth
rates remain high, total population increases significantly even without
immigration.

   From today's perspective, the demographic transition has five stages
(see Fig. 5). Strictly speaking, the demographic transition itself only
encompasses stages 2, 3 and 4:

Stage 1: From the Neolithic period to the 18th century, both birth and
death rates in pre-industrial agrarian societies were high. Mortality fluctuated heavily from one year to the next. Average life expectancy was low.
The population only grew very slowly, if at all.

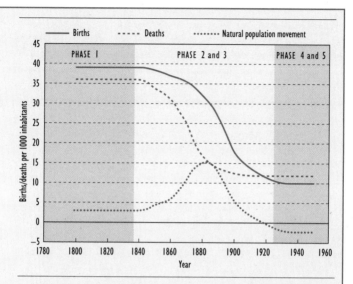

Figure 5   Demographic transition (idealized course) in Western Europe

Stage 2: The death rate first dropped as a result of social modernization processes. Life expectancy began to increase. At this point the demographic transition set in. As average numbers of children per family remained high at first, the population began to grow significantly during this stage.

Stage 3: Over time, although delayed for one, two or even three generations, families reacted to changing living conditions as well as to sinking infant and child mortality. They had fewer children. The birth rate began to sink, curbing population growth.

Stage 4: Birth and death rates in many countries stabilized at a lower level, ending the transition. When formulating the concept of the demographic transition, Notestein, Davis and other researchers had envisaged the process ending with a new demographic "equilibrium" between fertility and mortality.

Stage 5: Over the past forty years, data from Europe and other developed industrial societies – including Japan, Canada, Singapore and South Korea – shows, however, that demographic transition does not necessarily lead to a new equilibrium between births and deaths. In a number of highly developed countries, birth rates have fallen below the level of death rates. In other industrial societies, this development has yet to set in. Consistently low fertility levels seem typical for modern and postmodern societies. There are no clear indications pointing towards a reversal of this trend.

In most industrial states, as well as in some emerging economies, the average number of children is smaller than two per family. As a consequence, the share of native-born populations will shrink in the long term. In a few countries, this process of demographic shrinking is already under way. Thus far, the expected demographic contraction in almost all highly developed countries has been offset by increased immigration. Some authors refer to this as the sixth stage of the demographic transition.

The demographic transition model has to be understood as an analytical concept. It allows a greater understanding of the ways in which demographic patterns have systematically changed over the past one and a half centuries. It is questionable, however, whether we can speak of an almost universal process. Some demographers have argued that a second demographic transition takes place in stage 5. One criticism is that the model is too abstract, schematic, and imprecise. Abstraction, however, seems to be the essence of such models. Nevertheless, there are weaknesses linked to certain basic assumptions. The term "transition" might imply the departure from one "equilibrium" and the emergence of another "equilibrium." Discussions about a second transition do, however, prove that such a new equilibrium is far from certain.

Demographers in the 1940s assumed that in several developed countries the transition had been completed in the 1920s. At that time, the average number of children in many European countries was close to replacement level. In the long run, an average of approximately 2.1 children per family leads to the full quantitative replacement of the parent generation by their offspring. The Great Depression then brought about an even lower fertility level. A short baby boom at the beginning of World War II and an extended baby boom during the 1950s and 1960s did not bring about a lasting reversal of trends. These were times when people who had postponed having children decided to have them during the "better times" of the post-war years. Later on, fertility below replacement levels emerged as a new equilibrium following socio-economic modernization, especially the transition to industrial and service-oriented urban societies. Individualization and secularization were the consequences of unprecedented material well-being. Children took on a different value for their parents when a majority of people did not own a farm or family business where children could have served as additional labor. In most industrialized countries, universal social security coverage also severed the traditional link between offspring and material well-being in old age. New motivations to reduce the number of children or to remain childless emerged. And new contraceptive methods were developed that facilitated restricting the number of children. From the 1960s onwards, the decline in birth rates coincided with the introduction of the contraceptive pill.

The first transition (1800–1920) can be viewed as adapting the number of children to falling infant mortality in order to optimize life opportunities for both parents and offspring, the majority of whom now survived. The second transition (since the 1960s) is evidently a development of a different kind. It can no longer be explained as an adaptation to reduced child mortality. Now children are increasingly viewed as being an obstacle to parents' other goals in life; in particular to the gainful employment of women. This, however, leads to a birth deficit. Under such conditions, population size can only be stabilized through migration.

The concept of the demographic transition does not offer any explanation for its causes: sinking mortality and lower fertility. But it does describe the emergence of an imbalance between births and deaths – the two most important determinants of population growth or decline. And the concept describes the shift from growth to possible decline. Based on available data, this transition can be used to describe the situation in a large number of countries. a large number of countries. In part, though, the real order of events in individual countries diverges substantially from the concept. This especially applies to differences between richer and poorer countries. In this context one observation is of particular relevance:

In Europe and North America, the transition to lower death and birth rates essentially gained momentum once modern, urban, and industrial societies emerged. This is not, and has not been, the case in many developing countries. Mortality in developing countries initially dropped as a result of better nutrition following the large-scale cultivation of highly productive crops ("Green Revolution") and the use of chemical pesticides. Mass vaccination and effective medication imported from industrialized nations also play a key role. A high proportion of the contraceptive devices used in developing countries also come from Western Europe and North America. They are partially financed through development assistance programs and private charities. These "imported" advances have led to a demographic transition in developing countries that is taking place at an earlier stage of socio-economic development and far more rapidly than was the case in Europe and North America.

Interventions from outside the socio-economic system are not taken into consideration in the demographic transition model. Yet they have clear and recognizable consequences. Between 1800 and today, the population in European countries quadrupled during the course of the demographic transition. In contrast, most developing countries reckon with a seven to ten-fold increase before the population stabilizes. Several of these countries experience population growth of 1.5% to 3% annually. In Europe and North America population growth of the 19th and 20th centuries never gained such momentum.

the beginning of the 19th century, which was also quite early. In both societies, this transition took a long time. We can assume that the birth and mortality rates only redressed their balance in the middle of the 20th century (the end of the fourth phase). The transition period in both countries lasted a period of five to six generations.

The country where the demographic transition first became

reality was France, setting in during the early 1800s. Countries like Germany, Italy, and Austria only saw the start of their demographic transitions during the final quarter of the 19th century. In each case, it took about three generations before natural population growth had come to a halt. In some Central and Eastern European countries, the transformation started at the turn of the 20th century, but only lasted for two generations. A similar contraction in time can be observed in several developing and emerging economies.

The frontrunners needed longer to arrive at low death and birth rates than societies in which the demographic transition commenced later on. In order to do so, these pioneers first had to "invent" appropriate behavioral patterns. Societies evolving at a later date were able to "import" or copy social change and individual knowledge that allowed them to reduce mortality and the average number of children. This import or imitation not only applied to hygienic methods, health care, and life-prolonging measures, but also to methods of contraception and social attitudes towards modern family planning and birth control.

The demographic transition's significance stretches far beyond a mere adaptation with demographic consequences. When looking at the world as a whole, it is possible to speak of a global transition lasting three centuries. That transformation will only be completed in sixty to eighty years from now. We may well term it the Great Transformation of traditional to modern societies reaching from the mid-18th to the mid-21st century. At the same time, it triggers a fundamental transition in mentalities and attitudes towards the value of human life. This transition has brought about a phase of historically unprecedented population growth for individual regions and Earth as a whole.

Newborns to "Quality Kids"

Once humans had become sedentary, their lives were characterized by a demographic *"Ancien Régime:"* There was an enormous "waste" of human capital and a high degree of apathy
towards the value of individual human beings. From today's
perspective, this appears inefficient. On average, seven or eight
high-risk pregnancies and childbirths were necessary in order to
reach a modest population growth. When accounting for still-
births, infant, and child mortality, five children had to be born
to each woman of child-bearing age in order to barely maintain
the population stock. Of the children born, almost half did not
survive childhood, let alone reach a reproductive age. Many children died of infectious diseases, others starved to death. In some
cases, children were neglected because parents had produced
more offspring than they could raise and feed; or because the
father had remarried following the early death of the mother,
and the children from this new relationship were now favored.
This specific configuration led to the figure of the "wicked step-
mother" that is common to many fairytales.

Around 1800, women spent about three-quarters of their
adult lives procreating and raising children. Almost half of
these children did not survive to adulthood. The other half periodically suffered malnourishment caused by food shortages. A
vast majority of children generally remained uneducated. From
today's perspective, it would be a sign of grotesque apathy to
produce too many children – endowed with individual human
rights – and then to accept their premature deaths. We can
observe the changes that have taken place over the past 200 years
in our perception of family and reproduction as well as in our
attitudes towards our children.

Today, women in the developed world only devote on average

one-seventh of their lives to raising children. Measured against the number of surviving children the result is quantitatively not much smaller than in pre-industrial times, as the mere comparison of numbers of births per woman would suggest.

Yet the difference in the effect on development is arguably powerful: young people enter adult life far better equipped than in previous times. Qualitatively speaking, a small number of children enables loving parents – mostly mothers – to invest far more attention, care, and parenting in each of them. This not only increases the life expectancy of these children; it enhances their opportunities in life, their future productivity and income. As adults, these children can be much more productive as they are better prepared for their future lives. At the same time, mothers with fewer children and, of course, childless women have more time to pursue gainful employment outside their own households. They not only contribute to GDP and their societies' welfare; they, too, become more independent of their husbands' support. This empowers them to make decisions about their own lives. All these aspects underline the demographic foundations of prosperity and individualism in modern societies.

Within the highly developed modern societies of today, number of children is no longer the main focus. Instead, the "quality" of children has become a main concern. Some may find the use of terms such as "quantity" vs. "quality" with respect to children objectionable. The US-American economist Gary S. Becker first coined the term "quality children." In doing so, he attempted to find answers to the following question: why do lower-class families have more children on average than middle-class families, even though the latter have more money at hand?

If children represent an important life goal, the number of children should be higher if the level of income rises. Yet, on average, the number of children a family raises actually decreases

Household Size versus Large Numbers of Children

In many societies the number of children per woman was higher in the past than it is today. This can lead to the false conclusion that, in former times, families and households were also much larger than today. Alleged evidence was provided by novels and memoirs from the 19th century. Yet most of these novels and recollections concerned upper-class families. They usually had a larger number of people living in a common household. Lower-class households and even many middle-class households were significantly smaller.

In Western Europe, especially, there were also larger numbers of single persons with no other family members residing in their households. Complex households with many persons mainly existed among the aristocracy and among richer farmers. All other households usually only accommodated a few people. High mortality also meant that family households were much less stable than today. This was the case during the Middle Ages as well as in early modern times between the 16th and the 18th century.

An estimate for the year 1000 puts the average household in the Byzantine Empire at 4.3 persons. A further estimate for the early 1300s assumes a figure of 4.8 persons per household for the declining Byzantine Empire. Official government statistics in Italy show a household size of 4.5 persons in 1880. One hundred years later (1980) the Italian average stood at three persons per household. In Austria in 1951, the average household only comprised 3.1 persons.

Households during pre-industrial times were surely somewhat larger than those in developed countries after 1950. Yet they were by no means particularly large. Furthermore, in contrast to the cultural pessimism expressed by some commentators, cohesion among family members and household configurations today are probably more stable than they were in earlier times. The average number of children is probably not an accurate measure of family stability. Fewer people live together in present times, but these people tend to live together for longer periods of time than ever before. This is a result of a much higher life expectancy. The consequences for our family lives and our attitudes towards life in general are considerable.

with rising income. Neoclassical economics would suggest that only "inferior goods" are less desirable when income rises. But our sensitivities are in opposition to the notion that this logic might also apply to our children. Becker therefore came to the conclusion that children are not all created equal. Some parents, at least, attempt to give their children a better start in life by ensuring attentive parenting and the best education possible. The middle classes, especially, are not focused on having many children but on having "high-quality" children. Time and money are invested in them, assets that can only be afforded if the number of children is limited.

As a result, families and households start to shrink, as conspicuous lifestyles become increasingly common. The impact on population dynamics is obvious. Yet at least as important is the prevalence of a new philosophy of life that has developed in the recent past.

4 1950 to 2050: Peak and Slowdown of Global Population Growth

Categorizing states and nations

The categorization based on levels of material development, as used by the UN and affiliated organizations, differentiate between highly developed countries (*developed countries*; *high-income countries*) and less developed countries (*developing countries*). The latter subdivides into emerging markets (*middle income countries*) and developing countries (*less developed countries*; *low-income countries; LDC*); among these are notably the group of least developed countries (*least developed countries; LLDC*). This differentiation summarizes the gap between economic and political centers that have emerged during modern times, the peripheries lagging behind in economic terms being excluded from trade, foreign investment, and international politics. Such differences are relevant in demographic terms. There is a strong – but by no means total – interrelation between socio-economic development and demographically relevant behavior at individual as well as collective levels.

Country groupings allow for a synopsis of similar countries. Analyzing individual countries allows for more precise understanding of particular developments within the context of their own dynamics. Countries with large populations tend to have such leverage that they determine quantitative indicators in their world region (for example, China, India, USA). After all, eleven countries with populations of more than 100 million inhabitants collectively are home to 61% of the world population.

Highly developed countries/regions include Australia, Europe, Japan, North America, and New Zealand. At the beginning of the 21st century, the group of high-income countries accounted for a total of 1.2 billion people with an economic performance (measured by 2007 Gross National Income/GNI per capita) of US $37,566 per capita per year. Measured in purchasing power parity (PPP), this was a GNI of US $36,050 per capita and year.

Developing and emerging countries: Africa, Asia (except Japan), Latin America and the Caribbean, Melanesia, Micronesia, and Polynesia. Developing countries and emerging markets – comprising the less and least developed countries – currently have slightly more than 5.3 billion inhabitants with an economic performance (GNI per capita) of US $2872 per year. Measured in purchasing power parity (PPP), this was a GNI of US $5920 per capita and year (2007).

The fifty-one least developed countries include: Afghanistan, Angola, Bangladesh, Benin, Bhutan, Burkina Faso, Burundi, Cambodia, Cape Verde, Central African Republic, Chad, Comoros, Congo (DR), Congo (R), Djibouti, East Timor, Equatorial Guinea, Eritrea, Ethiopia, Gambia, Guinea, Guinea-Bissau, Haiti, Kiribati, Laos, Lesotho, Liberia, Madagascar, Malawi, Maldives, Mali, Mauritania, Mozambique, Myanmar (Burma), Nepal, Niger, Rwanda, Samoa, São Tomé and Príncipe, Senegal, Sierra Leone, Solomon Islands,

Somalia, Sudan, Togo, Tuvalu, Tanzania, Uganda, Vanuatu, Yemen, and Zambia.

In 2007, the world's fifty-one poorest countries had 800 million inhabitants with an economic performance (GNI per capita) of US $578 per year. Measured in purchasing power parity (PPP), this was a GNI of US $1471 per capita and year (2007).

PPP (Purchasing Power Parities) are a statistical artifact which account for different price-levels in highly, less or least developed countries. Comparing the material well-being of countries by measuring their annual production in US $, or in other words taking the exchange rate, biases the differences in the "wealth of nations." A comparison at current exchange rates understates the poor countries' national product and living standard while grossly overestimating that of the rich countries. The figures given above clearly show this. Using exchange rates, inhabitants of developed countries are sixty-five times richer than inhabitants of poor countries. Using purchasing power, the former are only twenty-four times richer than the latter. There are several reasons for this. On the one hand, exchange rate fluctuations have an influence. On the other hand, the equivalent of US $1 usually buys the same amount of "tradable" goods (for example, commodities sold at the world markets) while "non-tradable" goods and services (for example, housing, food at restaurants, domestic services) display large price differences within and between countries. In this case the equivalent of US $1 buys different amounts of comparable goods and services in different economic environments. This is why we have to take purchasing power parities into account when comparing productivity and material well-being across nations.

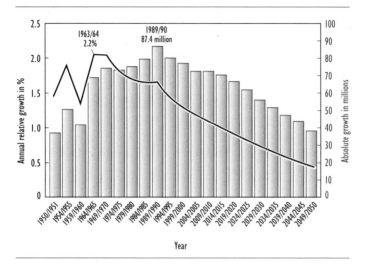

Figure 6   World population growth 1950–2050
Annual relative growth (in %) and absolute growth (in millions)

Dynamics of growth

In 1950, some 2.5 billion people lived on our planet. By 2008, the number had increased to more than 6.7 billion. In the year 2050, the number of people on our planet is expected to reach over nine billion. In between lies the period of the highest population growth in the history of humankind. In the mid-20th century (1950–1951), the annual growth rate of 1.9% was already considerable. In the early 1960s, the growth rate had reached an historic peak with an increase of 2.2% (1963–1964). Absolute growth, however, only reached its peak in 1989–1990 with an increase per year of 87 million.

During the period 1950 to 2050, global population growth has been and will be distributed unevenly among countries and world regions. In the two decades following 1950, highly developed regions reported significant population growth. Today, developing countries and emerging markets account for almost all population growth. Relatively speaking, it is strongest in the least developed countries. This is why the number of people living in the fifty-one poorest countries of the world will again double between 2009 and 2050. In some very poor countries, even a tripling of population size can be expected.

The most important reason for the demographic shift between richer and poorer regions is the different pace of change in fertility and mortality. Most less developed countries have a considerable excess of births over deaths leading to natural population growth. At the same time some rich countries are reporting more deaths than births, leading to natural population decline. Migration from poorer to richer countries is counterbalancing such diverging trends.

Global decline in numbers of children

During the past five to six decades, the birth rate (births per 1000 inhabitants) fell both in developed regions of the world as well as in present-day emerging markets and developing countries. In sum, a higher starting point in less developed regions led to a higher decline in birth rates and numbers of children. As a result, birth rates in less developed regions today are on average the same as birth rates of industrial countries sixty years ago. By 2050, birth rates in less developed regions will presumably sink by another 30% compared with today's rates.

The driving force behind lower birth rates is the change in fertility, or the number of children per woman or per family. In 1950, average global fertility was around five children per woman. It remained at this level for about twenty years. After 1970, it began to sink rather quickly. By 2007, global fertility had reached 2.6 children per woman. This is only half of the family size of the 1950s and 1960s. If this trend continues, there will be on average just over two children per woman in 2050. The main variant of the UN population projection is based on the assumption that global differences in fertility and family size will become smaller until reaching a level of two children per family. Even if this does not occur, the average number of children will continue to decline.

The drop mainly has consequences for the number of children in developing countries and emerging economies. Fertility decreased by more than half in these regions over the last six decades, from 6.1 (1950) to 2.9 children per woman (2007). This has not been a steady process, however. After 1950, several countries even experienced growing numbers of children. At the beginning of the 1950s, India and China – the two countries with by far the largest populations in the world – recorded high levels of fertility. At 6.2 children per woman, the rate in China was even somewhat higher – and it remained high until the end of the 1960s – than in India, which shortly after independence reported on average six children per woman.

Significant drops in fertility in Asia and Latin America

Fertility in China remained at a high level until 1970. During the 1970s, the number of children per family dropped sharply. Chinese political leaders not only made efforts to better the status of women, but started a policy of encouraging, and soon, even urging and forcing people to marry late and restrict procreation. Access to family planning and abortion was granted.

Since the post-Maoist period of the 1980s, a one-child policy was implemented including incentives as well as extremely repressive strategies. There are currently signs that a cautious reorientation might be under way as this policy has highly undesirable side-effects: in particular, an alarming number of early terminations of pregnancies carrying female fetuses, leading to a disproportionate number of male births.

In India, the Indira Gandhi government of the 1970s also implemented forceful measures in order to reduce the number of births. These programs met with considerable public resistance. As a result, Gandhi and her Congress Party were voted out of power in March 1977. This illustrates that there are very different population policy alternatives for authoritarian regimes and democratically elected governments. In China, fertility sank to 1.75 children per woman by 2007. In other less developed countries, the rate only sank to 3.1 children per woman (2007).

In total, fertility in Asia dropped from 5.9 (1950) to 2.3 children per woman (2007). Disregarding China and Japan, Asian women on average still have 2.9 children. India now falls right into this average (2007: 2.9 children per woman). Yet there are several Indian states – from West Bengal to Kerala – where governments emphasize the importance of social development as opposed to pure economic growth, where fertility is already below 2 children per woman.

Other parts of Asia, including – surprisingly – some developing countries and emerging markets, have also seen a drop below replacement levels in the number of children. These include Iran (2007: 1.7), Japan (1.2), Brunei (2.0), and Thailand (1.6).

Fertility in Latin America and the Caribbean has also dropped to a similar degree as in Asia. In 1950, women there had 5.9 children; in 2007, the rate had dropped to 2.5 children. The only countries in this region that still record high numbers of births are Haiti

(4.9), Guatemala (3.7), and Honduras (3.5). Countries that have
seen their fertility falling below replacement levels include: Cuba
(1.6), Uruguay (2.0), and Chile (2.0) as well as several small territories and states in the Caribbean such as Barbados, Dominica, Mar-
tinique, the Dutch Antilles, Puerto Rico, and Trinidad.

Fertility rates in Asia (2007)			
Highest		Lowest	
Afghanistan	6.6	Macau	0.9
Yemen	6.5	Hong Kong	1.0
Oman	5.7	Singapore	1.1
Gaza Strip	5.4	Taiwan	1.1
		South Korea	1.2

Table 2 Countries with the highest and lowest fertility in Asia – number
of children per woman

High fertility in Africa

During the second half of the 20th century Africa has seen a
significantly smaller drop in fertility than other world regions.
In 1950, women in this continent had on average 6.7 children. In
2007, the average was still 4.8. To date, some African societies
continue to remain largely unaffected by the global drop in fertility. All these countries belong to the poorest in the world. Even in
South Africa, the richest country of sub-Saharan Africa and at
the same time the country with the widest inequality in income
distribution, fertility in 2007 still remained at 2.5 children. Fertility at or below replacement level can only be found in Algeria
(1.9), Mauritius (1.8), the Seychelles (1.7), and in Tunisia (1.7).

Fertility rates in Africa (2005)			
Highest		Lowest	
Mali	7.38	Tunisia	1.73
Niger	7.37	Seychelles	1.74
Uganda	6.84	Mauritius	1.84
Somalia	6.68	Algeria	1.86
Burundi	6.48		
Burkina Faso	6.41		
Congo-Kinshasa	6.37		

Table 3   Countries with the highest and lowest fertility rates in Africa –
number of children per woman

Highly developed regions – low number of children

Between 1950 and 1955, the number of children in the world's
highly developed regions stood at 2.8 per woman. This was
already half of the global average. In 1975, fertility fell below 2.1
children per woman. By 2007, it had sunk to an average of about
1.6 children among all highly developed regions.

Fertility in Australia and Oceania in 1950 was comparatively
high at 3.9 children. Today, the rate lies at 2.1, primarily due
to the low rates in Australia (1.8), and New Zealand (2.1). In
contrast, a number of Pacific island states with relatively small
populations still have an average of four to five children per
woman: Kiribati, the US-governed Marshall Islands, Micronesia,
the Solomon Islands, and Vanuatu. The only larger country in
this group is Papua New Guinea (2007: 3.8 children). Almost all
of these countries and territories belong to the poorest in the
world; only three-fourths of Oceania can be considered part of
the developed world.

In North America, fertility was still at 3.5 children in 1950.
The American baby boom boosted this rate to 3.6 (1961). By

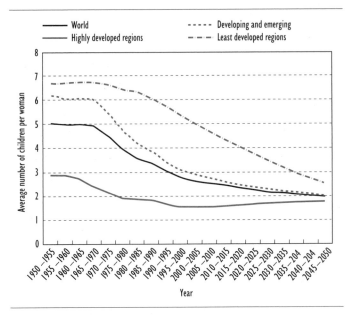

Figure 7   Average number of children per woman (TFR)
The UN predicts slightly increased numbers of children for highly developed
regions in 2050. There is little empirical evidence to support this, however.
Source: UN Population Division (2005)

2007, fertility had declined to 2.05 children. This level is largely
influenced by the USA (2.1). This number of children makes the
USA one of only a few industrial societies today whose fertility
is close to replacement level. The American population would
therefore remain stable even without immigration.

The number of children in Canada falls well below the American figure (1.6 children). This is notable when taking into consideration that the region had an exceptionally high fertility rate
in the 18th and 19th centuries and therefore enjoyed enormously
high natural growth rates.

Europe: the continent with the lowest number of children

In the 1950s, the average number of children in Europe was still 2.6 per woman. It increased slightly during the baby boom that followed in the mid-1960s, and since then has experienced a continuing decline. Today (2007), Europe reports 1.4 children per woman. It ranks at the bottom end, not only historically, but also when compared with other continents. Along with East Asia, Europe has the societies with the lowest number of children per woman globally. Southern Europe, as well as large parts of Central and Eastern Europe, fall below the European average. The lowest fertility rates have been recorded in relatively highly developed Slovenia (1.3) as well as in poorer Ukraine (1.2), and Belarus (1.2). In Germany (1.4) and Russia (1.4) fertility is somewhat higher.

In Central and Eastern Europe, low fertility can be explained by a rapid change in values, a transformation crisis during the 1990s, and an unprecedented economic upturn. During Communist times, women in this region usually had their children shortly after their twentieth birthdays. Since jobs as well as childcare facilities in kindergartens and pre-schools were guaranteed, most women did not have to choose between work and raising children. Many young adults became parents before they had established themselves professionally and some countries, such as the German Democratic Republic, even encouraged such patterns. In the event of an early pregnancy, the regime provided young people with an apartment as a motivation to have children shortly after completing school.

Once these conditions changed many young women delayed childbirth. This led to a sharp decline in births. At the same time, the average age of first-time mothers increased dramatically within a few years. In Central and Eastern Europe this marked the onset of increased individualism based on a Western model. Founding a family now takes place in a different life phase – if it takes place at all. Similar developments have been observed in Western societies at a slower pace since the end of the baby boom.

One could say that postponing children does not mean abandoning the idea of having children altogether. Yet this is only partly true. Experience shows that, in the end, many "delayed children" are never born.

All of the EU's Central and Southeast European member countries have similarly low numbers of children. The same applies to the large countries of Western and Southern Europe, such as Germany, Italy, and Spain. Without immigration, the populations of these countries would have been shrinking for several years or even decades now.

Region	Years		
	1950–55	1980–85	2000–05
World	5.02	3.58	2.65
Europe	2.66	1.88	1.40
North America	3.47	1.81	2.00
Africa	6.72	6.45	4.97
Asia	5.89	3.67	2.47
Latin America	5.89	3.93	2.55
Australia/Pacific	3.87	2.62	2.32

Table 4 Average number of children per woman by world regions,
1950–2005
Source: UN Population Division (2005)

In several northwestern European countries, the average number of children is well above the European average. Among them are France (2.0), Ireland (1.9), Norway (1.8), Sweden (1.7), the United Kingdom (1.7) and Iceland (1.9). Only countries at the margins of Europe, such as Albania (2.0) and Turkey (1.9), still have fertility near replacement level.

Delayed slowdown in growth

Between 1950 and 1955, fertility on average was five children per woman. Globally, this led to a mere 99 million births per year. In 2007, fertility had dropped to 2.6 children per woman, or half the level of the 1950s. Because of a much larger number of potential parents, the world recorded nearly 135 million births in 2007. And even though the average number of children will most likely continue to decline, the annual number of births will still reach 120 million in mid-21st century.

This clearly shows that the number of births in a particular region is not only determined by the average number of children, but also by the number of potential parents. The latter mainly depends on the number of births in the past decades. Conversely, the current numbers of births will influence the age structure well into the 21st century. This is also referred to as the demographic momentum. The high birth rates of the 1980s are currently producing a very large number of potential parents. Conversely, declining numbers of children today will lead to smaller numbers of potential parents in the future. This ultimately reduces the number of births. We can therefore assume that, in the second half of the 21st century, global population growth will come to an end.

Today, the average number of children per woman is still higher than four in seventy countries. These countries are home to 16% of the world population. Yet, in seventy-one countries, the average number of children per woman is below two. The total population of these countries accounts for 43% of the world population. In the future, this group of countries will continue to increase.

Enhanced reproductive age – lower number of children

Multiple factors played a role in the secular decline in fertility. Fundamental changes in living conditions first in the developed parts of the northern hemisphere and later in other parts of the world raised both the value and the costs associated with each individual child. This considerably reduced the desire to have many children. At the same time, the availability of better education for women resulted in delayed entry into the labor market. This led both to an increase both in the age at which women give birth to their first child and in numbers of women remaining childless.

Children per woman	2.0 and lower	2.1–3.9	4 and more	In total
Countries and territories* (absolute numbers)	73	81	41	195
Share of world population residing there (in %)	43	38	19	100

Table 5 Distribution of countries and world population by level of fertility, 2003.

*Only countries and territories with more than 100,000 inhabitants
Source: UN Population Reference Bureau (2007)

Until approximately 1860, only men with gainful employment, occupation, or proven wealth were allowed to marry in most parts of Western and Northern Europe (a rule that did not apply in the South and Southeast). By the time they had secured stable income and employment, they had usually reached midlife. They then tended to marry women from their own class. A fairly large proportion of the adult populations was forced to remain single. They were either too poor or held occupations and social positions incompatible with marriage and family formation. This pattern gradually disappeared with the industrialization of Western European societies, even though social restrictions on marriage remained effective in certain areas for a long time. Until the middle of the 19th century, women tended to give birth to their first child between age twenty-five and age thirty as a result of the traditional Western European marriage patterns. As legal and social restrictions on marriage gradually disappeared during the first half of the 20th century, the reproductive age moved to the early twenties. The pattern of marriage and family formation described above only applied to Western and Northern Europe, not to Central, Eastern, and Southeastern Europe separated by the so-called "Hajnel line". To the south and east of this line, early marriage and early family formation had already been the norm before the 20th century.

After the end of World War II, the reproductive age remained lower for more than two decades. In Western Europe at least, it then began to rise again from about 1965 onwards. In contrast, the phase of family building in Central and Eastern Europe continued to set in among twenty-year-olds. It was only after 1989 that this changed dramatically. Today, women in Europe on average give birth to their children about eight years later than in the early 1960s.

The reproductive age is also rising in poorer countries, although not at the same speed as in Europe, Japan, and North America. Shorter school attendance among girls than in the developed world, lower educational levels, and fewer opportunities for women in the labor market contribute to early marriage and childbearing. In many developing countries, fewer young women delay marrying and family formation, and fewer married women use effective birth control. However, this does not apply to all poor countries and emerging markets, as low birth rates in Iran, Thailand, and Tunisia and several states in India demonstrate.

There are significantly more young mothers in developing countries who give birth to their first child below age twenty than is the case in richer industrial countries. There are also higher numbers of older mothers giving birth beyond the age of forty – none of them for the first time. In Europe and North America, a considerable number of older mothers can be interpreted as a sign of social modernization. Yet in developing countries older mothers are an indication that fertility is high and birth control less effective.

Mortality is declining almost everywhere

During the past five to six decades, crude death rates in present-day emerging markets and developing countries have dropped by two-thirds. In 1950–1955, there were twenty-five deaths per 1000 inhabitants. By the early 21st century, this rate had fallen to eight deaths per 1000 inhabitants. This decline mainly took place between 1950 and 1980. In the 1980s, the crude death rate stood at ten. Since then, mortality rates in Asia, Africa, and Latin America have fallen insignificantly.

Mortality, or the risk of dying at a given age, has fallen in most developing countries and emerging markets. In other words, there have been fewer deaths. The main exception, however, are countries in southern and eastern Africa, which have been seriously affected since the 1990s by HIV/AIDS. On the other hand, high birth rates and a growing number of surviving children have led to a structural shift in age composition. Younger societies with decreasing infant and child mortality have few older people now represent the age group with the highest mortality. Societies with such an age structure have a lower crude death rate (deaths per 1000 inhabitants) than societies with similar socio-economic conditions but an older population.

This is the main reason why – despite growing life expectancy – the crude death rate in the world's most developed regions has risen slightly since the beginning of the 1960s. In 1960, there were nine deaths per 1000 inhabitants in Western Europe and North America. The current crude death rate in developed countries is about ten and will most likely rise to thirteen per 1000 inhabitants by 2050. Infant and child mortality no longer play a role in more developed parts of the world. The number of deaths now depends on the increasing number of people over age sixty. Thus, the mortality rate tends to be higher today in rich countries with aging populations than in poor countries with young populations. And the crude death rate will continue to rise in rich countries with increasing development and rising average age, despite continuously increasing life expectancy.

In contrast to the highly developed nations, developing countries and emerging markets represent a much larger share of world population than in the 1950s and 1960s. Demographic changes in these countries have considerably more impact on the size and structure of the world's population. As people in less developed countries are living shorter lives, there are fewer people above age sixty. This, however, will change during the coming decades. From 2020 onwards, crude death rates will most likely rise in the developing countries and emerging markets, despite expected further decline in mortality. Large birth cohorts of the 1970s will gradually enter the 50+ age group.

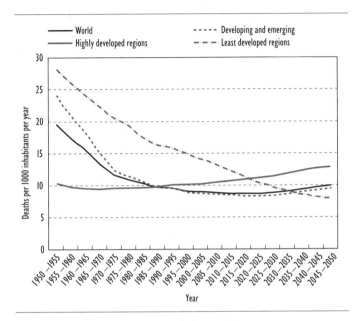

Figure 8 Mortality rate (per 1000 inhabitants), 1950–2050
   Source: UN Population Division (2005)

The difference can best be seen when we compare the major variant of UN population projections with an alternative scenario. If mortality remains at today's levels, global population in 2050 would not reach nine billion people, but roughly one billion less.

Reduced infant and child mortality

In most parts of the world, the increase in life expectancy at birth and average life span was mainly driven by declining infant and child mortality. In Europe and North America, this process started in the 19th century. In less developed regions, the newborn mortality has only declined since the 1950s. The most important reasons for this favorable development were better nutrition and improved hygiene, large-scale vaccination programs, and improved remedies for gastrointestinal infections. Furthermore, breastfeeding has been promoted since the 1990s, giving newborns and infants better chances of survival.

In 1950–1955, 157 of 1000 newborns died before their first birthday globally, and a further eighty died between age one and age five. By 2007, global infant mortality had dropped to forty-nine per 1000 newborns, and child mortality between age one and age five is at 26 per 1000 children.

In the mid-20th century, 180 of 1000 newborns in less developed regions died during their first year. Today, child mortality in the first year is fifty-four deaths per 1000 newborns. An extrapolation of this trend by 2050 would lead to only twenty-six deaths per 1000 newborns in developing and emerging economies.

Infant and child mortality continues to be highest in Africa. Today, eighty-seven out of 1000 children die during their first year. Another sixty-one per 1000 African children die between age one and age five. In Asia, too, mortality in younger age groups continues to be high, even if it is only half the African level. Infant mortality during the first year of life is forty-three per 1000 Asian newborns; child mortality between age one and age five is seventeen per 1000. Latin American infant mortality during the first year is twenty-two per 1000 newborns; child mortality between age one and age five is as low as six per 1000.

In the world's highly developed regions, infant mortality levels of fifty-nine per 1000 in 1950 were roughly the same as today's rate in Asia. Today, the mortality rate in rich countries – including Eastern Europe and Russia – is only seven per 1000

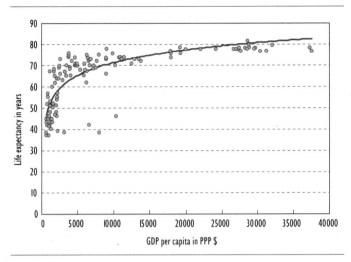

Figure 9   Life expectancy and GDP per capita, 2002–2003
Source: UN

births. In the most prosperous countries such as Austria (4.4 per
1000 births), the Netherlands (4.7), Switzerland (4.1), as well as
in Scandinavia and Japan (3.2), infant mortality has reached a
level that can hardly decrease any further. Deaths among children above age one barely occur in rich countries any longer.

Rising life expectancy

Life expectancy summarizes the development of mortality at all
ages by answering a question that interests almost every individual: "How long will I live?" or "What are my chances for
reaching a certain age?" Declining mortality means an increasing life span. This gain, however, is very unevenly distributed

between and within societies. In almost all regions of the world, gender has a significant influence on life expectancy. Women, on average, live longer than men. In addition and for obvious reasons, material well-being has a substantial influence on life span. People with higher incomes and privileged social or professional positions tend to enjoy a longer life expectancy. Access to health care and medical services plays a significant role. Yet differences in lifestyle, nutrition, working conditions, and available leisure time as well as the way this time is spent are apparently just as important. This does not only apply to individuals but to societies as a whole. There are, after all, effects that increase mortality at the societal level but are not taken into account in the calculation of life tables and life expectancy. Such effects include wars, political violence, and natural disasters that can claim a high number of lives in a short time.

In the mid-20th century, world average life expectancy was forty-six years. By 2007, it had increased to sixty-six years. In the coming forty years, world average life expectancy will most likely rise to seventy-five years. Particularly striking is the growth in less developed countries and regions (1950–1954: forty-one years, 2007: sixty-five years). Without the HIV/AIDS epidemic, this gain in average life span would have been even greater.

Clear differences between men and women remain significant. Historically speaking, this is a relatively new phenomenon. In earlier times, women had a high risk of dying during pregnancy, delivery, or shortly after giving birth. Today, women on average live four to six years longer than men. Yet this also varies depending on whether a person lives in a highly developed or in a less developed society. In five countries, men continue to enjoy higher life expectancy. In another twenty-eight less prosperous countries, the difference of 0–2 years in favor of women is still very small.

We do not know all the reasons for such differences. Yet historical data on mortality in Asia, Africa, and Latin America give a clear hint: rapidly rising life expectancy among women is linked to the declining numbers of pregnancies and births per woman. Child-bearing posed and still poses life-threatening risks to mothers associated with child bearing were considerable and continue to be so in quite a few poor countries. Fewer pregnancies per woman, however, directly reduce such risks. In India, for example, life expectancy among women has only been higher than that of men for the past two decades.

As long as fertility in this country after 1950 stagnated or even rose, Indian men tended to be the ones who profited more from gains in material well-being. Since the average number of children per family has decreased considerably, female life expectancy has become higher than that of men. Similar discrepancies have been observed in the more prosperous of present-day markets as well as in some of the poorest countries.

Yet, it is not only the risk to women caused by pregnancies and childbirth that has an important influence. Different lifestyles can affect the average life span. In this respect, there are also significant differences between men and women. Nutrition as well as paying attention to one's body and health play a decisive role. Consumption of alcohol and smoking strongly influence life expectancy. Both are more widespread among men than women. Since the 1980s, countries such as Russia and Ukraine have seen a drop in male life expectancy that is likely to be caused in part by increasing alcohol abuse.

In the coming decades, we may expect a further decline in the number of children to have a positive impact on women's life expectancy. Yet the UN forecasts for 2050 assume an average life span of seventy-nine years for men and eighty-five years for women. Compared to 2007, this would be a gain of seven years

	Infant mortality (age 0–under 1 year per 1000)			Child mortality (age 2–5 per 1000 at age 1)
	1950–1955	1980–1985	2005–2010	2000–2005
World	157	78	49	26
Europe	72	18	8	2
North America	29	10	6	2
Africa	179	114	87	61
Asia	182	82	43	17
Latin America	126	57	22	6
Australia/Pacific	62	37	26	9

Table 6 Infant mortality (during the first 12 months per 1000 live births) and child mortality (per 1000 children age 1 to 5) in macro regions, 1950–1955 to 2005–2010.

Source: UN Population Division (2008); PRB (2007)

for men, but only six years for women. The latter would therefore lose part of their comparatively better position during this period of time. The underlying assumption is that gender differences will generally decrease over time. This is an assumption not fully supported by empirical evidence. We may well come to the conclusion that convergence between genders as well as between regions, until now, is more based on the political desire of governments than on evidence. Such assumptions, therefore, have to be viewed with much caution.

Babies born in the early 1950s who had the luck to live in highly developed countries already had a life expectancy that was as long as the present-day world average. Since then, global average life expectancy has risen by twenty-one years. Since World War II, a rapid decline in mortality has helped developing economies

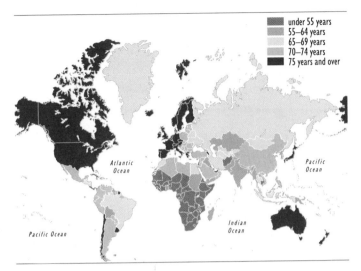

Figure 10 Life expectancy at birth in years, 2002
      Source: World Bank 2006

to catch up with highly industrialized parts of the world. In the 1950s, life expectancy in highly developed countries (1950–1955: sixty-six years) was on average twenty-five years higher than in developing countries (1950–1955: forty-one years). Today, the difference is only twelve years (highly developed countries 2007: seventy-seven years; less developed countries: sixty-five years).

During the second half of the 20th century, the pace of mortality decline in developing countries was significantly greater than in 19th century Europe. It took Europeans seventy years to increase their average life expectancy from 40 to 60 years. Developing countries as a whole only needed half that time: thirty-five years between 1950 and 1985.

Among inhabitants of highly developed countries, residents of Russia (2007: sixty-six years; males fifty-nine, females

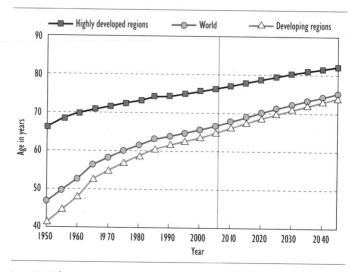

Figure 11 Life expectancy at birth, 1950 to 2050, by region
Source: UN Population Division

seventy-three) and Ukraine (sixty-eight; males sixty-two, females seventy-four) have by far the shortest life spans. Furthermore, since the collapse of the Soviet Union, life expectancy in these two countries has dropped considerably below former Soviet levels.

The countries with by far the shortest life expectancy are those most affected by HIV/AIDS, other epidemic diseases, and long-term consequences of political violence. In Africa these are Lesotho, Swaziland, Zambia, and Zimbabwe (40–43 years). Next in line are Angola, Liberia, Mozambique, and Sierra Leone, (44–45 years). The Asian country with the shortest life expectancy is Afghanistan (45 years). In the Western hemisphere, inhabitants of the Caribbean poorhouse of Haiti have the short-est lives (52 years).

In total, life expectancy for both sexes in present-day emerging economies rose from just below forty-two to just above sixty-six years between 1950 and 2007. This was a gain in life span of twenty-four years. During the same period of time, average life span in the poorest countries rose more modestly: from thirty-six to fifty-one years, spelling a gain of fifteen years in almost six decades. In both groups of countries, growth was somewhat higher among women than among men.

Life expectancy (in years; 2007)	Total	Men	Woman
Japan	82	79	86
Switzerland, Iceland	81	78	83–84
Australia, Sweden, Spain, Hong Kong	81	77–78	83–84
France, Israel, Canada, Norway, Singapore	80	77–78	82–84

Table 7 Countries with the highest life expectancy worldwide

Such results clearly show that material well-being plays a key role in determining life expectancy. Average GDP per capita explains a large portion of differences in life expectancy, particularly among poorer countries (see Fig. 9). About two-thirds of existing differences can be explained that way. The rest may be attributed to lifestyle, nutrition, the quality of the public health system, medical infrastructure, etc. Thus, most political decisions only affect the latter. As a result, politics surely has less influence on average life span than economic development and social structure – at least in the short run. In the long run, this relation is far more complex as political decisions may have a lasting impact on socio-economic development.

Amartya K. Sen – the 1998 Nobel Prize Laureate in Economics

– pointed to some other important factors especially the degree to which basic needs of humans, including food, shelter, and basic medical services, are provided within a society. This not only depends on the level of per capita income, but also on income distribution and welfare state intervention. This also applies to the industrialized nations. At the beginning of the 21st century, a report published by the World Health Organization (WHO) observed that, considering their high level of prosperity, it was not surprising that Americans with good health standards live 4.5 years less on average than the Japanese. According to the WHO, lower life expectancy in the USA is based on the fact that living conditions among minority groups in the USA are closer to those in a developing country rather than an industrial nation. The lives of these people are marked by poverty and a lack of medical care. A high degree of socio-economic inequality therefore also lowers national life expectancy.

From births and deaths to population growth

In the short term, the number of births and deaths analyzed here determines the size of "natural" growth, leading to an increase or decrease of "native" populations. Beyond this, total population change can also be heavily influenced by migration. At a global scale, however, births and deaths are the only determinants, as the sum of all international immigration and emigration is, of course, zero. If we look at particular countries and macro regions, immigrants and emigrants do, in fact, contribute heavily to population change and with that to growth or decline (Chapter 5). In this context, migration often has an equalizing effect: developing countries with growing populations exhibit more emigration than immigration. In contrast, highly

Life expectancy (in years; 2007)	Total	Men	Women
Swaziland	40	40	39
Lesotho	43	43	42
Zambia, Zimbabwe	44	44	43
Botswana	51	50	51

Table 8 Countries with the lowest life expectancy worldwide

developed countries with low fertility almost entirely belong to the demographic "winners," attracting international migrants. In total, though, mobility between countries is of much lower magnitude than most people think. Globally, only three out of 100 global citizens live outside their country of birth. The large majority of people still live in the countries they were born in; many of them, however, no longer at their place of birth.

In total, population change depends both on the balance between births and deaths (natural population balance) and the balance between immigration and emigration (migration balance). The sum of these two balances can be positive or negative. The former means population growth, the latter decline. Whether a population grows or shrinks and how quickly it grows or shrinks depends heavily on the degree to which the number of children per woman (TFR) differs from replacement level. In order for a parent generation to reproduce itself completely, the average number of children has to be somewhat higher than two, as slightly more boys than girls are born; and some girls die before they reach a reproductive age. In Western industrial societies where child mortality is very low, an average of 2.1 children is sufficient to entirely replace a parent generation in the long run. In many developing countries, higher infant and child mortality rates shift the replacement level to 2.2 to 2.3 children per woman.

	1950–1955			1980–1985			2005–2010		
	Total	Men	Women	Total	Men	Women	Total	Men	Women
World	46.3	45.0	47.8	61.3	59.4	63.2	68.5	66.3	70.8
Europe	65.6	62.9	68.0	71.9	67.9	75.8	74.6.	70.5	78.8
North America	68.8	66.1	71.9	74.2	70.7	77.7	78.5	75.9	81.0
Africa	38.2	37.0	39.6	50.1	48.5	51.7	52.8	51.7	53.8
Asia	41.1	40.4	41.8	60.3	59.4	61.3	69.0	67.2	71.0
Latin America	50.9	49.4	52.6	64.4	61.5	67.5	73.3	70.1	76.6
Australia/ Pacific	60.4	58.1	62.9	69.3	66.5	72.1	75.2	72.6	77.9

Table 9 Life expectancy at birth by world regions (in years), 1950–2010

Source: UN Population Division (2008)

Northern and Southern hemispheres: variable population growth

In 1950, our planet had some 2.5 billion inhabitants. One-third of them – 813 million – had the privilege of living in one of the world's highly developed countries. The remaining two-thirds – approximately 1.7 billion – were people living in European colonies and already independent countries in Asia, Africa, and Latin America. At that time, not all countries of the southern hemisphere were poor and part of the so-called "Third World." During the interwar period and in 1950, living standards in Argentina, Chile, and parts of Brazil were higher than in many parts of Europe. This, however, was not true for 201 million people – representing 8% of the world population – who lived in the least developed countries and colonies of that time.

At 1.2% annually, the highly developed countries exhibited a significant population growth during the 1950s. Since then,

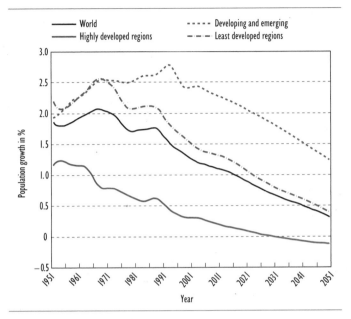

World ---- **Developing and emerging**
Highly developed regions --- **Least developed regions**

Figure 12 Population growth, 1951–2051

though, their annual growth rate has been on the decline. By the mid-1960s, it had been reduced to 1%, and by 1990 to +0.5%. Since then, the annual growth rate has again been cut in half. In 2007, the population of all developed countries grew by only +0.25%.

Today, a large part of the modest population growth in the rich countries of the northern hemisphere is due to migration, and this has a twofold effect. On the one hand, immigrants directly increase the number of people living in a particular country. On the other hand, young adults of reproductive age are more likely to migrate than older people. As a result immigration boosts the birth rates in migrant-receiving countries. This is particularly true when migrants come from low and middle-income countries with higher fertility. In the long run, however, migrants align their number of children with the – usually lower – levels of local population.

According to the main variant of the UN projection, population growth in present-day high-income countries will come to a standstill shortly after 2030. In the following years, the number of inhabitants in the world's richest countries would then start to fall. The UN projection forecasts a drop of -0.1% annually by the mid-21st century. Whether it actually reaches this level will depend on the extent of migration from less developed to more developed world regions. From a present-day perspective, it is more likely that immigration to rich countries with shrinking domestic populations will continue. As a result, it seems less probable that the number of people living in these regions will actually shrink.

Developments in the world's less industrialized countries and regions have taken a completely different course since the end of World War II and continue to do so. In the mid-20th century, the population in Asia (excluding Japan), Africa, and Latin America grew by +2.2% annually. At that time, the growth rate was almost twice as high as in Europe and North America. By the end of the 1950s, this growth began to accelerate.

During the second half of the 1960s, the population of the so-called "Third World" grew by 2.6% per year. The growth rate had reached its historical peak. At this pace, the total population of all emerging economies and developing countries would have doubled within twenty-seven years. Since then, growth rates have consistently declined. The growth rate in this now very heterogeneous group of countries is currently only +1.4% (2006/07) annually.

Such a growth rate does not seem large. In absolute numbers,

however, the population of all emerging economies and developing countries still grows by +76 million people annually. To
compare, the population of the so-called "Third World" only
grew by +64 million people annually between 1966 and 1977,
despite a growth rate that was twice the size of today. At that
time, developing countries with a higher growth rate had much
smaller populations.

In future, demographic growth in emerging economies and
developing countries will continue to decline. The UN projection for 2050 puts it at +0.4%. In absolute numbers, this would
still be an annual growth of +32 million people living in poorer
countries.

During the early 1950s, higher mortality rates meant that
growth in the world's poorest countries (1950/51: +1.9%) was
somewhat weaker than in today's emerging economies, but
it began to increase. With +2.8% in 1991–1992, demographic
growth in this group of countries finally reached its historic
maximum. This would have led to a doubling of populations in
least developed nations within twenty-five years. Currently, populations of the poorest countries still grow at a rate of approximately +2.3% per year (2006/7). In absolute numbers, this is an
annual increase of sixteen million people – creating additional
stress for the world's societies most burdened by poverty and
despair.

At an annual growth rate of +2.3%, populations would
double within a period of thirty years. Nonetheless, growth
rates in the poorest countries of the world will most likely also
slow down during the coming decades. The UN projects a reduction to 2% annually in 2025. For 2050, an annual growth rate of
+1.2% is still expected for the world's poorest countries. This
is half the growth rate of today. In absolute numbers this would
mean an annual increase of +22 million people in the world's

	Absolute					In %				
	1900	1950	2000	2007	2050	1900	1950	2000	2007	2050
World	1,650	2,519	6,071	6,600	9076	100	100	100	100	100
Developed countries	539	813	1194	1,216	1236	33	32	20	18	14
Europe	408	547	728	730	653	25	22	12	11	7
North America, Japan, Australia, and New Zealand	131	269	466	486	583	8	11	8	7	7
Less developed countries	1111	1706	4877	5,411	7840	67	68	80	82	86
Africa	133	221	796	951	1937	8	9	13	14	21
Asia without Japan, Pacific	904	1315	3561	3871	5120	55	52	59	59	56
Latin America, Caribbean	74	167	572	566	783	4	7	9	9	9

Table 10 Population (in millions) and their distribution (in %) by world
regions, 1900–2050

Source: UN Population Division (2008); PRB (2008); US Census Bureau. Data
for 2050 are based on the UN medium variant; the upper variant estimated 10.6
billion, the lower variant 7.4 billion

	1950–1955	1980–1985	2000–2007
World	+1.8	+1.7	+1.4
Europe	+1.0	+0.4	−0.0
North America	+1.7	+1.0	+1.0
Africa	+2.2	+2.9	+2.7
Asia	+2.0	+1.9	+1.4
Latin America	+2.7	+2.1	+1.6
Australia/Pacific	+2.2	+1.5	+1.7

Table 11 Average rate of population growth (in %) by world regions,
1950–2005

Source: US Census Bureau, International Data (2008)

poorest nations. Two-thirds of world population growth will then take place in these fifty-one poorest societies.

A shift in the demographic balance

Variations in growth rates are causing a shift in demographic gravity. In 1950, one-third of the world population lived in highly developed countries. Today, the share of Europe, North America, Japan, and Australia in the world population is less than 19% (2007). In demographic terms, the relative weight of the economically and technologically advanced part of the world has therefore almost halved within less than six decades. Until 2050, the share of all highly developed countries will further drop to one-seventh (13%) of the world population.

In the mid-20th century, people living in colonies and developing countries represented two-thirds of the global population. To date, the relative weight of these world regions has risen to 82% (2007). In 2050, according to the main variant of the UN population projection, some 87% of all future inhabitants of our planet will live in today's developing countries and emerging economies.

Today, 12% of the global population lives in the fifty-one poorest countries of the world. In 1950, their share had only been 6%. In the near future, disproportionate growth will continue to take place in countries with the lowest level of prosperity. By the mid-21st century, almost one-fifth of the world population will reside in these fifty-one countries (2050: 19%). In most of these nations, population growth will continue well into the second half of the 21st century.

Differences between the continents

When looking at differences at a regional level, we see significant variation between continents.

In 1950, Europe had 547 million inhabitants. This figure includes Russia and other European republics of the former Soviet Union. This continent's population grew by an average of +1.1% annually in the 1950s and early 1960s. This was a respectable growth by present-day benchmarks – especially when taking into account that more people emigrated from Europe until the mid-1960s than immigrated to the continent. The annual growth rate later decreased to +0.4% in 1984–1985. After 1989, political events in Central and Eastern Europe had considerable demographic consequences. Birth rates and numbers of children declined on an enormous scale and, since then, remain below the European average. Since 2000, Europe as a whole has seen a stagnating population despite higher immigration from other parts of the world. The losses in population size are almost entirely concentrated in Central and Eastern European countries. In the years since 2002, the populations of Germany and Italy have also been stagnating.

Today, Europe including Russia and the European successor states of the former Soviet Union has 732 million inhabitants. The UN projects a decline to 653 million by 2050. As the UN's demographers tend to make conservative estimates regarding future migration, Europe's total population in 2050 could also be larger.

The present-day EU with its twenty-seven member states has almost 500 million inhabitants. The total population is growing. Since 2000, EU population growth has been in the order of +1.5 to +2 million per year. For the larger part (some 80%), this growth in the EU can be explained by immigration from surrounding non-EU countries and other continents.

Demographic change in Africa is in sharp contrast to the European situation. At the beginning of the 1950s, Africa had 221 million inhabitants. Today, 951 million people are living on this continent. The annual growth rates were high during the period 1950–1955 (+2.2%). Growth reached a peak of +2.9% per year during the period 1980–1985 when Africa became the macro region with the highest population growth ever recorded in human history. Growth only began to slow down during the 1990s. Between 2000 and 2007, however, the annual growth rate still reached +2.7%, the same level as in the early 1950s. During the coming four decades, it will most likely fall to approximately 1% annually. The HIV/AIDS epidemic and other infectious diseases are contributing to this slowdown, but have not yet led to declining population numbers. This is true even in the most affected countries.

One of the weak points in Malthusian thought can be identified in this context: epidemics leading to the death of tens or hundreds of thousands of people can surely be viewed as a catastrophic influence in the countries and societies concerned. In most cases, however, even such catastrophes only have a minor impact on long-term demographic developments. In any event, the impact is far less than Malthus assumed. This, for example, applies to the period after the European plague epidemics – the so-called Black Death of the late Middle Ages (see Chapter 2). Almost none of the cyclical mortality crises that, until the mid-19th century, occurred on a more or less regular basis curbed population growth long-term. There are only a few exceptions. One is the decimation of Native Americans since the 16th century partly caused by infectious diseases "imported" by Europeans. Another is the Irish potato famine of the 1840s, when the British let approximately one million people on the island starve to death. Yet even in Ireland it was not only the catastrophic famine that hindered population growth for one and a half centuries. Large waves of emigration starting in the 1850s had a much larger influence. Emigration from Ireland continued well into the 1980s. Until 1924, the primary destination for Irish emigrants was the USA. During the 20th century, the UK became the main destination.

In 1950, some 1.4 billion people lived in Asia (including Japan). During the early 1950s, annual population growth was relatively high (2.0%), but never reached African levels. Asian population growth peaked between 1965 and 1970 (2.4% per year). A shift towards modest growth took place during the early 1970s. Since then, the annual growth rate dropped to +1.4% (2000–2007). This is only half of the historic maximum.

Barring the special case of China with its very restrictive population and family policies, Asia's annual growth during the years 2000–2007 still averaged +1.6%. In absolute numbers, annual growth in Asia at the beginning of the 21st century amounted to +48 million people. In comparison, Africa had a growth rate that was twice as high. During the same period, it only contributed +18 million to the annual growth of the world population.

In 2008, Asia had 4.0 billion inhabitants. Estimates assume that by 2050 Asia will have a population of about 5.3 billion. In East Asia, population growth will then come to a standstill. South and West Asia will most likely see further growth. India will then be the most populous country in the world.

From 1750 onwards, North America enjoyed strong population growth mainly as a result of large immigration waves. After 1924, this came to a temporary standstill. Mass immigration only regained momentum after 1945. In 1950, 172 million people lived in North America. The annual growth rate was 1.7%. In 2007, the two countries of North America had 334 million inhabitants and an annual population growth rate of 1.0%. In mid-2008, the

US Census Bureau assumed 304 million people to be living in the United States alone.

Forty percent of North American population growth is due to immigration. In 2050, North America is expected to have 462 million inhabitants. Immigration and a slightly positive balance of births will provide for a growing population well into the second half of the 21st century.

Until the mid-20th century, Latin America was one of the main destinations for international migrants. After 1950, the trend shifted. Poverty and high population growth in several countries led to a considerable emigration, mainly to the USA, but also to Europe. In 1950, Latin America and the Caribbean had 167 million inhabitants and an annual growth rate of +2.7%. Growth then began to slow down at the end of the 1960s. In 2007, 572 million people lived in this region. The growth rate amounted to 1.4%. In 2050, Latin America and the Caribbean will have a total of 783 million inhabitants. Population growth in this region of the world will then most likely come to a standstill.

In 1950, Australia, New Zealand and the Pacific island states (Oceania) only had thirteen million inhabitants. The annual growth rate averaged +2.2%. This was mostly due to immigrants settling in Australia and New Zealand. In 2007, the population of the whole region had almost doubled in size to thirty-four million. The annual growth rate stood at +1.3%. UN forecasts predict a population of forty-six million in 2050. Immigration will most likely continue to cause population growth beyond this period.

From a growing to a shrinking population?

Between 2000 and 2015, the population of our planet will grow by about one billion people. More than half of the growth is occurring in Asia: mainly South Asia (+330 million) and East Asia (+227 million). During the same period, the population of sub-Saharan Africa will rise by +227 million. More modest growth will occur in Latin America and the Caribbean (+108 million) as well as in North Africa and the Middle East (+88 million).

Globally, population growth will mainly take place in less developed regions. Between 2000 and 2015, the total population will grow by +642 million in developing countries and by +347 million in emerging economies. Developed countries and regions will only contribute +52 million to global population increase.

In some countries and regions, populations are already decreasing. In other countries, a decline is expected to set in over the coming decades. Two completely different circumstances can lead to population decline in the near future.

On the one hand, a shift in values and lifestyles towards individualism and a materialistic and post-materialist orientation is taking place. In this context, striving for personal fulfillment can go together with an altruistic approach towards (potential) offspring. A growing group of people has come to the following conclusion: they want to have children, but also they want to ensure that these children can have a decent life. Usually this is a strong argument in favor of limiting the number of children, in order to give each of them access to education and material well-being during childhood. Gary Becker (1986) in his discussion of this topic spoke of "quality kids" (see Chapter 3). Other people in modern societies have more individualistic reasons for limiting their number of children or remaining childless. They do not wish to forgo opportunities to maximize income, improve their own standards of living, and achieve self-fulfillment, all of which competes with the time-consuming duties facing parents. In many emerging economies and most developed societies, a combination of both individualistic and altruistic motives has led to a strong decline in the number of children per family. In almost all developed societies, fertility has fallen below replacement level on average. Sooner or later, this inevitably leads to a declining domestic workforce. In many countries, the resulting "gap" will not be completely filled by permanent immigrants. Population decline in parts of Europe and East Asia is therefore the most probable scenario.

How will this process further evolve? One could conclude that present-day highly developed countries represent the future of less developed countries. *De te fabula narratur* (the story is about you) was the punchline of a satire by the Roman author Horace. This could well apply to population developments (Fig. 13). If this is true, global population growth will come to a halt during the second half of the 21st century.

On the other hand, population decline can occur as result of a crisis. This is certainly the case with regard to the "African population crisis" in the southern and eastern parts of that continent. HIV/AIDS has affected significant shares of the population in Botswana, Malawi, Mozambique, and Lesotho, and has led to unusually high mortality even by the standards of poor and developing countries. In the medium term, this might lead to population declines as the HIV/AIDS epidemic mainly affects younger people.

A second type of crisis seems to affect East European societies. Russia, Ukraine, Belarus, Georgia, and several other post-Socialist countries are struggling with the demographic consequences of rapid social and economic change following the political transformation in 1989–1991. The most obvious sign is stagnating or even falling life expectancy – especially among middle-aged men. At the same time, the average number of children per woman in Eastern Europe is now about 1.2, far below

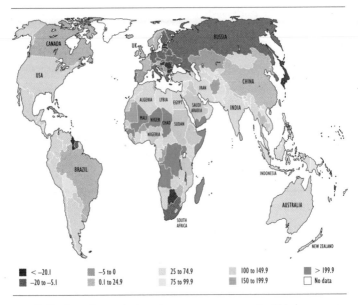

Color	Range	Color	Range	Color	Range
■	< −20.1	■	25 to 74.9	■	> 199.9
■	−20 to −5.1	■	75 to 99.9	■	150 to 199.9
■	−5 to 0	■	100 to 149.9	□	No data
■	0.1 to 24.9				

Figure 13 **Projected population change, 2004–2050 (in %), by country**
          Source: UN Population Division

replacement level. This is not only due to economic change and sometimes insecurity, but is also in line with a rapid adoption of Western values and lifestyles. This led to a situation in which young adults were having fewer children and family formation was being postponed to a later stage in life. This intensified the decline in absolute numbers of births ("tempo effect"). Even if delaying childbirth to a later biographical phase will eventually, in sum, lead to a higher number of children again, births will remain below the levels recorded between the 1960s and the 1980s. The consequence will be a considerable decline of domestic populations in parts of Europe.

Based on the continuation of current trends, in 2050, the

Balkans, Central and Eastern Europe, and possibly also Germany, Italy, and Spain, will be less populated than they are today. Yet, as the demographic system only reacts very slowly, even a considerable rise in the – currently very low – numbers of children would influence population size only in the distant future. With this in mind, long-term projections can give us an idea of what we are heading for.

This leads to the question of whether or not it is possible to alter this process of demographic change; to steer growing, stagnating or even declining populations.

1. Our comparison between India and China makes it clear that politics counts even in the case of a personal matter of choosing the number of one's children. Certain development goals can be much more rapidly reached when purposeful and adequate demographic policies are implemented (Chapter 7).

2. There is, however, a difference between convincing and coercing people. An authoritarian developmental strategy – such as in present-day China – is rooted in command-style politics. It involves a blueprint defined at the top that is enforced top-down using the instruments of political power, persuasion, material incentives, public naming and shaming, sometimes even violence. From a Western point of view, we tend to classify such politics as a violation of basic human rights. Yet this is a question of perspective. If one sees eradication of famine and stabilization of total population as main goals then, to date, the Indian approach has been much less promising than the Chinese.

3. This brings us to the question of the "costs" and trade-offs between competing policy goals. Based on Western culture, we assume that the values of democracy stand above

a government's particular political goal, even if it is an important one. China's government calculates that its policy has "saved" the country 400 million births to date, along with a great amount of misery. This has been – in its opinion – the only successful way of improving the quality of life for 1.3 billion Chinese.

In sum: how many people have ever lived?

The previous three chapters dealt with the natural and cultural history of humankind. A wrap-up leads us to the following question: how many people have ever lived over the course of the whole period analyzed in these three chapters?

The American demographer Carl Haub in a contribution to "Population Today" that calculated 106.5 billion humans were born between 50,000 BC and 2002. As a basis, he assumed extremely high crude birth rates – up to 80 per thousand – until 1800 and steady increases in life expectancy. His colleague Nathan Keyfitz calculated a total of 96.1 billion people for the period of 1,000,000 BC to the year 2000. In doing so, he took a constant average life expectancy of twenty-five years as his calculation base. His model included a further mathematical simplification. His calculation takes two people as a starting point, who then start to reproduce – two "prehistoric parents" based on the biblical image of Adam and Eve.

What does the entire number of all people ever alive depend on? First of all, a starting point in time has to be chosen. From that distant point in history onwards, our ancestors are defined as human beings to be counted. The respective population stock during earlier time periods can be calculated or estimated more or less accurately. At the end of the day, we need a plausible assumption for the life time of all people who have been born on our planet to date. We have to make assumptions about life expectancy in historic and pre-historic times. Our own calculation assumes a life expectancy of twenty years from humanity's beginnings to the start of the 1st millennium AD; we assume a life expectancy of twenty-five years between 0 and 1600; and until 1850 a life expectancy of thirty years. From then onwards and through to current times, we have access to data that allows us to calculate life expectancies based on real life tables.

Our own calculations provide a figure of fifty billion people for the last 160,000 years of the evolutionary history of *homo sapiens*. If we include a further two million years of our human existence alongside other species of the genus of homo, we can add just short of a further five billion to our calculation of fifty billion. This, however, also includes the population of Neanderthals and other extinct human species. This result is based on the assumption that the average human population was 50,000 people during these two million years. An average of 100,000 people would mean almost ten billion people during this era before the emergence of *homo sapiens*.

Today (2009), 6.8 billion people live on our planet. According to our own calculation, they represent 12% of all humans who have ever lived. In the event that N. Keyfitz is correct, the current world population would represent only 7% of humankind in total.

5 Spatial Mobility and International Migration

Humans have always been spatially mobile. We were nomads for the larger part of pre- and early history; changing the location of one's residence only became something special from the Neolithic period onwards, when humans first became sedentary.

However, a nomadic way of life did not mean that humans roamed about the Earth's surface without any boundaries. These early human groups were strictly limited in their areas, which were maintained through bitter rivalry.

Colonization and migration in the ancient world

From the ancient world to early modern times, migration was often synonymous with conquering land or expanding an existing culture's sphere of influence. Celtic people were an early example in Europe. They expanded their habitat, and with that their language, culture, and religion, from the northern foothills of the Alps to present-day France, the British Isles, Spain, Upper Italy, the Danube basin, the Carpathians, and the Black Sea region. Large present-day cities such as Paris, Turin, Budapest, and Ankara were all founded by the Celts. The remainder bear names like Gallia, as present-day France was called during Roman times, Galicia in Northern Spain, or Galatia in present-day Turkey. The latter was populated by the so-called Galatians,

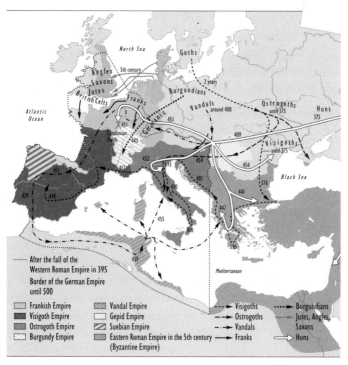

Figure 14 Euro-Mediterranean migration in the 4th and 5th centuries

or Celts, to whom St. Paul wrote one of his famous "epistles."

Ancient city-states in the Mediterranean region expanded in a different manner. They channeled their population growth by founding cities along the Mediterranean coast. Phoenician migrants founded Carthage, that later became Rome's most important rival in the Western Mediterranean. Today, Carthage is a suburb of Tunis. Greek settlers founded cities such as Syracuse in Sicily, Marseille, and Lisbon (see Chapter 2). Such colonization became necessary once local populations exceeded

certain limits, set by food and water supplies that the surrounding landscape of a particular city could provide.

Within the Roman Empire, production and shipping of food
as well as channeling of water via aqueducts was so well organized that growing populations in Rome – where the number of
inhabitants may have peaked at 700,000 – and other large cities,
were able to be fed, with no one having to leave. Nonetheless, the
Romans continued establishing cities and garrisons and securing
control over conquered territories. At the same time distribution
of land and the settling of veteran legionaries were used as a
retirement plan.

Despite this, not all migration in the ancient world was voluntary. Locals often had to flee from intruding foreign armies and
nomadic tribes. There were also deportations: Sargon of Akkad
founded the first territorial state in Mesopotamia. Chronicles
report that he resettled entire Bedouin tribes from the northern
border of his empire and gave them new pastures in the southern
part of Mesopotamia. Mass deportations took place in the Neo-
Assyrian Empire from 900 BC that affected tens of thousands of
people. Such an incident is mentioned in the Bible. The "Second
Book of Chronicles" speaks of a "Babylonian imprisonment of
Jews." It began in 586 BC with the seizure of Jerusalem by troops
of the Babylonia King Nebuchadnezzar II. In 19th century Italy,
the famous composer Giuseppe Verdi used the story for his opera
"Nabucco."

Actually, only a relatively small number of people were
affected by the famous "Babylonian exile," namely members
of the Jewish upper class. Among those kidnapped were the
prophets Daniel and Ezekiel as well as King Jehoiakim himself.
It was during the Babylonian exile that Jewish priests and schol-
ars finally emphasized the singularity of the Jewish faith. The
Torah became a central focus and the monotheistic faith centered

on Jahveh was established. The Babylonian exile thus became a most influential era in the emergence of the Jewish religion. Many centuries later in Mesopotamia, the Babylonian Talmud was developed in a strikingly similar setting. Second only to the Bible, it became an important source of Jewish theology.

Germanic, Slavic, and Asiatic "tribal" migrations

During late antiquity, Germanic tribes migrated to the Mediterranean region, the Black Sea region, and Western Europe. They were partly enemies and rivals of Rome, and partly integrated into the Roman Empire. Some were employed as mercenaries; others were tolerated as settlers and allies. The loss of internal military strength increasingly forced the Roman Empire to rely on such allies. Entire tribes were settled on the borders of the Roman Empire as confederates to create "buffer zones" against foreign enemies.

With the decline of the Western Roman military and administrative structures, the Germanic tribes established their own rule in various territories. This included the Crimea (Ostrogoths), Upper Italy (Ostrogoths, Langobards), present-day France (Franks), England (Angles, Saxons, Jutes, Danes), Spain (Vandals, Visigoths), and North Africa (Vandals). These "tribes" did not, however, exclusively involve communities of the same lineage or even homogenous ethnic groups. The so-called tribes were rather groups sharing loyalty, military organization, and social structures. They could fluctuate considerably in size and composition, and they were mostly composed of completely different ethnic groups and linguistic communities. The roving "Ostrogoths," for example, were actually a community of "real" Goths, Huns, Gepids, Persian-speaking Sarmathes, and Alans.

This also applied to other "tribes" during the period of the great migrations. In that sense, the names of some of these "tribes" are telling: Alemans (all men), Franks (free men), Saxons (people using a particular axe), Norsemen (men of the north).

Shortly after the fall of the Western Roman Empire, from the 6th century onwards, Slavic tribes first settled in Eastern Europe. They also migrated to present-day Greece and the Balkans, ruled at the time by the Byzantine Empire; and finally into many parts of Central Europe abandoned by Germanic tribes and Roman authorities. Slavic settlement stretched from the Elbe river and the Baltic Sea through Central Europe to the Adriatic and the Black Sea.

During this period of history, nomads on horseback edged forward from Central Asia to Europe and Asia Minor. In the 5th century, the Huns and Avars arrived in the Danube basin. During the 7th century, the Proto-Bulgarians – an ethnic group of Turkish origin – reached the Balkans from the Volga region. Between the 8th and the 10th centuries, the Hungarians came from the central Urals and finally settled in the Carpathian basin. Different groups of Turkish origin moved to Western Asia and present-day Turkey. Another group of horse-riding nomads first expanded their territory from the Arabian peninsula into eastern and then western Mediterranean regions; the Arabs had already crossed the Straits of Gibraltar during the 8th century, and had established Moorish control over the Iberian Peninsula.

All of these cases – from the invasion of Germanic tribes and Asian equestrian nomads in late antiquity to the proliferation of Arabs in the Mediterranean region and to Mesopotamia – had something in common: a mix of conquest and settlement migration. Yet only a few tens of thousands of people at most participated in each of these conquests.

The final immigrants to Europe in the Middle Ages were the

Ottoman Turks. Their forefathers also originally came from Central Asia. They expanded their sphere of influence from Anatolia to the Balkans. Then, in 1453, they conquered Constantinople, and larger parts of southeastern Europe soon thereafter. As a result, the Ottoman Empire became an influential European power. Bosnia and Bulgaria remained under Turkish control until 1878, and Albania and Kosovo even until 1912–1913. As a result, nation-states in the Balkan region – including Greece – generally established modern statehood during the 19th century as a way of emancipating themselves from the Ottomans.

What became of the conquerors and conquered?

In many cases, conquests and colonization meant that the language and culture of the immigrants became dominant. The integration of Iberia, Gaul, and Dacia into the Roman Empire as well as the settlement of Roman colonists led to a romanization of the resident majority population. This is why Spanish, Portuguese, French, Romanians and Moldavans amongst others, speak Roman languages today.

At times, newcomers suppressed the majority of the local populations. After the Angles and Saxons migrated to England, many British Celts fled to Wales, Cornwall, Scotland, and across the Channel to Brittany, which received its present-day name at that time. Celts remaining on the British Isles were later anglicized to a large extent. Today, only a minority of the Welsh, Scots, and Irish still speak a language that was once widely used from the Atlantic to the Black Sea and beyond: Gaelic. The same is true for French Bretons.

In other cases, the conquerors established themselves as the political and military elite; yet they assimilated with the majority of the conquered population when it came to language and culture. A small upper class of Germanic Langobards in Northern Italy became Romanized Lombards. The Francs dominated in Gallia. Their rule also led to a romanization of the Germanic upper class. A similar fate befell the Scandinavian Norsemen, who conquered the northwestern part of France that still bears their name: Normandy. There, the Norsemen became French speaking Christians. The Turkish-speaking Bulgarians were even forced by their own rulers (khans) to assimilate with the Slavic majority when they introduced a European-style feudal system in the country they had conquered.

Only rarely did the conquerors of Late Antiquity and the Middle Ages establish themselves as a small ruling elite that did not assimilate and was able to cling onto its own culture as a predominant minority. The Swedes in Finland are the most important example. Romanized Normans who conquered England in 1066 also retained their adopted language – French – during the Middle Ages.

The Modern Era: Europe's colonial and demographic expansion

Since the beginning of early modern times, migration was characterized by overseas military and economic expansion of European naval powers. This was triggered by the discovery of a seaway to India by Bartolomëu Diaz, who sailed to the Cape of Good Hope in 1488, and by Vasco da Gama, who reached the Indian coastline in 1497. Christopher Columbus' journey to America in 1492 was also instrumental. He actually meant to go to China and India and, at first, believed that he had in fact reached India. Based on this error – which Columbus recognized before the end of his life – the indigenous peoples of North and

South America are still referred to as "Indians." Following these events, Spain and Portugal were given Pope Alexander VI's blessing in the Treaty of Tordesillas (1494) to divide the known and unknown world between them. The Netherlands, England, and France largely ignored the Treaty of Tordesillas in competing efforts to establish their own colonies in North America, Africa, Asia, and Oceania.

During early modern times, the nature of this expansion was primarily of a military and economic nature. Under protection of their homeland fleets, a small number of European pioneers and adventurers established "footholds:" trading posts, fortified ports, garrisons, and plantations. Many of them hoped for rapid wealth and a subsequent return to Europe. In present-day northeastern USA, however, a number of settlers – religious zealots who intended to lead their lives as free citizens – already established permanent communities in the early 17th century. These so-called Pilgrim Fathers became pioneers of the pan-European emigration movement that started some 150 years later.

It was only from the mid-18th century onwards that the European expansion led to proper settlement colonization at a larger scale, changing the composition of the prevailing populations. Before this, Europe's colonial powers had already "shipped" slaves from West Africa to the Americas as well as the Caribbean. They were to replace the rapidly dwindling numbers of indigenous manpower. This resulted in approximately 11–12 million people arriving in America as slaves between the 17th and the 19th centuries. These people of Western African origins are the ancestors of today's Afro-American populations in Brazil, the Caribbean, and the USA. A further two million Africans at the time were shipped as slaves to the Arab world.

From 1750 onwards, Europe's population started to grow at increasing pace (Chapter 3). This unprecedented growth became the demographic basis for the mass emigration that set in at the end of the 18th century. Significantly improved means of transportation – especially the invention of rapid clipper sailing ships, steam ships, and the establishment of railway lines – were the other prerequisite. In the end, the Industrial Revolution also altered the nature of the migrations. Agrarian settlers became less important than laborers for overseas mining and manufacturing.

In contrast to the migration of tribes marking the transition from Late Antiquity to the early Middle Ages, European overseas migration did not involve entire populations but individuals and families. Many Europeans emigrated for religious or political reasons. This especially applied to various Protestant groups, in particular to religious dissenters and members of so-called "free churches." Furthermore, Jews experiencing discrimination or persecution in Central and Eastern Europe tried to escape their fate. Finally, liberals and exponents of the European left, including several prominent figures involved in the revolution of 1848, left Europe for good, often in an attempt to save their lives. Some later had great careers in the USA. Carl Schurz, for example, was born in the German Rhineland. In 1848–1849, he participated in the uprising against Prussian rule. During the American Civil War (1861–1865), he became a general in the Union's army. He was later elected to the US senate, and finally became Secretary of the Interior in the administration of the US President R. B. Hayes. Most migrants were, however, motivated by economic reasons. Emigration was the only chance for many Europeans to escape poverty, a shortage of arable land, and restrictions imposed by the guilds.

Migrations motivated by intolerance and persecution also played a role in intra-European migration. Since early modern times, hundreds of thousands of affiliates of ethnic or religious minorities were persecuted and eventually fled abroad. In the

16th century, Jews and Moors had to leave Spain and Portugal. Many of them sought refuge in the Netherlands and in the Ottoman Empire. In the 17th century, French Huguenots found exile in Prussia, as did Protestants from Habsburg territories in the 18th century. In the 19th and early 20th centuries, Eastern European Jews had to flee Tsarist Russia, including present-day Ukraine, present-day Poland, and the Baltic States.

These migrations had significant demographic consequences, regardless of their predominant motivation. In North America and the Caribbean, in parts of South America, and in Australia, indigenous peoples were either wiped out, eradicated by infectious diseases contracted through contact with colonizers or ousted from their original habitats by European settlers. This is why the term "Indian" today is often associated with inhabitants of inhospitable territories in southwestern USA or with hunter-gatherers in the Brazilian rainforest. The fact that advanced Indian civilizations – such as the Aztecs, Incas, Mayas, Olmecs – existed prior to European colonial expansion is hardly rooted in western cultural memory.

Today, the descendants of European immigrants and African slaves represent the demographic majority in most parts of North and South America as well as the Caribbean. In Australia and New Zealand, the majority of the population is also of European origin. The same applies to Siberia, northern Kazakhstan, and the northern part of the Asian Far East, where Russians and migrants from other parts of Europe settled between the 18th and the 20th centuries. Some Europeans even used this route to settle in Alaska, which Russia eventually sold to the USA in 1867.

Settlement colonization also took place in southern Africa, in the Maghreb, and, from the beginning of the 20th century onwards, in Palestine. In former Rhodesia (present-day Zambia and Zimbabwe) as well as South Africa, Angola, Mozambique, and Namibia, European settlers and their descendants dominated both politically and economically. Nonetheless, they remained a demographic minority. In Algeria, almost all European settlers and their descendants had to leave the country when it gained independence from France in 1962 (Treaty of Évian) following a bloody colonial war.

In contrast to North and South America, Australia, New Zealand, and southern Africa, European settlers did not play a significant role in other territories dominated by European colonial powers. In Western and Central Africa, East Africa, South and Southeast Asia as well as in the Pacific and parts of the Caribbean, colonial presence was restricted to soldiers, administrative officers and a small class of entrepreneurs, plantation owners, and adventurers.

Intra-European migration between the Industrial Revolution and the Great Depression

With industrialization came modern forms of labor migration. Migrants found work in trade and manufacturing. Sooner or later, many of them started their own businesses. Intra-European migration gained momentum from 1850 onwards.

The 19th century saw the onset of a substantial wave of migration to the new centers of coal mining and industrial steel production. These included the British Midlands, French Lorraine, and the German Ruhr region, as well as some industrialized areas in Bohemia and Switzerland. At the same time, mass migration within only a few decades turned several European capitals into cities with well over a million inhabitants – including London, Paris, Berlin, Vienna, and Budapest (Chapter 6). Many people regarded moving to one of these economically and culturally prosperous metropolises as an alternative to emigrating overseas.

Labor migration within Europe and immigration to the USA generally slowed down during and immediately after World War I. The main reason for this was that most nation-states – including traditional immigration countries like the USA – began to restrict immigration step by step from the turn of the 20th century onwards. In Central Europe as well as in the Balkans, the build-up of new nation-states reduced the mobility that had been possible within the German, Austro-Hungarian, and the Ottoman Empires. The end of the 1920s saw the onset of the Great Depression, which eventually led to national labor markets in Europe being completely sealed off.

Deportation, forced migration, and "ethnic cleansing"

Global migration reached a historical peak during the 20th century. For a large part, it involved involuntary migration: forced migration, expulsion, or a state-enforced exchange of populations. In Europe, at least sixty million people were forced to leave their countries or regions of origin because of their ethnic descent or their religion over the course of the 20th century – partially as a result of deportation, "ethnic cleansing," and attempted genocide. Forced migration and expulsion was, for example, triggered by World War I (Armenian massacres in Ottoman Turkey); the Russian October Revolution of 1917 (1.5 million refugees); and the Turkish–Greek war of 1922. In the 1923 peace treaty of Lausanne, the Turkish victors and the defeated Greeks – who had started the war – agreed to a large-scale population exchange based on religious criteria. Approximately 1.5 million Greek-Orthodox Christians from Turkey were expelled and resettled in Greece while some 450,000 Greek Muslims had to leave for Turkey. The United Kingdom and France gave this treaty their blessing.

Forced migration and expulsion, collective resettlement, deportation, and forced labor dominated Europe during the period of National Socialism, Stalinism and World War II. In sum, the Nazi regime forced nearly twelve million people from occupied parts of Europe to work in German agriculture and manufacturing. With the large majority of working-age German and Austrian men serving in the army, forced labor became the backbone of Nazi Germany's wartime economy. In certain cases, deportation and forced labor were linked to genocide. This was especially true for Jews as well as Sinti and Roma in Central and Eastern Europe. Six million people perished in concentration camps or became victims of genocide in territories occupied by Germany. A large number of people fell victim to Stalinist deportations inside the Soviet Union. In the end, approximately twenty million Soviet citizens were internally displaced. To a large extent this affected members of ethnic minorities, such as Crimean Tatars, Chechens and Ingushetians, Volga Germans, ethnic Poles, Estonians, and Latvians.

The new political order following World War II was also based on large-scale displacement, forced migration, and mass expulsion. Millions of people were displaced during the immediate postwar period. In Europe, this primarily affected twelve million Germans living in Central and Southeastern European countries (Czechoslovakia, Hungary, Poland, Romania, Yugoslavia) as well as ethnic Germans living in a few other countries. At the same time, 1.5 million Poles as well as hundreds of thousands of Ukrainians, Italians, and Hungarians were subjected to state-sponsored resettlement into territories of their own countries recently cleansed of their former inhabitants. These measures also largely took place with the blessing or even upon the orders of the victorious Allies.

Outside Europe, the foundation of India and Pakistan in 1947 led to the involuntary migration of an enormous number of people. Estimates speak of eleven million expelled Muslims, Hindus, and Sikhs. The same applies to the foundation of the state of Israel in 1948. This led to the forced migration and expulsion of 800,000 Palestinians as well as of 1.5 million Jews leaving Arab states and Iran from the late 1940s to the 1970s.

Mass exoduses from Communist countries took place on several occasions between 1949 and 1990: from the German Democratic Republic (East Germany, 1949–1961, 1989), Hungary (1956), Cuba (several years), Poland (1956, 1980–1981), Czechoslovakia (1968), and Vietnam (1975–1980). In 1949–1950, after Chiang Kai-shek had lost the Chinese civil war and fled with his army to Taiwan, he was followed by a large number of civilians. Bulgaria tried to force ethnic Turks and other Muslims to assimilate; its government set two waves of mass migration in the direction of Turkey – one in 1950 and the other between the mid-1980s and 1990 – that were partly voluntary and partly forced. During the 1970s and 1980s, the Ceauşescu regime "sold" tens of thousands of Romania's German-speaking citizens to the Federal Republic of Germany. The collapse of Communist regimes in the Balkans also led to mass migrations to Western countries: this was the case in Bulgaria (1989–1990), Romania (1990–1992), and Albania (after 1990). During the Cold War, such migrants were recognized by Western governments as political refugees, although economic considerations played an important role for many of those who left. Since 1990, persons leaving Central and Eastern Europe no longer qualify as political refugees.

In the late 20th and early 21st centuries, civil wars and violent political conflicts in Afghanistan, Bosnia, Kosovo, Iraq, Rwanda,

Sudan, and Chechnya resulted in substantial displacement and refugee flows.

Only a small minority of the refugees and expellees of the 20th century were later able to return to their former home countries. Most remained abroad permanently; many lived in refugee camps for years and sometimes even for decades. The UN High Commissioner for Refugees (UNHCR) estimated that there were ten million international refugees at the start of 2008, and the number is currently on the rise. Today, the majority of people recognized as refugees live in poor countries. Moreover, there are the many millions of Palestinian refugees who do not fall under the mandate of the UNHCR.

In the past, the most important host countries for refugees were Iran, Pakistan, Germany, the USA, and several Central and East African countries. The conflicts in Iraq and Darfur have led to Chad, Syria, and Jordan becoming countries hosting new refugee populations.

Between 1989 and 2007, approximately 7.6 million applications for asylum were submitted in Western and Central Europe. Since the end of the Cold War, there has been a clear tendency in Western countries to no longer automatically recognize asylum seekers and victims of civil war as political refugees. In many cases, asylum seekers are turned away or given only temporary protection. In contrast, the number of refugees accepted in the poorer countries of Asia and Africa has dramatically increased since the 1980s. Poorer countries that are located in the neighborhood of violent conflicts therefore carry the main burden presented by refugees.

Internally displaced persons also belong to the category of involuntary migrants. In 2008, more than twenty-five million (end of 2007) had to move to another part of their own country out of fear for their lives. Most of them were victims of civil

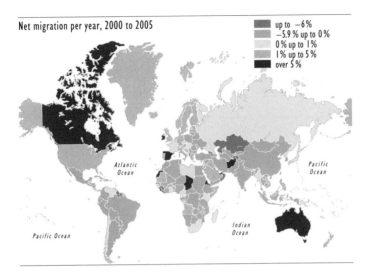

Net migration per year, 2000 to 2005

- up to −6%
- −5.9% up to 0%
- 0% up to 1%
- 1% up to 5%
- over 5%

Atlantic Ocean

Pacific Ocean

Indian Ocean

Pacific Ocean

Figure I5 Immigration and emigration countries, 2000–2005
Source: UN Population Division 2006; authors' estimates for Russia and South Africa

wars. The people involved are frequently members of ethnic or religious minorities or sympathizers of repressed factions, and they are often members of a civilian population that is being terrorized or collectively held hostage by one of the parties involved.

Decolonization and postcolonial migration

Immigration from other world regions is a quite recent phenomenon in modern Europe. In quantitative terms, it did not play a role before the late 1950s and 1960s. In the cases of the United Kingdom, France, the Netherlands, and later also Portugal, this was caused by decolonization. Following the end of European colonial rule in Africa, the Middle East, South and Southeast

Asia, and the Caribbean, many millions of former settlers of European origin as well as civil servants and soldiers who had worked for the colonial administrations remigrated to their respective homelands. In some cases, the migration of "white" settlers was explicitly or implicitly part of the agreements between former colonial powers and the newly independent nation-states. The Évian treaty between France and the Algerian liberation movement FLN (1962), for example, comprised an agreement on the complete resettlement of approximately one million Algerians of European origin – the so-called "Pieds-Noirs" – to their French "motherland." The return migration of five million ethnic Russians from Central Asia, the Caucasus, and the Baltic states to Russia, which has taken place since the 1980s, may also be interpreted as a consequence related to a process of decolonization.

Among the "colonial" return-migrants were many who had never lived in their respective European "motherlands." In addition, many locals from former colonies also migrated to Europe. Great Britain became the destination mainly for Indians, Pakistanis, Bangladeshis, and Anglo-Caribbeans; France received Algerians, Tunisians, Moroccans, as well as Vietnamese and West Africans. Christian and Muslim Indonesians as well as Surinamese and Dutch Antilleans went to the Netherlands. In the 1970s and 1980s, Angolans, Mozambicans, and Cape Verdeans migrated to Portugal in larger numbers. They all came to Europe in search of work and better educational opportunities for their children. Many also wanted to flee civil wars and political repression in their countries of origin. Many of these conflicts had started in the period following decolonization. To a certain extent, this migration was also promoted by Western Europe's increasing demand for less qualified labor.

Postcolonial migrations were initially facilitated by former "mother countries" allotting citizenship to the inhabitants of their former overseas regions or at least giving them priority to enter. It was also helpful for these migrants that they already spoke English, French, Dutch, or Portuguese. New ethnic minorities thus emerged in the former colonial powers, and today their presence marks the cityscapes of the large metropolises of Western Europe. These minorities, nevertheless, continue to encounter difficulties in their social and economic integration. In many places, immigrants from former colonial areas of the "Third World" find themselves at the lowest social stratum in the "First World" of today.

Labor migration

Systematic labor recruitment already took place under colonial auspices. Within the British Empire, Indians were brought from South Asia to work in Mauritius, East Africa and South Africa, the Caribbean, Guyana, and the Fiji Islands from the 19th century onwards. In Southeast Asia, both the British and the Dutch recruited larger numbers of Chinese laborers to support the rapidly growing plantation economy.

In North America, labor recruitment also started during the 19th century. Chinese were brought to the western parts of the USA and Canada. They were hired as construction workers on the transcontinental railroad lines and as lumberjacks. Later, manual labor mainly came from Mexico. Between 1942 and 1964, Mexicans were recruited on a temporary basis within the so-called Bracero Program. In contrast to regular immigrants, these laborers were not expected to settle permanently in the United States. Since 1964, irregular migrants to the USA mainly come from Mexico, the Caribbean, and South America. Over eight million were able to legalize their status between 1986 and 1989. According to a 2008 estimate, ten to thirteen million irregular labor migrants were living in the United States of America; mainly workers from Mexico and other Latin American countries, but also a growing number of Asians.

In Europe, France and Switzerland have a tradition of recruiting foreign workers that goes back to the 19th century. During the late 1950s and 1960s, other Western European countries – including Belgium, Germany, and Austria – began to recruit unskilled labor abroad. At that time, the most important countries of origin were: Italy, Spain, Portugal, Greece, Turkey, Morocco, Tunisia, and later Yugoslavia. In addition, there was considerable Finnish immigration to Sweden, Irish to Britain, and Austrian to Switzerland and Germany.

Between the late 1950s and the early 1970s, most migrant workers in Europe eventually returned to their home countries. A sizeable minority, however, remained and established themselves in northwestern Europe. Today, Europe is confronted with new minorities resulting from that period of labor migration. The recruitment stop at the beginning of the 1970s provided an important turning point. Switzerland initiated the halt in 1972; Germany and Austria followed in 1973–1974. In those years, the wealthier countries of Western Europe wanted to signal "we don't need you any more;" and "please go home." Many labor migrants chose to read the signal in opposite terms: though the labor market had become less favorable, it was better not to go back home as a later return to Europe would prove difficult.

The end of immigrant recruitment shifted the focus from labor to family reunion. Those who were determined to stay on in Western Europe now encouraged their spouses and children to join them. This was initially seen as a process that would soon be completed. The opposite was true. Younger immigrants often only started families in their destination countries – although usually with partners from their region of origin and from their extended family network. The same applies to the children of immigrants. They, too, often seek partners from their parents' home countries, ethnic groups, and family networks. Or their parents arrange a marriage by choosing an "appropriate" partner from their community. As a consequence, family migration continues until today. In many European countries, this now is the most important means of entry for legal immigrants. It could also be said that many use the option of marriage and family migration because they have no other legal options.

The process of family reunion and marriage migration confronted many European countries with the lack of social and economic integration of immigrants. The degree to which immigrants and their children are able and willing to learn the language of the receiving country and to accept the values of liberal democracies became issues of political debates. Several EU states – for example, Austria, Denmark, Germany, and the Netherlands – introduced mandatory language and integration courses for new immigrants.

Today, labor migration also takes place outside Europe and North America. The oil-producing Gulf States recruit labor migrants from other parts of the Middle East, and from South and Southeast Asia. People from neighboring countries migrate to South Africa in large numbers. Within Southeast Asia, Malaysia and Singapore have become the most important destination countries. In the South American context, people from poorer countries in the Andes primarily move to Brazil and Argentina.

Political refugees and ethnically privileged migrants

Between 1949 and 1990, a particular form of European east-west migration resulted from the ideological division of Europe and the Cold War. Citizens of Communist countries attempted to reach the West in considerable numbers. The largest migration flows were recorded between East and West Germany. In 1961, the German Democratic Republic closed the last gap in the Iron Curtain by building the Berlin Wall. In other Central and Eastern European countries, crisis years of Communist dictatorship led to spontaneous mass emigration: from Hungary in 1956, Czechoslovakia in 1968, Poland in 1980–1981, and the German Democratic Republic in 1989–1990. Until 1990, immigrants from countries behind the Iron Curtain were usually recognized as political refugees by Western Europe and the USA. At that time, economic motives that may have played a role in the decision to leave a Communist country were not used as an argument against granting political asylum. East-West migration was of a magnitude that seemed manageable at the time; and Western politicians often welcomed these refugee flows as they publicly demonstrated the superiority of Western democracies and market economies.

It was only after the fall of the Iron Curtain that immigration and the stream of asylum seekers became controversial. Instead of dwindling down after the fall of Communism, the numbers of European east-west migrants rose. On the one hand, travel restrictions had been abolished, giving citizens of Central and Eastern Europe an opportunity to travel and even seek employment in Western countries. On the other hand, political transformation after 1989 led to crises and the outbreak of violent ethnic conflicts. This was particularly the case in Bosnia, Croatia, Chechnya, and Kosovo. Since the early 1990s, large numbers of asylum seekers have also come from Afghanistan, Iraq, Iran, Turkey, and more recently from different African countries.

Western European countries reacted to this influx by reinstating visa requirements for neighboring non-EU countries as well as tightening their asylum laws. In addition, the EU and Schengen member states began to cooperate on asylum and visa issues. As a reaction, people now arrive in growing numbers by boat at the shores of Spain (Canary Islands), Italy (Sicily, Lampedusa), Malta, and Greece.

Some states have special immigrant programs or at least preferential treatment for members of their "own" co-ethnic or religious diaspora. The best-known example is Israel: all persons of Jewish descent or Jewish faith have the right to immigrate and also bring their non-Jewish family members. Between 1948 and 2006, some three million people made use of this right. There are also a considerable number of migrants in Europe whose ethnic affiliation gave them the right to immigrate to a particular European country. The largest group is ethnic Germans who remained in Poland, Romania, and the Soviet Union after 1945. They and their non-German family members were given the right to settle in Germany in great numbers (1950–2008: 4.6 million people). Since the 1990s, however, Germany has been trying to curb this migration.

Many other countries also offer privileged access to certain groups. Greece welcomes Pontian Greeks from Eastern Europe and the Black Sea region; Hungary accepts ethnic Hungarians from Transylvania, Serbian Vojvodina, and western Ukraine as immigrants; Poland welcomes ethnic Poles from Lithuania, Ukraine, and Belarus; Serbia admits ethnic Serbs from Croatia, Bosnia, and Kosovo; Croatia welcomes ethnic Croats, especially those from Bosnia and Serbia; and Turkey welcomes ethnic Turks and other Muslims from Bulgaria and Greece. During the 1990s, Russia accepted citizens from other Soviet successor states as immigrants. Between 1990 and 2000, approximately five million people made use of this provision, the majority of whom were ethnic Russians.

Irregular migration to Europe

Since the late 1980s, irregular migration in Europe has gained a quantitative momentum. The most important countries of origin were Poland, Romania, Moldavia, the Ukraine, and Albania, as well as Morocco and Tunisia, and some West African and Latin American countries. The trigger for this migration was the fall of the Iron Curtain, cheap transportation, and the emergence of a new smuggling industry. In addition, the evolution and spread of informal labor markets in Western Europe as well as the economic boom in southern Europe played a decisive role.

Irregular migrants find work in agriculture and construction as well as in hotels and restaurants. Others find work as household helpers, nannies, and care-givers. In many regions, locals are no longer willing to work for the mediocre wages paid in these branches of the economy. In other regions there is simply not enough local labor available. Several European countries – notably Belgium, Greece, Italy, Portugal, and Spain – reacted to this influx of irregular labor with "amnesty" programs carried out at a wide scale. In total between 1995 and 2008, some 3.5 million irregular migrants received work and residence permits in the EU and Switzerland as a result of such programs.

At the same time, EU enlargement in 2004 and 2007 automatically led to the legalization of hundreds of thousands of Poles, Romanians, Slovaks, etc. who had already lived and worked in the "old" EU member states before EU accession of their home country. Countries such as the United Kingdom, Ireland, and Sweden immediately opened their labor markets to these new EU citizens; Finland, France, Greece, Italy, and Spain did so in 2006–7. In contrast, Austria and Germany grant these EU citizens access to residence, but not to legal employment.

Elite migration – retirement migration

In the past decades, economic globalization and the internationalization of educational systems have led to many more managers, specialists, researchers, and students moving from one country to another or being placed by their companies. For most researchers and students, the first country of choice is the USA. At the same time, the number of foreign students at European universities is rising. The number of American, European and Asian transnational companies that are doing business in more than one country is also on the rise – with staff prepared to work in various countries during their careers.

Elite migration also partially includes tax evaders who deliberately settle in places where the tax rate is low or portions of the income or assets do not have to be declared.

In the USA, retirement migration has a long tradition. Those involved in this type of migration usually move to Florida, Southern California, Arizona, or New Mexico. Mild winter and spring seasons are the most important factor determining the choice of destination. In Europe, retirement migration is also of growing importance. Until now, the main destinations have been the coastal regions of the western Mediterranean and the Iberian Peninsula. Retired persons mainly from the United Kingdom, Germany, the Netherlands, and Scandinavia settle in these areas. Greece has seen a much smaller influx of retirees to date. In contrast, Turkey's southern coast has recently seen a rise in numbers. In the meantime, this type of "retirement migration" has been widening in scope, stretching as far as Sri Lanka and even Indonesia. Mobile American pensioners are internal migrants within their own country whereas North European pensioners have to go to other states.

A growing number of retired people engage in a kind of seasonal migration, recalling a traditional type of seasonal commuting between lower winter residences and higher or cooler summer residences. In other cases, people do not migrate for climatic reasons but because of their own migrant background. Some former labor migrants return to their countries of origin. This comprises retired persons, but also a growing number of individuals who become professionally active in their countries of origin – or their parents' former home countries.

Global migration in the 20th and early 21st centuries

Settlement colonization – the taking of arable land in order to establish farms, villages, and cities – was a typical form of migration until the mid-19th century. Currently, politically motivated and often violent settlement colonization no longer plays a significant role. Among the few exceptions are Jewish settlements on the Golan Heights and the West Bank; large-scale resettlement of Javanese people on other Indonesian islands; and the resettlement of Han Chinese in regions like Tibet and Xinjiang. Instead, the 20th and early 21st centuries have been dominated by other forms of migration: namely labor migration, family reunion, ethnic migration, migration for educational purposes, state-sponsored resettlement, and forced migration triggered by civil wars, violence, "ethnic cleansing" or ecological disasters.

Year	World (millions)	High income countries* (millions)	Share (in %)	Low and middle-income countries (millions)	Share (in %)
1960	75	32	43	43	57
1970	81	38	47	43	53
1980	99	47	47	52	53
1990†	120	56	47	64	53
1995†	165	95	58	70	42
2000	177	105	59	72	41
2005	191	116	61	75	39

Table 12 Total number and geographic distribution of international migrants, 1960–2005

Source: United Nations Population Division (2006): International Migration Database
*Europe, North America, Australia, New Zealand, Japan, Soviet Union/CIS.
†Since 1991, the dissolution of the former Soviet Union, former Yugoslavia, and Czechoslovakia has led to an increase in the number of international migrants, because internal migrants from earlier periods suddenly became international migrants.

Demographers working for the UN Population Division estimate that there were seventy-five million international migrants in the early 1960s. At that time, they represented 2.5% of world population. Their share of the population was 3.4% in industrialized countries and 2.1% in less developed countries. In absolute numbers, more international migrants and refugees lived in the Third World than in rich countries of the Northern hemisphere. On the one hand, this was the result of large refugee flows related to post-colonial nation-building in Asia and Africa, such as Palestine/Israel, India/Pakistan. On the other hand, this reflected a historical situation in which Europe was a region of emigration while, between 1921 and 1965, US immigration

	World	High-income countries*	Low and middle-income countries
1960	2.5	3.4	2.1
1970	2.2	3.6	1.6
1980	2.3	4.2	1.6
1990†	2.3	4.3	1.8
1995†	2.9	8.1	1.6
2000	2.9	8.8	1.5
2005	2.9	9.5	1.4

Table 13 International migrants as a percentage of the total population,
1960–2005

*Europe, North America, Australia, New Zealand, Japan, Soviet Union/CIS.
†The dissolution of the former Soviet Union, former Yugoslavia and
Czechoslovakia led to a rise in international migrants following 1990, because
internal migrants from an earlier period subsequently became international
migrants.
Source: United Nations/Population Division (2006): International Migration
Database

policies were quite restrictive, leading to a decline of its foreign-
born population.

Until 1990, the global population grew faster than the number
of international migrants while their geographic distribution
shifted from poorer to richer countries. In 1990, there were 120
million international migrants – some 2.3% of world population. Their share of the population was 4.3% in industrialized
countries and 1.2% in less developed countries.

After 1990, the number of international migrants rose quickly.
We must distinguish two different reasons for this increase. On
the one hand, far more people have changed their country of
residence during the last two decades – some voluntarily, others
forced by prevailing circumstances. Among the latter were ethno-
political conflicts and civil wars – such as in Afghanistan, Burma,

Region	Immigrants (million)	Share of total population (in %)	Distribution across world regions (in %)
Africa	17	1.9	9
Asia	53	1.4	29
Europe	64	8.8	32
Latin America and Caribbean	7	1.2	3
North America	44	13.5	23
Australia/Pacific	5	15.2	3
Total	191	2.9	100

Table 14 Absolute number, share and regional distribution of
international migrants, 2005

Bosnia, Chechnya, Iraq, Kosovo, Lebanon, Rwanda, and Sudan.
At the same time, the fall of Communist regimes and the dis-
mantling of the Iron Curtain led to more East-West migration
while rising commodity prices increased the demand for skilled
and unskilled workers in oil and gas exporting countries. The
main destinations for international migration were Western
Europe, North America (USA, Canada), the Gulf States, and
Russia, but also countries in the neighborhood of conflict zones
– for example Chad, Iran, Jordan, Pakistan, and Syria.

On the other hand, to a certain degree the rise in numbers
of international migrants was a statistical artifact. Since 1991,
the collapse of the former Soviet Union, former Yugoslavia, and
Czechoslovakia automatically led to rising numbers of international migrants. By establishing new international borders,
the twenty-four new nation states in Europe and Central Asia
defined many people as international migrants who had previously simply been internally mobile Soviet, Czechoslovak,
or Yugoslav citizens. For some of them, this turned out to be

not just a "statistical effect" but a change of status with material consequences. People became stateless overnight because they belonged to the "wrong" ethnic group: among these were hundreds of thousands of ethnic Russians, who had moved to Estonia and Latvia during Soviet times; and also tens of thousands of Roma who had lived in countries like the Czech Republic and Slovenia for a long time. As a consequence, they lost their civic and political rights. Other former internal migrants became minorities in their own country. Some were treated as "unwanted people" or encouraged to emigrate.

Today, more than 190 million people live outside their countries of birth. They account for 3% of the world population. Of these international migrants, 116 million live in industrialized countries representing one-tenth of the total population (2005: 9.5%). In less developed countries, an estimated seventy-five million people are international migrants, constituting only 1.4% of the total population. Many of them are refugees and displaced persons.

Over one-third of all international migrants live in Europe (34%). Two poles of attraction can be identified on this continent: more than one-fifth of all international migrants live in one of the twenty-seven EU member states (22%), notably in the EU states in northwestern and southern Europe. The second major pole of attraction in Europe is Russia, where some 8% of all international migrants reside. There, the early 1990s saw an influx mainly of ethnic Russians from other successor states of the former Soviet Union. Since 1998, immigration has been dominated by migrant labor coming from Ukraine, Central Asia, and the Caucasus. The number of Chinese living in Russia is also growing.

More than one-quarter of all international immigrants (28%) live in Asia, mainly in the Gulf States, in India, and in East and

Southeast Asian "tiger states," which include South Korea, Hong Kong, Taiwan, Malaysia, and Singapore. These are the most important destination countries for labor migrants from poorer Asian countries. Israel is dominated by Jewish immigration, but also recruits migrant labor from Southeast Asia. The number of migrants is also high in the vicinity of two large-scale political conflict zones: Afghanistan and Iraq. A total of 6–7 million Afghans live as refugees in Pakistan, Iran, and Uzbekistan. And in recent years, more than two million Iraqi citizens have moved to neighboring countries such as Iran, Jordan, and Syria.

Almost one-quarter of all migrants (23%) live in North America. The USA is by far the most important single destination country. It is home to a fifth (20%) of all international migrants. Canada (3%) plays a smaller role. Other important international migration destinations are Australia and New Zealand, Brazil, South Africa, Libya, and several West African states. Beyond this, civil wars and ethnic violence have led to large refugee populations in different parts of Africa.

According to the International Labor Organization, more than half of all international migrants participate in the labor force of their new country of residence.

Migrants in traditional immigration countries

For the past 150–200 years, population censuses in the USA, Canada, and Australia have collected information about immigrants, their numbers, and origins. This allows for an analysis of changes in immigration covering a longer period of time.

International Migration

International migration is a specific form of spatial mobility. By definition, both the place of origin and the destination of the migrants are located in different countries. This distinguishes international migrants from internal migrants. Only persons who leave their country for a minimum or unspecified period of time – sometimes for good – are included in this category. The UN suggests a minimum period of twelve months. According to this definition, tourists, commuters with a workplace in a neighboring country who return home on a daily or weekly basis, and expatriates working in another country for a short-term period are not considered to be international migrants.

In fact, the definition of international migrants differs from country to country. In Germany, migration statistics include persons who remain in the country for three or more months. In Switzerland, only persons who remain in the country for at least twelve months are counted as immigrants. In the USA, students and temporary labor migrants can remain in the country for many years without being officially counted as immigrants. In several Asian, African, and Latin American countries, immigrants and emigrants are not documented as such in official statistics. Many countries lack population registers that would allow distinguishing between native-born and foreign-born residents. Others – like the UK, Ireland, and many developing countries – have no population register at all, which makes migration statistics even less reliable. These are reasons why it is impossible to specify the exact number of international migrants at a global scale. UN population experts came up with a figure of 191 million international migrants in 2005. Obviously, this is an estimate.

International migration not only depends on distance between places of origin and destination. On the one hand, a change of domicile, even over a short distance, falls into the category of international migration if there is an international boundary in between. On the other hand, migration over thousands of miles does not count as international migration if it takes place within the same country; for example, from the east coast to the west coast of the USA, or from Vladivostok to Moscow. Whatever the distance, crossing an international border is of relevance as migrants become foreigners in the destination country and therefore have fewer rights. The question of citizenship is therefore always closely related to international migration. Today, the decision to leave one country and to settle in another one is usually not an irreversible decision. Today, migrants who leave their countries of origin for good are a minority. This not only includes seasonal laborers and other labor migrants who regularly return to their countries of origin. Even individuals who migrate with a long-term perspective may return to their home country.

USA

In the 19th and early 20th centuries, North America was the main destination for Europeans migrating overseas. Between 1820 and 1920, a total of thirty-one million immigrants arrived in the USA. A long period of restrictive migration policies lowered the number and share of the immigrant population in the USA during the first half of the 20th century.

In 1950, 10.1 million people born abroad lived in the USA (7% of total population). Of these, almost all had come from Europe. By 1970, the number of immigrants further decreased to 9.6 million and its share of the total population fell below 5%. After that time, fundamental changes in US immigration law started to show their long-term effects. The new immigration law enacted in 1965 made it much easier for citizens of non-European countries to acquire the so-called "Green Card." Since then, immigration to the USA has mainly taken place from Latin America, and increasingly also from Asia. And the number of immigrants rose significantly. In 2008, almost forty million legal and irregular migrants lived in the USA. This is a share of 13% of the total US population. In absolute terms, the immigrant population quadrupled between 1965 and 2008.

Canada

Between 1820 and the 1920s, about seven million people immigrated to Canada. During the latter half of the 20th century, the number of immigrants in Canada rose continuously: from 2.1 million (15% of total population) in 1951 to 6.5 million (20% of total population) in 2008. Between 1951 and 2008, Canada's immigrant population tripled in absolute terms. At the same time, its composition changed significantly. Until the 1950s, almost all Canadians were of European stock. Since then, the share of Asian, North African, and Latin American immigrants and their children has increased considerably. Today, Canada recruits a proportion of its immigrants with the help of a points system. Potential migrants interested in working and living in Canada are assessed according to age, language, skills, etc. The aim is to test how well they might "fit" into the Canadian economy and society as a whole. Applicants meeting the required minimal number of points are accepted as immigrants and given a residence permit.

Australia

From the 18th century onwards, Britain deported convicted criminals to Australia. Later, this country became a destination for immigrants from all parts of Europe. Between 1800 and the 1920s, some four million people came to Australia. Immigration dropped during the 1930s and World War II, however, and in 1945 only 9% of Australia's total population was foreign-born. Since then, their absolute number and relative size has been on the rise again: from 1.0 million (12%) in 1951 to 4.0 million (24%) in 1991. Since then, the immigrant population has remained stable, while its share is sinking as the total population continues to grow (2007: 4.2 million; 21%).

Until 1973, Australia almost exclusively admitted persons of "European origin" as immigrants. The elimination of these restrictions immediately led to increased immigration from Asia. Australia also employs a point system to recruit some of its immigrants.

Europe – the new immigration continent

Until the 1950s, Europe was the most important source of inter-national migration. Between 1750 and 1960 some 70 million Europeans had left for good. In 1950, only 3.8 million foreign immigrants lived in the western part of Europe. The majority of these foreigners were labor migrants. Many of them had been recruited by France and Switzerland. Large numbers of foreign troops stationed in Europe did not count as migrant populations. Post-war expellees, displaced persons, and some refugees were also not included in these figures.

Only since the mid-1960s has there been more immigration to Europe than emigration of Europeans to overseas destinations. Since then, the size and share of the foreign-born population has increased considerably: first in Western Europe, later in Southern Europe, and most recently in parts of Central and Eastern Europe as well. Since the 1990s, Russia has become an important destination for international migrants, especially for people from other successor states of the former Soviet Union.

Today, almost 510 million people live in the EU-27, Norway, and Switzerland. Among these are some forty-four million people who live outside their country of birth. One-third of them have come from one EU member state to another. Two-thirds have come from non-EU countries. These figures are partly based on estimates, as some European countries do not distinguish in any detailed way between native-born and foreign-born residents, but only between their own nationals, citizens of other EU countries and third country nationals.

In sum, the absolute number of immigrants is larger in Western and Central Europe than in the USA. If, however, migration between EU member states is not taken into account, then the USA continues to be the most important destination country. In a way, migration between EU member states can be seen as equivalent to internal mobility within the USA. Nonetheless, there is a significant difference: a person migrating from New York to California remains a US citizen. Yet a person migrating from Romania to Italy or from Poland to the UK remains an EU

citizen but is, at the same time, a foreigner with restricted political rights. Persons emigrating to the EU from third countries
have even fewer rights.

In the past few decades, Germany has been Western and
Central Europe's most important destination country. Today,
some 10.1 million immigrants live here. After the USA and
Russia, this is the third largest immigrant population in the
world. Other important destination countries in Europe are:
France (6.5 million), Great Britain (5.4 million), Spain (4.8
million), and Italy (2.5 million). In a few other countries, the
foreign-born population is also of a considerable size: Switzerland (1.7 million), the Netherlands (1.6 million), Austria (1.3
million), Sweden (1.1 million), and Greece (1.0 million).

On average, Europe's immigrant population is about 8.7%
of the total population. The share of immigrants is largest in
small countries such as Luxembourg (37%), and Liechtenstein
(34%). Next is Switzerland, where one in four residents (23%)
is foreign-born. Significantly above the European average are
also Austria (15%), Ireland (14%), Sweden (12%), Germany
(12%), and Spain (11%). Cyprus is a special case. Since 1974,
the northern and eastern parts of the island have been occupied
by Turkish armed forces. In the meantime in Northern Cyprus,
settlers from Anatolia together with Turkish troops and civilian
personnel make up more than 50% of the total population. Con-
currently, there has been substantial immigration to the Greek
southern part of the island.

The Baltic States also represent an atypical case. Latvia (20%)
and Estonia (15%) have relatively large foreign-born populations. Yet most people now classified as migrants came to the
Baltics during Soviet times. They were internal migrants and,
like the ethnic Estonian and Latvian population, citizens of the
Soviet Union. These people only became international migrants

as a result of the collapse of the Soviet Union and the foundation
of independent states in the Baltic region. The majority of them
became foreigners in a country that was no longer their own.

Europe and North America compared

Traditional immigration countries – namely the USA, Canada,
Australia, and New Zealand, and historically also Argentina,
Chile, Brazil, and other Latin American countries – differ
from European nation-states in one important point: the overwhelming majority of their populations has consisted of immigrants and their descendants since the 19th century. Immigrants
during the 17th, 18th, and 19th centuries are now seen as "pioneers" who founded and built these nations. And most people
born in traditional immigration countries refer to their ancestors
as successful immigrants. This is not the case in Europe, and this
is the main reason why citizens of Britain, France and Germany
do not view these countries as "immigration countries" despite
the fact that their populations include as many immigrants as
Canada or Australia.

It is therefore the share of immigrants rather than their absolute number that draws a line between "immigration countries"
and countries that do not see themselves that way. In the context
of large-scale migration this has substantial consequences.

It is obviously more difficult for immigrants to integrate into
a society that defines itself as descent-based. By the same token,
integration is somewhat easier in societies that accept different ethnic, religious, and cultural backgrounds as part of their
national identity. This is one of the reasons immigrants in many
European countries experience above-average rates of unemployment, occupy lower socio-economic positions, are paid less,

and have inferior housing conditions compared to the majority of locals. Some of these disadvantages are passed on to the next generation. In Europe, children of immigrants have fewer chances of becoming upwardly mobile. Not all of this, however, can be attributed to a lack of socio-economic integration. It is also the result of a certain form of adverse selection. Australia, Canada, and the USA attract highly skilled migrants; Europe – at least in the past – attracted semi-skilled and unskilled migrants.

Today, the clearest indication of the low level of integration of immigrants is the fact that significant numbers of residents have lived in an EU country for many years while remaining foreign citizens. In some EU countries, naturalization rates are either low or declining. As a result, more than half of all immigrants in Europe – an estimated twenty-four million – retain the citizenship of their country of origin. This means that these migrants are subject to the laws and taxation of the country in which they are resident. Yet as foreigners they are not represented in the political process.

In Europe – depending on the country – between 3% and 20% of the population are excluded from political representation. At the local level, the share is often higher. Conversely, many states grant their citizens living abroad the right to vote, even though many of these voters are only marginally affected by the consequences of legislation in their country of origin.

The situation is different in the USA, Canada, and Australia. In these societies, social mobility for migrants is higher. On average, individuals settling in traditional immigration countries are economically more successful than those coming to Europe. In the USA, Canada, and Australia, immigrants can apply for citizenship after three to five years of residence. Nonetheless, it usually takes longer even in these traditional immigration countries before people decide to apply for naturalization. Changing citizenship is a highly symbolic act touching on one's personal and political identity. Some people are reluctant to make such a decision. Others prefer to retain their old citizenship even after becoming citizens of the destination country. As a result, the number of dual citizens is on the rise.

Without any doubt, traditional immigration countries are more attractive destinations for many potential migrants than the wealthy European countries. This especially applies to qualified, upwardly mobile, and highly motivated migrants. This means that the EU and its member states are in a less favorable position regarding global competition for talent and skills. As a consequence, Europe attracts many fewer highly skilled immigrants than the USA, Canada, and Australia. And these migrants are less likely to be successful, as they, on average, bring less "human capital" with them than those moving to North America and Australia.

Prospects for the 21st century

Annual population growth in the USA is about three million people, and two million in the European Union. Immigration is responsible for 40% of US growth and more than 80% of EU growth. In Russia, annual population decline is one million people. Without immigration, that loss would be almost twice as high. These figures highlight the importance of international migration for the future of aging societies in the Northern hemisphere. Most of them report more immigration than emigration. As a result, their populations not only turn "gray" because of demographic aging. Immigration, at the same time, makes them more "diverse" at ethnic, cultural, and religious levels. This inevitably leads to questions of identity and belonging.

From a legal perspective, this is a matter of citizenship defining political rights and responsibilities. At the societal level, the main question is the following: which common values, rules, and perspectives will immigrants of completely different backgrounds and native-borns be able to share? Predominantly Christian societies in Europe and North America now have growing Muslim, Hindu, and Buddhist minorities which will continue to increase. At the same time, terrorist attacks by Muslim extremists in New York, London, and Madrid as well as occasional calls for jihad against all non-believers have led to skepticism towards immigrants with non-Christian backgrounds.

What does immigration mean for cultural identity in Europe and America and for both natives' and immigrants' sense of civic belonging? Unlike the USA and Canada, most European societies do not have national identities that include both natives and immigrants. Rather, the "foreigners" who come to Europe are seen as challenging national identity. At the same time, integration is more narrowly defined in Europe than in North America. An immigrant can easily become an "American" during the course of his/her life, but becoming a European does not happen as easily.

During the 21st century, we can expect more immigration. There are several reasons for this:

First, demographic aging in rich countries will continue. A growing number of countries will also experience a decline in native populations. In a few countries, this decline has already begun. Others will follow.

Low birth rates today will lead to fewer people leaving the educational system and entering the labor market in the future. Sooner or later, this translates into a lack of younger, qualified labor. At the same time, the demand for skilled labor and for personal services – especially in the health care system – will grow. It is therefore most likely that the European Union and its member states will switch from a restrictive to a pro-active migration policy.

Second, there are regions in Europe and North America with poorer, but youthful and rapidly growing populations. In North Africa and the Middle East as well as in Latin America and the Caribbean, the number of people of working age will continue to grow for a few more decades. Even larger increases can be expected in sub-Saharan Africa and South Asia. All these regions will continue to serve as a pool for potential migrants. Many of them will continue looking for opportunities in Europe and the USA regardless of whether or not they are welcome. It is unlikely that the USA and Europe will be able to counter this determination with only higher fences and stricter controls at external borders.

Third, in the future we will most likely encounter a growing number of so-called "environmental refugees" in addition to political refugees and expellees. Global warming will result in rising sea levels, dislodging people from coastal zones likely to be most affected. Climate change will also lead to an expansion of deserts as well as to the salinization of formerly fertile and arable land. Without any doubt, ecological degradation and the flooding of habitats will lead to higher numbers of internally displaced people and international migrants. To date, there is no appropriate legal framework for dealing with persons whose habitats have been destroyed by environmental degradation or rising sea levels.

6 Urbanization and Migration from Rural to Urban Areas

"A sunny midsummer day. There was such a thing sometimes, even in Coketown. Seen from a distance in such weather, Coketown lay shrouded in a haze of its own, which appeared impervious to the sun's rays. You only knew the town was there, because you knew there could have been no such sulky blotch upon the prospect without a town. A blur of soot and smoke, now confusedly tending this way, now that way, now aspiring to the vault of heaven, now murkily creeping along the earth, as the wind rose and fell, or changed its quarter: a dense formless jumble, with sheets of cross light in it, that showed nothing but masses of darkness ... The whole town seemed to be frying in oil. There was a stifling smell of hot oil every where."

This was how Charles Dickens described a 19th-century British industrial town in his novel *Hard Times*. In Europe, such towns now belong to the past, but not in China or India.

In 2008, for the first time in history, more people lived in cities than in rural areas. Around 1950, the share of urban dwellers was just below 30%. This trend is even more striking in absolute terms. In the mid-20th century, an estimated 730 million people lived in urban areas. Today, this figure has more than quadrupled: to 3.4 billion people.

In 1950, six out of ten urban dwellers lived in rich countries. Today, almost three out of four live in low- and middle-income countries; among them, a rapidly rising number resides in large cities. In 2004, 411 cities already had more than one million inhabitants.

Not all cities offer equal living conditions. Those who have ever been stuck during rush hour in Beijing (China), Karachi (Pakistan), or Mumbai (India) and have felt the impact of the local microclimate on their respiratory systems, understand Charles Dickens best.

In 1950, larger cities in more developed countries were still a mix of industrial locations and service centers that provided a plethora of social, commercial, and cultural opportunities. These cities, however, did not offer their inhabitants much living space per capita. Yet people living in rural areas also had little space. When a farmers' family had five children, and possibly also servants living under the same roof, even a larger house did not provide very much space for each individual.

Today, inhabitants of European and North American cities have twice the amount of living space as in 1950. And outside the cities, living spaces even for the lower middle classes are – from a historical perspective – almost luxurious.

The city in history

The first cities in history emerged about 7000–7500 years ago in the Middle East: Eridu, Jericho, Hamoukar, Mari, Uruk (see Chapter 2). They were centers of political power, hubs for early long-distance trading and sites of social, political and economic innovation. In comparison to today, they were sparsely populated and the areas covered by urban dwellings were not very large. Compared to the total population of the Middle East, only a small number of people lived in cities at that time. Nonetheless, the foundation of cities had overarching effects: they played a paramount role in the emergence of more productive societies without which the past millennia would not have seen such powerful population growth.

Three stages of urban development

Urban development took place in a number of stages. In Europe, the first stage was primary urbanization during the Middle Ages. The first medieval towns emerged as relatively small, fortified places whose inhabitants were mainly merchants and craftsmen. These cities became strategic centers of communication in societies in which aristocratic landowners had the political say. Cities became nodes within larger societies, and a social structure and character of their own emerged. Moreover, the capital and residence cities served as political steering centers. During primary urbanization, the populations of European cities remained limited. Agrarian societies produced only minor surpluses. They would not have been able to feed millions of city-dwellers. Added to that, a lack of transport infrastructure meant that it was impossible to bring large quantities of food to the cities.

At the end of the Middle Ages, one-tenth of the European population at most lived in cities. This share was higher in northern and central parts of Italy. From the High Middle Ages onwards, this was the most prosperous region in Europe and the world. The urban population concentrated in cities like Genoa, Florence, Milan, and Venice already made up 18% of Italy's total population. At the same time, in England, only 4% of the population lived in cities.

Over the next few centuries the situation changed radically. This is evident when comparing the same countries. By the mid-19th century, Italy had become one of the poorer regions in Europe. The economic center had shifted to the northwestern part of Europe already before the onset of the Industrial Revolution. In Italy in the 1850s, the share of the urban population was only 13%. In contrast, 40% of the populations of the United Kingdom and the Netherlands already lived in cities. A new period of urban growth had started – it was linked to industrialization. The same is true for North America.

Europe's and North America's large industrial cities emerged in the course of secondary urbanization. The character of these cities changed considerably. Within a few decades, large cities with several hundred thousand inhabitants emerged. Over the course of the 19th century, the capital cities of the European great powers – London, Paris, Berlin, Vienna, Budapest, and St. Petersburg – as well as New York and Chicago evolved into cities with more than one million inhabitants. In the 20th century, the metropolitan regions of London, Paris, Moscow, New York, and Los Angeles exceeded the ten million mark.

Steady population inflows from the surrounding areas of core cities and from remote peripheries, were the main demographic drivers for this growth. Another element of urban expansion was the administrative incorporation of growing suburbs into the old core cities. Many cities became metropolitan regions at that time. During secondary urbanization, cities exploded because they and their immediate surroundings became the centers of modern industrial production, and these industrial centers urbanized. The best examples of this are the English Midlands, the German Ruhr area and the metropolitan area of New York including parts of New Jersey. The people living in the rapidly growing agglomerations could now be supplied with food and other goods.

The prerequisite for this development was a significant

increase in agricultural productivity. In Roman times as well as during the Middle Ages, eight to nine agrarian producers were necessary to feed one urban dweller. In 1800, England's farmers were already producing enough food for themselves as well as for one additional non-farmer. Today, farmers in developed countries only represent 3–5% of total population. This development created the demographic potential for migration from rural peripheries into urban agglomerations.

However, cities hosted very different if complementary strata. They emerged as a common habitat for aristocratic and bourgeois upper classes, the middle class and the industrial proletariat. Europe's and North America's metropolises thus also became centers of political conflict. In turn, a host of literary and political critics of urban life emerged who linked all alleged and actual problems of modern life to big cities: from anonymity and loneliness through an uprooted existence to criminality and alcoholism. Since the second half of the 19th century a counter-image of the "idyllic country life" has emerged, a way of living previously viewed as destitute and characterized by hard work and poverty.

A new urban age has since begun. Post-industrial urbanization is fundamentally different from primary and secondary urbanization. Its most important characteristic is suburbanization. Inhabitants of large cities tend to leave the urban core and move to the surrounding areas even though the cities remain highly attractive as labor markets and commercial and cultural centers. The surrounding areas of bigger cities became prime destinations for young families and affluent urban classes. From there, people commute to work. There are at least two different causes for this process. Suburbanization, on the one hand, is linked to the search for affordable living space because housing is cheaper at the periphery than in city centers in most metropolitan

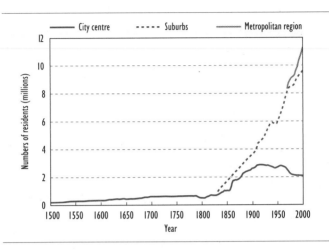

Figure 16 Population of Paris (in millions), 1500–2000

regions. On the other hand, many people want to live in a green, if not bucolic environment. The price for both is increasing time spent in commuting, as decently paid jobs usually do not move to suburban residential areas.

In early modern times, urban life was the exception. Most people lived and worked in the countryside. This continues to be the case in many poor countries of the world. In developed societies, however, the urban way of life has become the norm for society at large. This starts with the way people dress, eat or travel, but it is also reflected in today's family structures. Modernity in Europe and North America primarily organized itself as networks of urban centers that transformed and finally dominated previously agrarian societies.

Population density was very high in the cities of the Middle Ages and early modern times. This resulted in very limited living space for urban inhabitants, especially when taking into account that town houses at the time had far fewer storeys. Within the walls of an average European city, population density was in the range of 35,000 persons per km². In some cities, population density was even higher. Urban living conditions mainly meant terrible hygienic conditions, the risk of infection, and a danger of contracting epidemic diseases such as the plague and cholera. In 1740, more than one-third of London's children died within their first year. In Vienna, the share of newborns not surviving the first year was around 50% in 1790 and increased to 62% in 1800. Life expectancy in larger cities was even lower than that in surrounding rural areas, which itself was not impressively high. At the time, urban life included a kind of "mortality penalty."

During the course of the Industrial Revolution, immigration caused these conditions to worsen. As a result, some migrants moved to surrounding communities instead of settling in traditionally densely populated districts. For the same reason, affluent urban citizens also moved to newly developed suburbs. Because of prevailing westerly winds in Europe, suburbs primarily populated by the upper and upper-middle classes emerged to the west of densely populated city centers. Examples include Kensington and Chelsea (London), Neuilly and the 16th *arrondissement* (Paris), Dahlem and Grunewald (Berlin), and Rózsadomb (Budapest).

Large cities are dependent on migrants

Cities have always depended on their attractiveness – even if a number of today's megacities in the Third World are, presumably transient, exceptions (see below). No large city would have reached its present-day size without immigration. And without further immigration, most metropolises would immediately start to shrink, as most cities in Europe, North America, and East Asia register more deaths than births. The same now applies to several European and Asian countries as a whole. This clearly has to do with the fact that urban behavioral patterns and family forms have spread to the peripheries.

In the 19th and early 20th centuries, Europe's emerging metropolises were mainly populated by internal migrants from the agrarian peripheries moving to the economic and adminstrative centers located in bigger cities. Those emigrating to overseas destinations populated the emerging metropolises of North and South America. Since the mid-20th century, in contrast, large European and North American cities have mainly been a destination for immigrants from economically less developed countries. The consequences can be seen in the composition of present-day urban populations. Today, international migrants and their children make up 20–50% of the total population in Western Europe's and North America's urban agglomerations.

It is possible to speak of an urban demographic paradox. Despite originally unfavorable living conditions, cities in the Northern hemisphere became centers of attraction for a growing number of people from the 19th century onwards. At first, modern societies with their employment opportunities, communications structures, political participation, and a differentiated social stratification only existed in cities. This is why *civitas* in modern languages became *cité*, *città*, and *city*. Today, though, *citoyen*, *cittadino*, and *citizen* not only refer to inhabitants of a city but also of a country. This reminds us that citizens enfranchised with political rights at first existed in European cities, while the majority of rural dwellers were subjects of their landlords until the late 18th or early 19th centuries. Until 1865 in the USA, there was a similar difference between free citizens of European descent and enslaved African-Americans.

In Europe, relatively small, narrow and enormously over-crowded medieval towns evolved into comparatively large but almost as overcrowded industrial cities. This development spread across the Atlantic. During the late 19th and 20th centuries, some of these cities developed into today's large metropolises of the northern hemisphere. They no longer play host to industrial production but are now advanced service economies, many with central government functions. In Europe and the Americas, some 70% of the total population live in urban areas. Such a degree of urbanization marks the end of this development. In developed countries, the large majority of people now live in cities and their surrounding suburban areas. In Europe and North America, this development has driven the demographic transition from high to low mortality and fertility. Behavioral patterns of the urban middle classes have become universal patterns.

The final stage of demographic transition can best be witnessed in the big cities of Europe, North America, and East Asia. Almost all of them register more deaths than births. These cities are therefore losing native-born inhabitants. This is intensified by rapid suburbanization and urban sprawl, in which young locals move to surrounding areas and other nearby regions.

The picture therefore changes when analyzing urban and suburban regions as a whole. In Europe and North America, most agglomerations are gaining in population. In the meantime, a geographic "expansion" of the city that goes beyond suburbanization. This is particularly taking place along the east and west coasts of the USA, and in densely populated parts of Britain, Germany, the Netherlands, and Switzerland. Large urbanized regions with multiple centers are emerging.

Garden Cities

Today, we tend to view urban planning and the management of urban space as bureaucratic and technical affairs. Both are closely linked to decisions taken by politicians, private developers, and public administrations. Their origins tend to be forgotten. During its beginnings, urban planning was conceived as "spatial policy." Its promoters saw such planning as a contribution to social reform based on ideas of how living space would influence people's minds and behavior. Several theoreticians linked urban development to reformist or even revolutionary concepts. This is clearly the case in some classical utopias of early modern times. Thomas More (1478–1535) and Tommaso Campanella (1568–1639) designed their ideal societies as urban societies. They were inspired by Plato's Polis and the urban societies of antiquity. However, we should not overlook the fact that both Mores' "Utopia," and Campanella's "City of the Sun" even more so, contained totalitarian elements.

In 1898, Ebenezer Howard – a stenographer working for the British parliament – published his "Garden Cities of Tomorrow." His diagnosis read: "It's wellnigh universally agreed by men of all parties, not only in England, but all over Europe and America and our colonies, that it is deeply to be deplored that the people should continue to stream into the already over-crowded cities, and should thus further deplete the country districts." In his view, an analysis of this development was "not necessary." Instead, he came up with the metaphor of "magnets" attracting urban dwellers.

The fact that cities attracted rural populations in large numbers was evident to contemporary observers. Howard concluded that this attraction would have to be balanced with an even stronger "magnet." His aim was to end a situation in which "this unholy, unnatural separation of society and nature endures. Town and country must be married, and out of this joyous union will spring a new hope, a new life, a new civilisation."

Howard's answer was formulated as the "garden city" project, in which he designed a reformed society "en miniature." For him, this project was not just about urban planning. He wanted a society that fulfilled the "long dampened striving for a more beautiful and noble life, not in heaven but here on Earth. (…) The means by which these objects are to be achieved being a healthy, natural, and economic combination of town and country life, and this on land owned by the municipality." Howard saw the downsizing of big cities as the only solution to all urban deficits. For him, the upper limit for a viable city was 250,000 inhabitants. At the same time, Howard's garden city was to be economically self-sustainable. Less than three decades later, the French architect, urban planner and theoretician Le Corbusier was already planning new cities for three million people.

Howard's projects did materialize, although not exactly in the way he envisaged. The town of Welwyn is a half-hour journey from London's King's Cross Station. Letchworth can be reached by continuing on the same line a bit further. To the impartial eye, both towns – one would characterize them rather as suburbs – show no characteristics that fundamentally distinguish them from other suburban centers surrounding London today. If anything, they are somewhat more generously endowed with green space. And yet these two towns were the first results of a large-scale social reform project, the popular garden city movement. The development of Letchworth began in 1903, with Welwyn following in 1918. The piecemeal incorporation of this originally radical movement soon became evident. At the end of World War I, the British government promised housing for demobilized soldiers as part of a program called "Homes for Heroes."

The "New Townsmen" movement initiated by Howard thereupon asked for financial assistance to develop 100 garden cities. The new homes, however, were not built in newly founded garden cities but at the edge of London and other British cities. Yet according to the garden city idea, this was where they least belonged. Thus, the two model cities – Letchworth and Welwyn – did not evolve into the nucleuses of a future society living in self-sustained small towns, but instead into unostentatious suburbs of London with just a bit more green space between the family homes.

Urbanization in developing and newly industrialized countries

Urban development in the Third World has taken a different course where the situation today in large cities partially recalls the state of many European and North American cities during the Industrial Revolution. Primary and secondary urbanization processes that have taken place since the mid-20th century can be observed alongside one another in Asia, Africa, and Latin America. An apparently unstoppable spread of the economic and cultural model of the Western world is rapidly changing everyday life in these cities. The local elite and middle classes are quick to adopt urban life styles and patterns common in the wealthy "North."

However, growth in the cities of the "South" is curbed by low agricultural productivity. In China, farmers and agricultural laborers make up two-thirds of the workforce; this proportion is even larger in countries like Bangladesh, Ethiopia and Uganda. In India, farmers make up a somewhat smaller percentage of the population. Nevertheless, social and cultural change in these countries primarily takes place in the metropolises.

Urbanization is increasing in low and middle-income countries. In 1950, the share of the urban population in these areas was 18%. In 2005, this share was already 43%. Altogether, the cities of low- and middle-income countries hosted 2.3 billion people. Even in the group of the poorest countries the number of people living in urban agglomerations between 1950 and 2005 grew from 15 to over 200 million people, now representing 27% of total population.

Conversely, this means that three out of four people still live in rural peripheries in the poorest countries in the world. There, isolated subsistence farming continues to be a reality for a larger part of the agrarian population. In many places, this

City	1970 millions	2005 millions	Growth 2005-1970 in %
Tokyo	23.3	35.3	+52
Mexico City	8.8	18.7	+114
New York	16.2	18.7	+16
São Paulo	7.6	18.3	+141
Mumbai (Bombay)	5.8	18.2	+213
Delhi	3.5	15.1	+326
Kolkatta (Calcutta)	6.9	14.3	+106
Buenos Aires	8.1	12.6	+55
Shanghai	7.1	14.5	+106
Karachi	3.1	11.6	+270
Los Angeles	8.4	12.3	+47
Dhaka	1.4	12.6	+815

Table 16 Megacities 1975, 2005 (for the total agglomeration)

Source: United Nations (2007): "Population Growth in Selected Megacities, in Millions (1975; 2005)"

farming takes place under deteriorating economic and ecological conditions.

Many decide to leave this way of life behind and move to larger cities. Urban societies in developing countries have to bear the consequences. In Africa, Latin America, and South Asia almost half of the urban population live in slums. These slums paradoxically seem to offer more appealing living conditions than the surrounding rural peripheries. People move there with hopes for higher income, access to medical services, and generally a better life.

Indeed, average incomes of urban dwellers in Asia, Africa, and Latin America are higher than those of the rural populations. Yet only few migrants from the agrarian peripheries immediately find well-paid work in the modern industrial or service sectors.

At first, many remain unemployed or start with low-paid work in the informal sector. This forces newcomers into the slums at the edges of Third World cities. Over time, many immigrants do, however, succeed in obtaining better-paid positions in modern sectors of the economy. Their upward mobility and the related rise in income serve as a model to be emulated by people in their respective home regions, thereby attracting more immigrants.

From the countryside to the urban world of the slums

Almost two-thirds of urban populations in Africa live in slums. Their proportion continues to rise. In contrast, "only" 40% of urban dwellers in Asia live in slums. Latin America belongs to the highly urbanized part of the world. Even here, over 30% of the urban population lives in slums. As the global urban population is growing rapidly, the absolute number of slum dwellers is rising as well.

Today, a total of more than a billion people live in slums. This is almost one-sixth of the world's population. It is estimated that at the beginning of the 21st century, 72 out of 100 new households in middle and low-income countries are created in slums. The consequences are visible in many parts of the world. Today, the share of slum dwellers in cities like Kinshasa, Cairo, Ankara or Bogotá already reaches 60%. In Addis Ababa, Casablanca, and Mumbai this percentage is even higher.

In Europe and North America, the term "slum" refers to run-down neighborhoods with cheap apartments and poor or socially marginalized inhabitants. Living in a real slum – also termed *favela*, *bidonville*, *shanty town*, or *geçekondu* – means a hut made of cardboard, corrugated iron, or plywood with only a few square meters of space; cow pats might be drying outside as the inhabitants cannot afford any other heating materials. The dwellings are usually built single-handedly.

In many low and middle-income countries, urban renewal programs to date have not led to the disappearance of slums. Efforts to improve living conditions by upgrading the infrastructure have usually attracted new migrants to settle there. Yet this led to a vicious circle. The continued influx quickly overstretched the upgraded infrastructure. Urban planning and development policies often employ administrative means to curb the influx of migrants entering major cities. To be effective on a permanent basis, these countries need to adopt other strategies. They would have to increase opportunities in rural regions, create jobs in those locations, and invest in infrastructure. Making rural areas more attractive could remove the central causes behind large-scale migration to urban centers.

Rapid urbanization in many developing countries has only slightly improved the living conditions of millions of slum dwellers. In the short-term, it has brought about many new problems. Unlike in 19th-century Europe, the urbanization process in most developing countries took place at a pace with which local industrial production, labor markets, and the urban infrastructure could not keep up. This led to a significant rise in marginalized populations living in urban agglomerations. The rapid expansion of the slums allows the development sketched here to become especially palpable. These usually unplanned settlements mostly do not offer their inhabitants any public infrastructure. Frequently, these areas lack running water, sewage systems, garbage collection, schools, and hospitals. In many cases, connections to other parts of the respective cities via public transport are poor or non-existent.

Bad living conditions negatively affect the health of the inhabitants, and a lack of jobs promotes crime, alcoholism, and prostitution. Cities such as Lagos (Nigeria) are among the least secure places in the world. Johannesburg in well-off South Africa is also notorious in this respect – even more so than neighboring Soweto. The Soweto "township" originally emerged as a slum for black locals and immigrants who were needed during Apartheid as cheap labor but not permitted to settle or even spend the night in Johannesburg.

Even under very restrictive conditions, new identities emerged in the cities of the "Third World." While the British colonial power and private investors spurred mining in southern Africa during the interwar period, new cities emerged in the former Rhodesia – present-day Zambia and Zimbabwe. Black laborers came here from all parts of the region. Living conditions were frequently very poor. A new phenomenon soon manifested itself alongside crime and alcohol. New rituals emerged, such as the "Kalela dance" – which later became famous among anthropologists. Networks and social structures emerged around the dance which took on some specific ethnic characteristics. Initially, anthropologists assumed that the black laborers were members of old "tribes." It only later became clear that they came from entirely different regions. In other words, spontaneous new identity groups were formed. In a situation where old value systems were lost, new structures, solidarity, and self-help activities began to emerge. The white masters, however, were not particularly pleased about this development.

Global urbanization

In some regions, particular geographic features led to a high degree of urbanization. This was understandably the case in city-states such as Hong Kong, Singapore, and Djibouti. Yet it also applied to countries dominated by deserts restricting human settlements to a few places, such as Libya, Saudi Arabia, or Iraq. There are, however, also countries that have reached a high level of urbanization which cannot be explained by geographic particularities. Argentina (90%), Venezuela (87%), and South Korea (80%) have a similar degree of urbanization as the USA (81%), Britain (90%), and Germany (88%). As a world region, Latin America – with three-quarters of its population living in cities – has almost the same degree of urbanization as Europe and North America.

World region	Proportion of urban population (in %)	Proportion of rural population (in %)
Western Europe	80	20
North America	79	21
Latin America	76	24
West Asia	65	35
East Asia	43	57
Southeast Asia	38	62
Sub-Saharan Africa	34	66
South Asia	30	70

Table 17 Urbanization in selected world regions (in %), 2004

Source: PRB (2006)

In contrast, most African, South Asian, and Southeast Asian countries still have a strong rural population base. In these regions, only every third person lives in a city. In South Asia, the share of the urban population is 30%, in sub-Saharan Africa it is 35%, and in Southeast Asia 38%. UN projections assume that this will most likely change over the next decades. It is expected that by 2025 more than half the populations of Asia and Africa will be urban dwellers.

Figure 17 The 20 most populous urban agglomerations in the world, 2004
        Source: World Gazeteer
        Illustration: Mike Shibas

Megacities and global cities

In the 20th and early 21st centuries, one specific form of urbanization has been the emergence of megacities; these are defined
as large urban agglomerations with more than ten million
inhabitants. Today, almost 300 million people live in cities with
more than ten million inhabitants. In 1950, New York was the
only megacity in the world. In the early 21st century, there were
already twenty such large agglomerations, of which fifteen are
in developing countries. In 2015, there will be at least twenty-six
megacities.

Over the past decades, it has mainly been the urban

agglomerations of Asia and Africa that have grown dispropor-
tionately into megacities. The population of Lagos, for example,
grew from less than 300,000 inhabitants in 1950 to over ten million
in 2005. This was a thirty-four-fold growth within just over a
half century. The oil boom in Nigeria definitely contributed to
this growth. Dhaka, the capital of Bangladesh, grew thirty-fold
during the same period. Other present-day large cities – such as
Shenzhen in southern China – did not even exist in 1950.

The largest European metropolitan region in Western Europe
is Greater Paris with over eleven million inhabitants (Fig. 17). Yet
metropolitan Paris only occupies the 19th place in the 2005 large
city ranking. In Europe, Moscow's metropolitan area has more
inhabitants, with twelve million people in 2005. In the meantime,
some experts assume that because of heavy illegal immigration
from neighboring countries, Moscow now has fourteen million
inhabitants.

Present-day megacities in industrialized as well as developing
countries are not dependent on their immediate hinterland. This
distinguishes them from cities during medieval or early modern
times. They work together and – at the same time – compete
with each other globally. This division of labor was enabled by
global transportation facilities, rapid information sharing, the
availability of food and relatively cheap energy. In this sense,
metropolises are not only centers of regional or national integration but junctions in a globalization that has several layers,
one of them being globalized urban societies.

In Europe and East Asia, because of low fertility, large cities
mainly grew through immigration from rural peripheries. In contrast, urban growth in most emerging and developing countries
is the result of both immigration from rural areas and an urban
surplus of births. The latter contribute between 20% and 50%
to urban population growth. The more important contribution

to population growth in the megacities of developing countries, however, comes from migration. It explains 50% to 80% of this growth. During the past two decades, the largest migration movement from rural to urban areas was the internal movement of some 200 million Chinese who have left the hinterland for the coastal cities of East and South China.

Incentives to migrate to the city

In addition to presumed job opportunities, there are other reasons to move to larger cities. In many parts of the world, health care and education tend to be better in cities than in the countryside. The opportunities for sending children to a good school or university are significantly better in bigger cities than in rural regions and small towns. Young migrants also have other motivations. They leave rural areas not least for social reasons. Many of them want to escape social control within a village or an extended kinship network. Young adults rather enjoy the anonymity of urban space as traditional family ties are increasingly seen as restrictive. Modernization processes and the spread of non-traditional living arrangements via mass media contribute to this perception. Better education and the opportunity to earn money through gainful employment also play a role. The "promise" held by cities contains hope for upward mobility, less social control, and the chance to connect to modern civilization.

National policies have fostered large discrepancies between living conditions in cities and those in rural areas. Undoubtedly, the preference for cities has to do with the fact that this is where the political and economic elites live and fits closely with their desire to improve their own living conditions. Moreover, cities were and are focal points of social modernization. The political stability of many developing countries and the survival of the elite in power are more dependent on populations of the large cities, and especially on capital cities. The rural population is less organized and less often well politically engaged. Yet when the urban masses demonstrate in Manila, Kathmandu, or Kiev, governments do sometimes fall. The political elites of some countries therefore decide to move the capital to a newly-established town inhabited by hand-picked bureaucrats. Burma's new capital Naypyidaw, which replaced Rangoon, is the most recent example.

The global population of the future will mainly be an urban population, even if "urban" may not have quite the same meaning as in the past. It will continue to make a difference whether someone lives in a large city or a rural area.

7 Demographic Politics, Family Planning, Reproductive Health

Being able to make autonomous decisions about the number of children and the timing of their births is a basic human right. It was formulated for the first time in 1968 at the UN Human Rights Conference in Teheran. The Final Act states that "parents have a basic human right to determine freely and responsibly the number and spacing of their children."

This declaration was renewed at the UN International Conference for Population and Development (ICPD) in Cairo in 1994. In 2005, 150 heads of state took stock of the implementation of the Millennium Development Goals (Chapter 10) at a summit meeting in New York. Support for "reproductive health" was explicitly mentioned as an additional goal.

According to the definition adopted in 1994 by the UN World Population Conference's Program of action, reproductive health includes the criteria:

- "that people are able to have a satisfying and safe sex life,
- that they have the capability to reproduce, and
- that they have the freedom to decide if, when and how often they want to make use of this capability."

The implementation of these basic human rights is tied to several prerequisites. First, sexual education providing sufficient information is crucial. Second, and just as important is access to effective means and methods of contraception, assistance during pregnancy and delivery, and medical care for mothers and their children. These have to be seen as minimum requirements of national family and health policies.

Sexual education – a controversial issue

In the realm of demographic and family policies there are clear ethical boundaries: governments clearly have the right to promote certain politically defined objectives, such as the two-child family, the avoidance of teenage pregnancies, or HIV/AIDS prevention. Yet, from a human rights perspective, free decision-making on the part of couples and individuals has to be enabled and respected, for at least adults. When it comes to children and adolescents, family policies may, and perhaps should, go a step further. Most countries set a legally defined minimum age for sexual relations as well as for marriage. In most societies the aim is clear: adolescents, especially teenage girls, are to be protected from sex with adults, from unwanted pregnancy, and from starting a family too early.

Family policy, to a certain extent, deals with an ideological minefield. Different goals defined by such policies may easily contradict one another. Traditional opinion has it that sexual abstinence until marriage is the best protection against an unwanted pregnancy as well as against HIV/AIDS. This position is not only propagated by strict Islamic regimes and the Catholic Church, but also by some political parties and governments close to them. The same is true for conservative Protestant and evangelical groups. The latter are mainly active in North America and exert considerable influence on the rightwing political spectrum of the USA.

As a result, the religious groups, social forces, and political movements mentioned above are opposed to sexual education in schools and the distribution of contraceptive devices to adolescents and young adults. All of this is viewed as an "invitation" – or at least a "temptation" – to engage in premarital sex. Moreover, the Catholic Church is generally opposed to the use of "modern" contraceptive methods, such as the Pill, intrauterine devices (IUD), or condoms. The same religious or political groups are unified in their opposition to abortion. Crucial to these positions are not only theological arguments. Islamic and Christian proponents of such positions fear that sexual education and access to birth control might lead to "moral degeneration." Religious and civil authorities do not want to lose a key element of social control they have long exerted.

The alternative point of view emphasizes sexual education for adolescents and adults, family planning, and the empowerment of women inside and outside the family. They advocate three important benefits of contraception: it serves to avoid premarital pregnancies, to limit the number of children within marriage, and to promote reproductive health by protecting against sexually transmitted diseases and reducing the number of risks associated with pregnancy, birth or abortion.

Pro-natalist and anti-natalist policies

Modern population policies generally aim at influencing the number of births. In doing so, they want to achieve specific goals; usually limiting or stimulating population growth. In countries with high population growth, policies are generally designed to reduce the number of children per woman. These are referred to as anti-natalist population and family policies. In contrast, highly developed countries with aging populations tend to pursue the goal of promoting births and encouraging adults to become parents. Even if this is not openly declared, they are pursuing a pro-natalist population and family policies.

A global survey provides more specific information. The UN, in regular intervals, asks its member states about general perceptions and practical measures related to demographic and family policies.

The 2005 UN survey shows the following. In the European Union, Russia, Japan, and North America, encouraging births is a family policy goal. Indirectly, the aim is to stabilize or increase the number of children per family. The most common political measures are direct payments, tax benefits, state sponsored or subsidized childcare, and social services and employment-related benefits for pregnant women and parents with minor children. In contrast, direct support to family planning services and the promotion of contraception matters is decreasing. In 1976, two-thirds of all developed countries still supported such activities. In 2005, the UN survey revealed that only some 35% of developed countries earmarked public resources for this purpose.

In contrast, for many low- and middle-income countries the main concern is how to curb population growth by reducing the number of children per family. Governments can do this in two ways. First, they can try to influence their citizens' intentions in order to lower the desired number of children. Or alternatively, they can take steps to satisfy an unmet need for family planning. The main precondition is that women are empowered to make use of their rights, which in turn requires adequate economic and familial positions.

For and against more children

In traditional societies, children have always been an economic resource. In this sense, having children is seen as a fairly self-evident goal in life. Parents expected that their children would participate in agricultural, crafts, or trade-related family businesses. It was also expected that children would later take over their family's economic activities or find work elsewhere while continuing to support their elderly parents. A somewhat modified version of these expectations still exists today: successful migrants generally support their close relatives as well as members of their extended family by sending money back home. For poorer countries in particular, this has become a considerable source of national income. In 2008, more than US$200 billion in remittances was sent to developing and emerging economies, much more than the total development assistance given by all wealthy countries. Furthermore, children in traditional societies and in present-day emerging markets are still the most reliable resource sustaining elderly, sick or invalid parents. In the past, these were all reasons to have many children. During times of high mortality, it even made sense to have more children than were actually required or desired. In addition to economic considerations, many cultures are based on religious and social ideals that favor a large number of offspring. These rationales can hardly be kept separate, as many religions reflect the necessities of agrarian societies.

Once having as many children as possible no longer brings parents any advantages, the individual desire to restrict births emerges. Declining infant and child mortality can provide an impetus to restrict births. However, family planning can only become an option when potential parents manage to overcome the traditional notion that children are God-given or decided by fate. For people to restrict the number of children they produce, they must have a certain degree of rationality and willingness to engage in foresighted planning of their lives.

The desire to limit the number of children or to postpone their birth is, of course, not sufficient. Individual wishes pertaining to ideal family size can only be realized when potential parents have access to efficient methods of birth control.

In Europe, it was the upper classes who were the first to restrict the number of children they produced. They were motivated by a desire to maintain their family fortunes. In the 19th century, the urban middle classes followed suit, especially small producers, employees, and civil servants. For them, a large number of children held no economic advantage, and instead, carried additional burdens. Social security, in particular pension and health insurance plans for workers and civil servants, made it possible to expect a respectable standard of living in old age without being dependent on children. In a way, state-sponsored social protection replaced family solidarity by providing support during retirement as well as in the event of unemployment. This, however, was not achieved in one big step, but through the gradual expansion of social rights.

Over the course of the 20th century, workers also began to restrict births, with better educated and skilled workers and their families taking the lead. In Europe and North America, the last social group to reduce their number of children were peasants, who began to do so once modernization had reached rural peripheries. Their interest in having fewer children was encouraged by the widespread mechanization of agriculture. Their inclusion in public pension schemes also played an important role.

In general, children in Europe, North America, and Japan no longer bring their parents any economic advantage. Instead, these children generate substantial direct and indirect costs.

Direct costs are obvious: food, clothing, education, etc. Indirect costs refer to income and career opportunities that people forgo while raising children. Economists therefore call them opportunity costs. This is predominantly an issue for mothers, who remain at home or work part-time for as long as their children are young. At the same time, more and more time has to be invested to raise children, to support their education, and to help them start their professional lives.

Public pension systems allocate old age pensions according to earlier income, levels of contributions, and the period during which they were paid. In many countries, childrearing also has a positive impact on future pension levels. But periods of parenting are usually much less rewarded in terms of pension levels than periods of gainful employment. As a result, mothers who remain at home for a period of time or work part-time have to expect lower pensions. From an economic point of view, this serves as an additional argument for women to engage in a professional career rather than have children. This unintended consequence of public (first pillar) pension systems is currently strengthened by the growing importance of funded (second pillar) pension systems. The size of funds covering future pension claims depend only on individual contributions and the performance of capital markets, but not the number of children someone has born, raised, and socialized. Funded pensions systems therefore inevitably create an additional reason to have fewer children.

Global trend towards fewer children – continuing disparities

The frontrunner in the trend towards fewer children was France. Fertility in that country had already started to decline during the first half of the 19th century – and even earlier among higher social classes (see Chapter 3). Great Britain, Belgium, and Sweden followed this trend during the final twenty-five years of the 19th century, and from 1900 onwards Germany and Austria followed suit. The number of children born in Russia and many Balkan countries only started to decline in the 1920s. In the USA, an accelerated decline in fertility started in the 1870s, with a gradual decrease setting in even earlier.

In several Latin American, East and Southeast Asian countries, fertility trends can be compared with Europe and North America. Some countries – China being the most prominent example – have implemented restrictive population policies. In the case of China, the target set by political authorities is that young adults should only have one child. In many low- and middle-income countries, more rights for women and declining birth rates go hand in hand. Key to this is that women and children have access to education, professional training, and the labor market. Gainful employment and the possibility to have a personal income strengthen the social status of women, as well as their position within their own family. Access to efficient methods of contraception are a further prerequisite for smaller numbers of children.

Today, the average number of children per woman in the EU is 1.5. There are, however, significant differences between countries. France and Scandinavia report higher numbers of children per woman. In these countries, institutional childcare – including crèches, kindergartens, pre-schools – is highly developed and widely available for infants and children. All-day schools are the norm. All this makes it much easier for women to combine work with raising children. Greater participation in childcare among Scandinavian fathers also plays a role.

Crèches, kindergartens, and schools providing childcare and educational services from early morning to late afternoon continue to be an exception in countries such as Austria, Germany,

Greece, and Italy. This makes it more difficult or even impossible for mothers with younger children to be gainfully employed; or conversely, for working woman to have children. As a result, women with higher qualifications and better career opportunities are less likely to have children. In countries like France or Sweden, this is not the case.

Similar correlations exist in developing countries and emerging markets. For African, Asian, and Latin American women, gainful employment, professional careers, and increased self-determination hardly go together with frequent pregnancies and a large number of children. This is why well-educated and gainfully employed women tend to have their children at a later stage in life than those who had little or no education. In turn, being born into smaller families by mothers who are above the age of twenty provides better preconditions for children growing up in developing countries.

Social groups interested in restricting their numbers of children exist in almost all developing countries. This especially applies to the urban middle classes, but also to many slum dwellers. The social role model provided by these groups can influence other sectors of society. In such cases, appropriate family planning programs can help to accelerate the decline in births. Introducing compulsory education and school fees as well as a general ban on child labor have corresponding effects. In middle- and low-income countries, all this transforms children from a potential source of income to a cost factor, as has been the case since the Industrial Revolution in today's developed countries.

Modernization and its consequences

Not all aspects of modernization automatically lead to fewer children. Under certain circumstances, modernization can also trigger higher fertility. The positive effects of nutrition, health, and medical care are beyond dispute. When they improve, puberty sets in earlier and involuntary sterility becomes rarer. Sometimes, the dissolution of traditional social norms and taboos is an important factor, not in lowering but in enhancing fertility. Examples exist both in developing countries and Western societies.

Traditional marriage patterns in Western Europe and parts of Central Europe, for example, had a limiting effect on fertility. They reduced the number of children by imposing an appropriate age to marriage that was generally far beyond the twentieth birthday. There were also bans on marriage for persons without secure livelihoods, household staff, soldiers, and female teachers.

In some parts of Europe and in many other regions of the world, there was even a ban on widows remarrying. Instructions to abstain from sexual relations during religious fasting periods or following births and abortions had similar effects. These rules and taboos set limits on procreation. Many of those who respected these rules and taboos, however, were not fully aware of their effects. Social modernization has proven effective in removing many of these restrictions.

Shorter lactation periods had and still have a similar effect, as the risk of becoming pregnant again is very low as long as women breastfeed their children. As soon as women nurse their newborns for a few weeks or months only rather than for two to three years, natural protection against conception provided during the lactation period shortens considerably. At the same

time the use of milk powder and other pre-fabricated baby food
also decreases natural protection against infections.

Family planning: demand and applied methods

In the early 21st century, family planning is, or at least could
be, an issue for approximately 1.1 billion couples in which the
woman is between 14 and 50 years of age. Of these couples,
some 950 million live in low- and middle-income countries, and
the other 150 million in highly industrialized nations.

In the past, global studies have been conducted covering topics
such as the desire to have children, the actual number of children,
knowledge of family planning, and contraceptive methods primarily used.

These studies show the following: at the end of the 1990s and
the early 21st century, six in ten couples where the female partner
was below age fifty used some sort of family planning (Fig. 18,
Table 13). In almost a quarter of all couples, one partner – more
frequently the woman, less often the man – had been sterilized.
In 10% of all cases, the woman used hormone-based contraceptives (the Pill or a hormonal implant), and in another 14% the
woman used an IUD. In only 5% of cases did the man regularly use a condom. This is one of the reasons why HIV/AIDS is
spreading among heterosexuals.

During the period 1995–2004, slightly more than one in two
couples globally used a secure method of contraception. Approximately 7% of all couples still depended on traditional, but significantly less effective, methods – such as calculating fertile days
and the withdrawal method.

Contraceptive use among married and unmarried couples
was widespread in Australia, North America, South America,

Most frequently used method	Use among all couples with female partner age 15–49 (in %)
No method	39
Modern and safe methods	54
Female sterilization	21
Male sterilization	3
IUD	14
Hormonal contraception (such as the Pill)	10
Condom	5
Traditional methods	7
Calculating fertile days	3
Withdrawal method	3
Other	1

Table 18 Most frequently used contraceptive methods among women in the 15–49 age group and their (marital) partners (in %), survey period 1995–2004 (only women and men who are married or live together as couples)

Source: diverse national surveys, Demographic and Health Surveys, UN Population Division (2005): World Contraceptive Use

East Asia, and Europe. In these world regions, between two-thirds and three-quarters of all couples used some protection to avoid unwanted pregnancies. Some 60% of all couples in Central America, the Caribbean, and Southeast Asia used some contraceptive method. The share was somewhat lower in southern Africa, North Africa, South Asia, and Western Asia, where approximately half of all couples use some form of contraception. In many parts of Africa, contraception continues to be an exception. In the eastern part of the continent and in Central Africa, only one in four couples used some form of protection against pregnancies, and in West Africa the share was only one in eight couples.

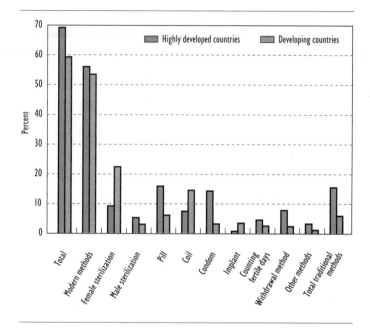

Figure 18 Comparison of contraception methods used by women
between 15 and 49 and their partners, in highly developed
and less developed countries, 1994–2005

Modern and safe contraceptive methods were widespread in
East Asia, Australia, North America, and northwestern Europe.
In contrast, traditional and less reliable methods played a larger
role in many Central and East European as well as West Asian
countries. Significant regional differences in the use of safe
methods were also observed.

The use of the Pill and condoms was most widespread
in wealthier countries. Second in line were male and female
sterilization. In developing countries and emerging markets,

sterilization of women is by far the most common among all safe contraceptive methods, followed by the IUD. At the turn of the 21st century, the use of condoms fell far behind at only 3%. This also provides an explanation for why HIV/AIDS continues to spread drastically in a range of poorer countries.

In some countries and regions, information on contraception and family planning among couples has been collected covering a period of more than half a century. Available results show that in the 1960s globally only some 10–15% of all couples systematically tried to protect themselves against unwanted pregnancies. Today, more than 60% of all couples do so. That represents a big increase, which is also reflected in a big drop in fertility that took place during the same period of time. Available information, however, only refers to married and unmarried couples. We still know very little about the majority of singles in the 15 to 50 age group.

Demand for family planning

At the turn of the 21st century, four out of ten couples (39%) did nothing to protect themselves against pregnancies. In South Asia, Western and large parts of Africa, this trend even represented the majority of all couples. There are different reasons for this behavior:

- Some very traditional groups in a number of societies consider a high number of children to be economically advantageous, or they still view the number of children as God-given or decided by fate. Contraception within marriage therefore barely plays a role. On the other hand, premarital sexual contacts are strongly prohibited, which

– at least in theory – make the use of contraceptives among unmarried teenagers and adults unnecessary. In most low and middle-income countries, increasing educational levels and growing prosperity is causing this group of traditionalists to dwindle.

- A second group of women and men may not consider a large number of children to be desirable, but they do not have access to effective means of protecting themselves against unwanted pregnancies. This second group has an unmet demand for family planning. This group decreases when access to contraceptive methods improves faster than additional demand grows among couples and individuals of fertile age. The size of this second group is of crucial importance when it comes to allocating additional resources for the promotion of family planning.

- A third group already practices contraception and birth control; either in order to delay the next birth or to prevent any additional children from being conceived. This third group includes all women who currently practice contraception, as well as women who have pregnancies terminated because of a lack of effective contraception. Abortions are often an indication for an unmet demand for family planning.

- And finally, there are women and men who are not interested in contraception during a given period of time because they want to have a child. In this group, it is usually just a matter of time until the desired number of children is reached – or even surpassed.

In sum, there is a considerable unmet demand for family planning – particularly in low- and middle-income countries. Experts assume that there are more than 200 million couples among whom at least the female partner either does not want to have another child or does not want to become pregnant during the coming years.

Married and unmarried couples are not the only target group for contraception and birth control. There are also unmarried adolescents and adults who are sexually active on an occasional or regular basis. Furthermore, there are married people having extramarital affairs. There are no internationally comparable studies on any of these groups. Yet it is precisely they who most likely hold an interest in avoiding pregnancies. At the same time, these groups have a substantial unmet need for information, contraception, and birth control.

Studies show a clear correlation between effective contraceptive use and the number of children per woman. It is also evident that women bear significantly fewer unwanted children when they have access to modern contraceptive methods (Table 15). The more children women already have, the more likely it is that the next child is unwanted (Fig. 19). And if intervals between births are very short, the subsequent child usually comes at an inopportune time or is unwanted by the mother.

Because of the HIV/AIDS epidemic, some contraceptives have taken on greater significance since the beginning of the 1990s. The use of condoms offers far-reaching protection against infection. Naturally, this also applies to other sexually transmitted diseases (such as syphilis, gonorrhea, and herpes).

Contraceptives and abortion

A lack of sexual education and the failure to use efficient contraceptive methods frequently lead to pregnancies. Experts estimate that every year between 80 and 100 million women globally face

Preconditions	Abortion legal in % of UN member states; highly developed countries	Abortion legal in % of UN member states; low and middle-income countries
To save the lives of pregnant women	96	98
To resist significant physical problems	88	59
To resist significant psychological problems among pregnant women	85	57
Following a rape	88	35
When the fetus is deformed	83	30
For considerable economic or social reasons	77	19
Upon request of the pregnant woman	67	15

Table 19 Conditions under which abortions are legal in UN member
         states (2005)

Source: UN Population Division 2005

unwanted pregnancies. At least half of all these unwanted pregnancies end in abortion. There is, however, a lack of empirical data. The latest global study on this topic was carried out in the 1990s. Researchers at the Alan Guttmacher Institute (New York) analyzed data from fifty-seven countries. From this they calculated about twenty-six million legal and twenty million illegal abortions for 1995. For comparison, 128 million babies were born in the same year.

In the mid-1990s, abortions were particularly frequent in Central and Eastern Europe as well as in East and Southeast Asia. At the time, relative to population size, Vietnam reported the largest number of abortions. In China, too, this was a widespread method of birth control. Japan also lay above the average in wealthier countries, as the Pill and other hormonal contraceptives were not legally available until 2004.

Conversely, it was evident that abortions are used less frequently as a method of birth control when more effective contraception is more widely available in both developed and developing countries.

Abortions are legal almost everywhere in the event that the pregnant woman's life is threatened by the pregnancy. Moreover, some 85% of highly developed countries and about 60% of low- and middle-income countries allow an abortion that prevents significant physical or psychological problems related to the pregnancy. Almost all highly developed countries allow abortion following a sexual assault or in the event of a malformed fetus; but only a third of low- and middle-income countries permit this. Two out of three wealthier countries, but hardly any low- and middle-income countries, give the pregnant woman a free choice during the first three to four months of a pregnancy (Table 14). Consequently, almost half of all terminated pregnancies are illegal, and are therefore carried out in unsafe conditions.

Pregnancy termination and gender preferences

Abortions also play a role for another reason. Some parents have a clear preference for boys especially in Asia. An examination of the amniotic fluid in the placenta has been available for some time in order to detect severe malformations of the fetus. This examination also reveals whether the child will be a boy or a girl. In a number of countries – especially in China and India, but also in South Korea, Japan, Pakistan, and Singapore – this has led to systematic abortion of female fetuses.

In China, the one-child policy has caused some parents to employ this method to ensure that they will have a son. This is not just a question of social prestige, but also a precaution taken in view of old age. In the absence of general social security, Chinese children are still responsible for their parents once they grow old and no longer have an income of their own. In this context, parents expect more financial support from a son than from a daughter – a deplorable but understandable reality.

In India and Pakistan, too, material considerations are at the forefront. Daughters can generally only marry when their parents are able to pay a considerable dowry. Even middle-class families can hardly afford marriage for a larger number of daughters without severely indebting themselves. This explains why many couples try not to have daughters in the first place.

The consequence of abortions following intra-uterine sex determination is obvious. Since the 1990s, far more boys than girls have been born in quite a few countries. Usually, 945–950 girls are born per 1000 boys. In 1991, this was also still the case in India and China. In 2001, however, the rate in India was only 927 girls. Among Indian women who have already had one girl, the rate among the second child dropped to only 759 girls for every 1000 boys.

In China, the sex ratio at birth is even more distorted. In 2005, only 850 girls were born per 1000 boys. In the province of Guangdong, the sex ratio was at a record low of 770 girls per 1000 boys.

Selective abortion in South and East Asia is leading to a long-term shortage of younger women. As a consequence, a large number of young men in the future will not be able to find a bride and not be able to start a family. In 2025, there will already be 32 million Chinese men in the age bracket 15 to 45

Country	Married women who used modern contraceptive methods (in %)	Average number of children per woman	Of which: unwanted children
Yemen	10	6.5	1.9
Uganda	18	6.9	1.6
Haiti	22	4.7	1.9
Kenya	32	4.7	1.2
Philippines	33	3.7	1.0
Nepal	35	4.1	1.6
Bangladesh	43	3.3	1.1
Zimbabwe	50	4.0	0.6
Peru	50	2.8	1.0
Egypt	57	3.5	0.6
Columbia	64	2.6	0.8

Table 20 Contraception and number of children in selected developing
countries

Source: Various national surveys, Demographic and Health Surveys (DHS)
1997–2001, German Foundation for World Population (DSW; 2004)

who will not be able to find a female of their age group within
the country.

Programs promoting family planning

Over the past decades, a significant number of developing countries and emerging economies have tried to influence families'
desires to have smaller numbers of children by offering material incentives or imposing sanctions. To date, China has implemented such incentives and sanctions in the most radical fashion.
European and American critics of China's one-child policy argue

that fundamental ethical boundaries have been crossed because of the use of repressive measures such as naming and shaming, penalties, transfer to a smaller apartment, etc. The long-term success of a policy restricting the number of births depends on continuing authoritarian rule. A move towards more democracy, in which the Chinese government would have to relinquish control over the private lives of its citizens, would most certainly lead to a "wave" of births.

The sterilization program practiced in India during the 1970s was also most contentious. Many sterilizations were carried out against the will of the men and women involved, and were underpinned by violent methods or incomplete information. They brought disrepute to state family planning initiatives in India as well as in neighboring countries.

Nowadays, most developing countries aim to offer better access to family planning and contraception rather than using coercive measures. Many women realize that it is not in their interest to have a large number of children or to have children at an early age. Many use contraception to a more or less effective degree. The best proof of this is globally declining numbers of children per family. Yet there are still many women who do not want to have a child at a given moment, but who also do not use effective contraception. There are different reasons for this. Comprehensive and transparent information on available methods, their particularities, and their side-effects are often lacking. For these women, sexual education and information campaigns could enhance the acceptance of modern contraceptive methods and facilitate access to them. Normally, however, campaigns are not enough. In addition, qualified individual counseling for couples, and particularly for women, is necessary.

In many parts of the world, poor people living in rural areas as well as in urban slums do not have sufficient access to sexual

Chinese One-Child Policy

Since the 1980s, Chinese population and family policies have been based on the curtailing of births. Official statistics state that the strict one-child policy only applies to 36% of the population. This is especially the case in metropolises such as Beijing, Shanghai, and Tianjin, as well as in rich provinces such as Jiangsu. More than half of the population (53%) is permitted to have a second child if the first one is a girl. More than 9% of the population may officially have two children. Officially, no restrictions limiting the number of children are imposed on ethnic minorities. These include Mongols, Tibetans, and Uigurs in particular, who represent less than 7% of total population; in absolute numbers, however, they still make up more than 100 million people. In practice, migrants, farmers, and party officials have more children than members of the urban middle classes.

China's policy is generally considered to be effective. Still, the most rapid decrease in fertility (children per woman) occurred in the 1970s, during a period before the restrictions were made obligatory and enforced by harsh measures. If we trust Chinese statisticians – who surely have no political motives to embellish the late Maoist period – the number of children per woman was 5.8 in 1970. Ten years later, just before the one-child-policy started in 1980, the figure was 2.7 children per woman. By 1990, it had dropped further to 2.2. Today, with 1.6 children per woman, Chinese fertility has reached European levels.

education and modern contraceptive methods. Not least is the financial aspect, which very often poses a significant barrier. In most developing countries, couples would have to spend 5–10% of their family incomes to purchase the Pill or condoms on the free market, or to have an IUD inserted. Many cannot afford any of these alternatives.

Access to effective contraception is especially important for couples who are considering but not using family planning methods, or who have not yet agreed on the number of children they wish to have – usually because the man would like to have a further child but the woman does not. Family planning programs can considerably increase access to more effective contraception by providing information, counseling, and making free or subsi-dized contraceptives available to particular target groups.

As an unmet demand for family planning exists in almost all developing countries, improving resources for such programs could curb population growth in the short run. Many develop-ing countries, especially in Africa, are dependent on financial support from wealthy industrialized nations in order to provide these resources.

For decades now, it has proven beneficial to link medical care for mothers and children with counseling on family planning issues. In the meantime, such outreach centers have been opened in many developing countries. It has been observed, however, that young women without children as well as men tend to visit such centers much less frequently than pregnant women and younger mothers. There is a second problem. In societies with rapidly growing populations, the expansion of health facilities for mothers and children can often not keep up with the rising numbers of births. Understandably, doctors, midwives, and nurses in poorer countries with rapidly rising populations have to concentrate on urgent care of pregnant women, newborns and their mothers, and sick children. Sometimes family planning services tend to be neglected, with further unwanted pregnancies as the consequence.

The most obvious evidence of the unmet need for family planning are the 100–120 million unwanted pregnancies each year and the estimated fifty million abortions globally.

In order to counter such problems, non-clinical forms of family planning are increasingly offered. Community-based services are now available in more than fifty countries. They depend on volunteers – the majority of whom are women – who manage a depot of hormonal contraceptives (the Pill) and condoms for their village and distribute them usually at no charge. At the same time, volunteers give family planning advice at the community level: at gatherings, during door-to-door visits, and within circles of friends and acquaintances. They are generally selected by their communities to take on this task and are given training. Experience has shown that this kind of family planning service is highly effective.

A further approach emphasizes the subsidized purchase of the Pill and condoms via commercial channels, such as in drugstores, kiosks, grocery stores, and restaurants. Commercial advertising methods are employed in order to provide information about these products and to market them. This method has proven especially effective in promoting the use of condoms as protection against HIV/AIDS.

Additional demand for family planning

The demand for family planning services will grow significantly over the next decades – quantitatively as well as qualitatively. In quantitative terms, the demand for family planning will grow at least as rapidly as the population increases, since large cohorts of

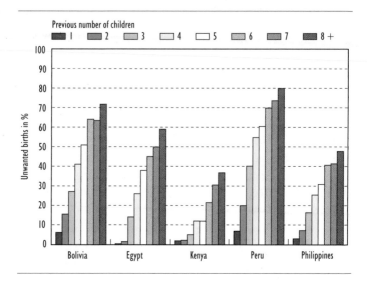

Figure 19 Rate of unwanted children (in %) to women who already
have children
Source: DHS

people born in the 1980s and 1990s are entering or have already
entered reproductive age. These individuals have the right to protection against unwanted pregnancies. Even in low- and middle-
income countries where population growth has already peaked,
the number of individuals and couples at reproductive age will
continue to rise for some time.

It is precisely in the world's poorest countries that a further
drop in fertility – as forecast by most population prognoses – will
not set in on its own. This target requires a more effective distribution of modern contraception, especially in those countries
in which only between 10 and 20% of all couples use protective
methods at all.

In developing countries, there is also a new demand for qualitative advances in sexual education and family planning programs. Improved counseling on the advantages and disadvantages of different contraceptive methods and their side-effects is necessary for those people who have not made use of existing programs even though they have access to them. Improved counseling is needed to reduce the discontinuance of certain methods.

The spread of HIV/AIDS is forcing family planning programs to expand their traditional tasks to prevent the spread of this epidemic and counseling for those who are already infected. In 2007, some 33 million people were infected with HIV globally, and an estimated 2.6 million new infections occurred. This inevitably poses new challenges for staff training and the propagation of safe sex methods. People need to be informed and empowered to protect themselves against HIV/AIDS. In this context, the containment of HIV/AIDS requires substantial changes in behavior, universal access to condoms, and the treatment of other sexually transmitted diseases that significantly increase the risk of infection.

Locally operating family planning programs often have the right preconditions to make a contribution in this direction. They cannot, however, do this without additional resources. A further qualitative challenge is the need to involve more adolescents and men in existing family planning programs.

And the results?

Does the promotion of family planning directly lead to fewer births? Or do investments in family planning only take effect when the desire to have fewer children is already part of a larger social trend? International experts have dissenting views on this issue.

The Dutch demographer John Bongaarts, who works in the USA, has strongly supported the thesis that a direct relationship exists. His evidence is based on detailed studies on selected regions in China and Bangladesh. Bongaarts claimed that in both countries the main cause of decreasing numbers of children per woman was national support for family planning and birth control. Better sexual education and improved contraceptive provisions led to a reduction in the number of unplanned and unwanted children within families. And at the same time, the number of abortions declined. According to Bongaarts, the decline in the number of children per woman can be directly attributed to more efficient family planning and birth control.

Developments in Ireland also seem to support this idea. After 1945, this country registered by far the highest numbers of children per woman in all present-day EU member states. It was only in the 1970s and 1980s that the sale of contraceptives was legalized. Today, fertility in Ireland is slightly below two children per women.

The most prominent critic of this view is the American development economist Lant Pritchett. He points to a significant number of unplanned births in developing countries with decreasing fertility. His opinion is that the effect of family planning programs depends on the desired number of children. Pritchett claims that this varies from country to country and accounts for up to 90% of differences in the actual numbers of children per women.

Regardless of how this contentious question is resolved based on future evidence, we can safely say the following: all measures to promote sexual education, family planning, and reproductive health in general create the preconditions for the implementation of an elementary human right. They give each individual the right to choose the number of children they have and the timing of their birth. These measures also have an important demographic consequence. If the unmet demand for family planning in developing countries is satisfied, global population growth could slow down more quickly and come to a standstill in the foreseeable future.

8 Health, Illness, and Death

At present, approximately fifty-five million people die each year. Almost one-fifth of all deaths – a total of ten million per year – occur among infants and young children below the age of ten. In developing countries, deaths of infants and children even now make up one-quarter of all deaths. This is, however, not only caused by higher infant and child mortality in poorer countries. It is also an effect of the younger age structure in these countries that are still home to many children, but few older people. In the majority of cases, deaths of infants and children could be avoided, as the most important causes of death include birth complications, diarrhea, and pneumonia.

Today, the survival rate among infants and young children largely depends on their place of birth and the social group into which they are born. The main differences are clearly between richer and poorer countries. They do, however, also exist within societies. We have accurate and reliable data for approximately thirty low- and middle-income countries. In rural areas in Asia, Africa, and Latin America, infant mortality on average is 50% higher than in the cities. In these regions, children of poorer women without formal education die twice as often as children whose mothers attended school. There have hardly been any change in these differences over the past fifteen years, even though mortality of infants and children in general is on the decline.

Access to clean water and better nutrition have been key elements in the fight against child mortality. Global vaccination campaigns have also had life-saving effects on a considerable scale. In 2004, almost 80% of all children were inoculated during their first year against diphtheria, whooping cough, and tetanus. In 102 countries, the vaccination rate against these three diseases had already reached levels of over 90%. In fifty countries, vaccination levels were still below 80%; and in ten countries they were below 50%. The latter group reporting particularly low vaccination rates includes very poor countries such as Haiti, Laos, Liberia, and Central Africa, but also oil-producing countries such as Gabon and Nigeria. In India and Pakistan, vaccination rates are at 65%, in Indonesia 70%. In China the rate has surpassed 90%, reaching European levels.

Unequal chances for survival can also be explained by significant differences in the quality of the respective health systems. A comparison between Africa and North America makes this very clear: 5% of the global population resides in the USA and Canada. More than one-third of all medical doctors and nurses work in these two countries. The USA and Canada consume 50% of total global expenditure on health care. For comparison: almost 15% of the world population lives in Africa, yet only 3.5% of all medical doctors and nurses are active in this part of the world. Africans consume only 1% of total global expenditure on health care. These discrepancies are further impacted by the fact that many rich countries directly recruit nurses, doctors, and caregivers from developing countries which inevitably worsens the performance of their health systems.

Most common diseases and causes of death

Globally speaking, there are two important causes of death: infectious diseases and other parasitic illnesses; and cardiovascular diseases. Each year some eighteen million people die of infectious and parasitic illnesses, accounting for about 30% of all deaths. Currently, deadly infectious diseases are common in developing countries and emerging markets. In wealthier countries, they barely play a role as a cause of death.

The second paramount cause of death is cardiovascular diseases, including heart attacks, strokes, and related vascular problems. Today, one in two inhabitants of industrialized countries dies from such illnesses. Yet they are responsible for only one-fourth to one-fifth of all deaths in low- and middle-income countries. Time series on causes of death show that cardiovascular diseases are also rising in the latter group of countries. In sum, they claim some eighteen million lives annually, making up another 30% of all deaths.

Third in line are different forms of cancer – or "malignant tumors" as they are referred to in medical jargon. In highly industrialized countries, they are responsible for one-fifth of all deaths (21%). In contrast, cancer is the cause of one-tenth of all deaths in Asia, Africa, and Latin America. Globally, approximately 7.5 million people die each year of cancer representing 13% of all deaths.

Lung diseases and other respiratory illnesses claim some four million lives annually, making up 7% of all deaths. Diabetes as well as all other chronic and degenerative illnesses are responsible for a further 11% of all deaths and fatal accidents and injuries are the cause of no less than 10% of global mortality.

Deaths are only the most visible manifestation of the prevailing spectrum of illnesses. At the same time, they are closely

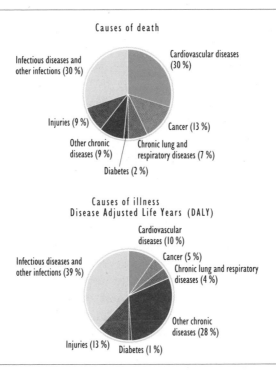

Figure 20 Main causes of death and illness (DALY) in %, 2005
Source: WHO, 2005

related to particular living conditions and the performance of healthcare systems. Yet, in most cases, accidents and diseases do not lead to death. Even illnesses that ultimately result in a person's death can last for many years. The actual impact of various illnesses can be measured by looking at the physical impairment of a normal, symptom-free life caused by illness and calculating the total amount of symptom-free life time "lost" due to this impairment. This leads to a measure called "disease-adjusted life

Causes of Falling Death Rates

In no period of human history has mortality dropped more rapidly than during the past 150 years. An interaction of different factors led to an intense decline in mortality. The most important factors were:

- the increase in agricultural outputs and improve nutrition (more calories per capita despite population growth)
- the transportation revolution allowing improved food could be distribution (i.e. prevention of famines)
- improved public hygiene (availability of clean drinking water, sewage systems, waste removal, etc.) as well as private hygiene (tap water, regular laundering of clothing, iron bed frames, affordable soap, modern housing in brick or stone buildings)
- medical and pharmaceutical progress (antiseptic treatment, antibiotics, widespread inoculations, reduction in infections diseases)
- a rise in educational levels and the changing status of children (ban on child labor, compulsory school attendance, acceptance of childhood as a separate phase in life).

years" (DALY), which gives a somewhat different picture. Calculated over the course of an entire life, infections and chronic degenerative diseases of all kinds have a significant impact on DALY, followed by injuries.

A shift in the causes of death

Until 150 years ago, deadly infectious diseases and parasitic infections were the norm throughout the world – including Europe and North America. English statistics for the years 1848 to 1854 confirm the dominance of deadly infectious diseases at that time. In the mid-19th century, they were the cause of the death for approximately 60% of all people living in England and Wales. These illnesses were transmitted in different ways, mainly via contaminated drinking water, garbage, and direct infection from human to human. At the beginning of the 20th century, tuberculosis was still the most common cause of death in Europe. Between 1918 and 1924, however, some twenty million people fell victim to Spanish flu.

During the second half of the 19th century, mortality in Europe and North America began to fall because deadly infectious diseases – especially among infants and young children, but also among adults – became less common. This was mainly the result of better living conditions, such as modern housing, tap water, sewage systems, and canalization, which intercepted earlier transmission paths of infections. Larger towns introduced communal waste collection. Better nutrition also led to infectious diseases causing fewer deaths. In Europe and North America, only a small proportion of the decline in mortality was due to medical and pharmaceutical progress during this period. Vaccinations became the most important medical contribution of the 19th and early 20th centuries. Antibiotics, which play a significant role in fighting bacterial infections today, only came into use after World War II.

In wealthier societies, most infectious diseases today can either be prevented or cured. Over the past decades, they have been replaced by cancer and cardiovascular disorders as the main cause of death. Since both of these groups of diseases only began to dominate once a certain level of prosperity had been reached, they are also referred to as "diseases of civilization." Today, the vast majority of Europeans, North Americans, and Japanese die of these illnesses.

With reference to the concept of demographic transition, fundamental shifts in the spectrum of illnesses and causes of death can be interpreted as an "epidemiological transition." We can consider the demographic effects of curing illnesses or even preventing them. In all societies, both possibilities are seen as progress. Historically, this transition was closely related to industrialization and modernization. This was particularly true for Europe, North America, and Japan, where the epidemiological transition went hand in hand with economic and social progress.

In the future, the epidemiological transition will proceed more intensely in developing countries. There, cancer and cardiovascular diseases will become more common as a result of demographic aging. At the same time, progress will be made in both the treatment and prevention of infectious diseases today are responsible for 30% of all deaths globally. The World Health Organization (WHO) predicts that in 2030 their share will go down to just over 20% of all deaths. This will also cause an increase in the average age of death.

In contrast to Europe and North America, the epidemiological transition in developing countries and emerging markets is not solely dependent on improved living conditions, but can also be the result – or by-product – of "imported" progress. One example is the vaccination campaigns that are partially sponsored by development assistance funds. An important contribution is also provided by software pioneer Bill Gates. He has invested the bulk of his private fortune in a foundation that

– among other things – finances healthcare and vaccinations in poorer countries.

In 2005, 19% of all deceased people were children and adolescents below age twenty. Another 29% of all deceased people were adults between the ages of twenty and sixty. Only slightly more than half of all deaths (52%) affected people above the age of sixty. For the year 2030, World Health Organization (WHO) experts estimate that deceased children and adolescents will only make up one-tenth of all deaths; in contrast, older people above age sixty will make up two-thirds of all deaths. There are two reasons for this forecast. First, the change in the spectrum of illnesses analyzed above will continue; and second, demographic aging will inevitably lead to more deaths among older people. As the number of elderly people is expected to rise considerably during the coming decades, more people will die at higher ages.

From "dying before one's time" to a nursing risk

In the EU, North America, Japan, and Australia, deaths before the age of sixty has become a very rare event. Men and women in Britain, France, and Germany, for example, have a 99% chance on their 59th birthdays of reaching their 60th birthdays. In Western Europe, half of all deceased are over seventy-five years of age. Inhabitants of wealthier countries no longer have to expect death below age sixty as an every day phenomenon. This has changed their attitudes towards life. Indeed, life and career planning as we know it today has only been enabled by the low mortality of adolescents and adults below age sixty. If someone in Britain or the USA today dies of cancer or in a car accident at age thirty-five, it appears to us as "premature death." We would say that "his/her time had not yet come." Historically speaking, this is a very recent phenomenon.

Until well into the 19th century, "dying before his/her time" did not exist. Death was on the agenda at any time. Until 1870, one-third of all newborns died during their first year and a further 10% died in the following four years. As a consequence, almost 45% of all children died before reaching their fifth birthdays. It was only those who survived these first years who had a good chance of later becoming adults – and, for some, growing old even by today's standards. Death was therefore part of everyday life. Many infectious diseases were deadly until the early 20th century. In less developed parts of the world, such illnesses still play a significant role today. Societies in Europe, North America, and Japan, but also in many middle-income countries, have managed to handle most infectious diseases.

In the past twenty years, wealthier countries have also succeeded in curbing the main causes of death. A heart attack today no longer necessarily means imminent death. Significantly more than half of all those affected survive their first heart attack. Early detection methods have been improved and promising therapies to combat cancer are being developed.

There is, however, a price to our success in prevention, early detection, and successful treatment of cancer and cardiovascular diseases. We are heading towards a future in which other illnesses will dominate: in particular dementia, Parkinson's disease, Alzheimer's disease and mature-onset diabetes. These are all illnesses that negatively affect our quality of life, but that do not cause death – at least not immediately. The additional years of life gained by increased life expectancy, therefore, do not necessarily translate into extra normal, symptom-free years unhindered by illness. These gains come at a price: we face an increased likelihood of spending a longer period of our lives impaired by chronic and degenerative diseases. As a consequence, many more people than today will need long-term care.

Infectious diseases

In Africa, South Asia, and Western Asia as well as in parts of Latin America, infectious and parasitic diseases lead to the death of many newborns, children, and adults of all ages. In sub-Saharan Africa, over 60% of all deaths are due to such illnesses. In Asia, they are the cause more than one-third of all deaths. But it is not only infections and the spread of tropical diseases that contribute to high mortality in developing countries. Malnutrition, especially among children and adolescents, has a significant impact as well as the often catastrophic conditions under which women in poor countries give birth to their children.

In highly industrialized countries, the situation is totally different. If we exclude infectious pneumonia, only 1% to 2% of all deaths are caused by various infectious diseases.

Of all infectious diseases, inflammatory lung diseases (including pneumonia) and other respiratory illnesses (3.9 million), as well as HIV/AIDS (2.9 million), claim the largest number of victims annually. Third in line are so-called gastrointestinal infections affecting digestion and causing – among other things – dehydration. Other infectious diseases claiming more than one million victims annually include malaria and tuberculosis. Measles, sleeping sickness, tetanus, syphilis, and hepatitis claim hundreds of thousands of lives each year. These illnesses also partially reinforce one another. Sexually transmitted diseases increase the chance of contracting HIV/AIDS. Fever during a malaria attack accelerates the multiplication of HIV viruses and thus make contacts with those already infected even more

Type of infectious disease	Annual number of deaths (estimates)
Lung and other respiratory diseases	3.9 million
HIV/AIDS	2.9 million
Gastrointestinal diseases, including dysentery	2.1 million
Tuberculosis	1.6 million
Malaria	1.0 million
Measles	800,000
Sleeping sickness	500,000
Tetanus	300,000
Whooping cough	300,000
Syphilis	200,000
Hepatitis	180,000
Meningitis	160,000

Table 22 Main types of infectious diseases by annual number of deaths
         (estimates)

Source: WHO

dangerous. As HIV/AIDS negatively affects the immune system,
it also facilitates the spread of other diseases. Another example
is hepatitis. This infectious disease often leads to both cirrhosis
and liver cancer.

As already explained, HIV/AIDS is by no means the only
widespread deadly infectious disease. Far more people fall
victim to other infectious diseases. These illnesses, however, are
less spectacular than HIV/AIDS. They do not appear to be as
threatening to Europeans and North Americans. This is why
global efforts to prevent and combat those illnesses are more
modest. The fact is that medical and pharmaceutical research
mainly looks at illnesses prevalent in wealthier countries. It is,
after all, only these countries that have highly developed healthcare systems, almost universal health insurance coverage, and

people who are able to pay for medication and therapies either directly or via taxation.

Many plagues and infectious diseases that we thought we had under control are again becoming more prevalent. This is especially related to the collapse of comprehensive healthcare in parts of Eastern Europe and Central Asia. This facilitates the spread of diphtheria, HIV/AIDS, hepatitis, and other infectious diseases because infected persons are neither treated nor informed about their condition.

Malaria is also on the increase due to irrigation systems and dams. Both offer the carrier of the malarial causing plasmodium protozoa – the Anopheles mosquito – new habitats.

The HIV/AIDS epidemic

Of all deadly infectious diseases, HIV/AIDS is spreading the fastest. In 2007, approximately thirty-three million people were infected with HIV. More than 90% of those infected live in low and middle-income countries. The most affected world region, with twenty-three million people infected, is sub-Saharan Africa. In South Asia and Southeast Asia, their number is about 4.2 million. In contrast, at the start of 2007 only 730,000 people with HIV lived in Western and Central Europe.

Globally, only 1% of all adults carry the virus that causes HIV. In sub-Saharan Africa, 6% of adults are infected. And in the most affected countries, more than 30% of young adults living in larger cities and along major roads used for mass transportation are infected with the virus. Among high-risk groups – such as prostitutes, intravenous drug users, and individuals who frequently change sexual partners – the share of infected people in some countries at times surpasses 50%.

In 2007, approximately 2.6 million people contracted HIV: on average, 7,100 per day. More than 90% were inhabitants of low- and middle-income countries. Over the last fifteen years, a rapid increase in new infections has taken place in Eastern Europe and Central Asia, especially in Russia and Ukraine. This led to a rise in the number of those infected with HIV from 1.2 million people in 2003 to 1.5 million in 2007. In contrast, relatively few people presently contract the virus in EU countries and in North America.

There are, however, EU countries in which the rate of infection is becoming more widespread again: among these are parts of Scandinavia, as well as Great Britain, and Ireland. The most important cause of this is unsafe sex and sex tourism "importing" the disease from overseas. In other EU countries, HIV is only spreading among homosexuals with multiple partners as well as among drug addicts. The latter mainly become infected by sharing non-sterilized needles.

In Eastern Europe, the HIV virus was first transmitted among drug addicts and prostitutes. It has been spreading among a wider group of people since the late 1990s. In Russia, only about 10,000 persons were infected in 1996. By 2007, the number had jumped to one million people.

Between the beginning of the HIV/AIDS epidemic in the 1980s and the end of 2007, approximately forty-one million people died of this disease, of which two million in 2007 alone. For a time, the demographic effect of this illness was underestimated. At the beginning of the 1990s, only ten million people were thought to be infected and at the time, AIDS was only responsible for 2% of all deaths in developing countries. In the meantime, HIV/ AIDS has become a more prominent cause of death in quantitative terms than tuberculosis and malaria. In view of the high number of infected persons and the rapid speed at which this immuno-deficiency disease is spread, it is clear that AIDS will become increasingly important as a cause of illness and death in many low- and middle-income countries.

To date, there is no vaccine and no other form of immunization against HIV. Nonetheless, effective medication has been developed since the 1990s that suppresses the multiplication of the virus within the bodies of infected persons. Medication that prolongs the lives of those infected with HIV/AIDS in Western industrialized nations, however, is often too expensive or completely unavailable for infected persons in developing countries. Today, in low- and middle-income countries only two million HIV infected persons received anti-retroviral therapy.

At the same time, the duration of an infection from contraction to the outbreak of the illness itself, and to the death of the infected person, is considerably shorter in Third World countries than in Western Europe and North America. Reasons for this are not only a lack of medical care but also lower hygienic standards and higher pathogenic virulence in tropical zones.

AIDS reduces average life expectancy in southern Africa – by twenty to thirty years, depending on the country we look at. Botswana, Lesotho, and Zimbabwe hold the worst records. There, HIV/AIDS has almost halved the average life span since the mid-1980s. This has not only affected younger adults. AIDS has also caused child mortality to more than double in these countries since the beginning of the 1990s. Many children whose mothers are HIV-positive become infected through contact with blood during labor or during breastfeeding. AIDS in the family turns many more children into orphans.

In 2005, American statisticians estimated a life expectancy of thirty-four years for nationals of Botswana. Yet this country, with its annual GNP per capita of more than US$10,000, hardly belongs to the poorest countries in the world. Without HIV/

AIDS, life expectancy in this country would be around seventy years of age.

Until now, the rapid rise in mortality has been limited to some thirty countries in which the HIV/AIDS epidemic is already in an advanced stage. In these countries, this infectious disease alone substantially reduces population growth; e.g. in Botswana, from a hypothetical 2.6% annually (without AIDS) to -0.1% (actual figure for 2005) or in Swaziland from 1.6% (without AIDS) to +0.1% (actual figure for 2005). In these countries, population growth has come to a standstill.

As the countries most affected by HIV/AIDS do not have a large share of world population, this dramatic development has not had a major effect on global demographic dynamics to date. This could change if the infection continues to spread in highly populated countries such as China or India.

Zero population growth is not advantageous for countries highly affected by HIV/AIDS today. On the contrary, the epidemic carries extensive disadvantages, as the economic and social consequences are almost as catastrophic as the illness itself. Urban and better qualified segments of the population are especially affected: these are often people at the beginning or in the middle of their professional lives. As a consequence, not only their manpower, but also their skills and expertise are lost. At the same time, approximately fourteen million AIDS orphans are dependent on close relatives or charitable organizations. When this support is missing, children often have to live on the streets. In the most affected countries, AIDS absorbs a significant proportion of health care services. In some countries, more than 60% of hospital beds are occupied by AIDS patients.

Maternal mortality

Globally, approximately 600,000 women die each year as a result of complications during pregnancy or childbirth. Among them are 70,000 to 100,000 girls and women who die as a result of illegal abortions that are conducted in an unsafe manner or under unhygienic conditions.

Ninety-eight percent of this mortality affects women in developing countries. In poor countries, along with HIV/AIDS, risks posed by pregnancy, delivery, and abortion are among the main causes of death for women between fifteen and forty years of age. On average, the risk of dying during a pregnancy or labor is forty times higher for women in developing countries than for women living in wealthy countries. The situation for pregnant women and mothers is worst in sub-Saharan Africa. In the early 21st century, the death rate in this region was 910 mothers per 100,000 births. The rate for North Africa, the Middle East, and South and Southeast Asia was 460 mothers per 100,000 births. In Latin America, 190 mothers died per 100,000 births.

Eighty percent of all cases of maternal mortality are related to five causes: bleeding, infections, high blood pressure, exhaustion before and during pregnancy, and abortions carried out under unprofessional conditions. In addition, over fifty million women annually suffer from complications and physical ailments caused by pregnancy or birth. These ailments become chronic in twenty million cases annually.

Teenage births and births beyond age forty significantly increase the health risks for both mother and infant. The same applies if pregnancies succeed one another too rapidly. Furthermore, frequent pregnancies not only weaken the physical conditions of expectant mothers. More children per family can often lead to a worsening of the health of all children as parents have less time to spend taking care of each individual. When a mother dies during or after childbirth, mortality for her surviving children is ten times higher than among children who grow up with their mothers.

Complications during pregnancy and childbirth also exist in wealthy countries. But they do not lead to maternal mortality at any significant level.

Whether mother and child are injured depends very much on the care available during the pregnancy and childbirth. Most women who die during childbirth received no medical assistance. For many of them, health services were too expensive or out of reach. In developing countries, midwives are only present at one in two births. In some very poor countries in Asia and Africa, there is only one midwife per 300,000 inhabitants. In these countries, one midwife on average would have to take care of 15,000 births annually.

In total, two-thirds of all mothers in developing countries receive prenatal care, and less than one-third receive any postnatal care.

What can we do?

We all have to die. The question, then, is when and of what? International comparison reveals significant differences: people living in highly industrialized countries of the Northern hemisphere have the highest life expectancy. This includes Western Europe, North America, and Japan, as well as Hong Kong, Singapore, Israel, and Australia. In other parts of the world, many people have shorter lives. They often die of infections and illnesses that could be prevented, or treated and cured, or that would not even spread in the first place if living conditions improved. The following strategies should be pursued in order to lower mortality at a global level.

First, better living conditions are essential. Those who are well-fed, have access to clean drinking water, and dry living conditions fall ill substantially less frequently. Those living in areas with adequate sewage systems exist and where waste water is filtered are less likely to contract infections. Furthermore, well-nourished individuals who have access to clean drinking water are more likely to survive an illness.

Second, an ecologically intact environment is crucial. Industrialized nations are faced with the task of reducing pollution as well as the contamination of soils and aquifers caused by traffic (especially cars and trucks), industrial production, modern farming, and private households. In developing countries, urban traffic also plays a role. But the main polluters are mines and industrial plants emitting unfiltered fumes and untreated wastewater. People in many poor countries suffer from toxic waste exported by rich countries. Uncontrolled use of poisonous herbicides and pesticides also creates major health risks – including the use of agents that have been banned in Europe and North America.

Third, medical prevention (such as vaccines), medical and paramedical care of patients, pregnant women, mothers and infants, as well as access to medication are essential. In order to achieve these goals, poorer countries not only need improved health care systems, but people living in these countries also need to be able to afford professional care and medication.

Fourth, information is vital. Those who are informed about risks of transmission and possibilities to protect themselves tend to become infected less frequently. The same applies to protection against pregnancies. Education and literacy are distinct advantages in achieving this goal. Access to education for girls, especially, has positive effects.

Fifth, behavioral change can be life-saving, as in the case of HIV/AIDS. Lives could be saved by changes in sexual behavior, the most effective method being the consistent use of condoms. People in industrialized countries could also live longer and better if they were to change their eating habits, avoid alcohol abuse and smoking, and become more conscious about their health in general. Without a doubt, reduced weekday working hours and a lower retirement age can have an impact on our life spans.

9 From a Growing to an Aging Population

The 19th century was characterized by strong population growth in Europe and North America. The 20th century was the period with the strongest population growth ever in human history. There were and still are considerably more births than deaths. Between 1900 and 2000, the number of people living on our planet quadrupled. Such growth has never taken place before, and it will never take place again.

During the 21st century, something very different will affect the development of humanity. We will be confronted with demographic aging. At a global level, rapid aging of the world population has never occurred before. Now it is becoming the most important feature of demographic change. At the same time, population growth will continue to slow down. This is not primarily the case because of declining numbers of births, but because of a growing number of deaths. Despite rising life expectancy, more and more people will reach older age groups that are characterized by high mortality. As a consequence, the annual number of deaths will increase from fifty-five million today (2008) to ninety-one million in 2050.

Global life expectancy has risen over the past 150 years. Despite this increase in average life spans, demographic aging is a relatively new phenomenon. For decades, chances of survival have mainly been increasing among infants and young children. Paradoxically, rising life expectancy initially led to younger populations as more newborns survived. After 1945, a baby boom in developed countries and high numbers of births in other parts of the world intensified this effect. This modern era characterized by a decreasing average age of the world population, only came to an end during the 1970s.

Since the 1970s, the average age of the global population is on the rise. Now in most countries, mortality among older people is declining. Therefore, the world population balance is increasingly shifting from young people to the elderly. This is the change referred to by the term demographic aging. It is not a biological process but a process of change in our society driven by shifting age structures.

Demographic and biological aging

In contrast to demographic aging, the aging of humans as individuals is a biological process with social consequences. This process determines the development, full maturation, and subsequent decay of our body and mind. Newborns become children, then youths, and finally adults. During the course of our life as adults, our vitality declines. Not only do our muscles weaken, but so too does our ability to procreate. Our intellectual and learning capacities are equally affected. Two factors are responsible for this: our genetic disposition and living conditions.

In the end, our age measured in years is of social significance. This can most clearly be seen in existing age groups. Pre-schools and kindergartens are only open to particular age groups of younger children. School attendance is compulsory for children starting at age five or six. The other side of the coin is a ban on child labor enforced in many societies. A minimum legal age is set for gainful employment, marriage, military service, and the right to vote. And finally, most industrialized countries have a mandatory retirement age set by social security laws.

Demographic aging

Demographic aging simply means an increasing number and share of older people and a decreasing number and share of younger people. This leads to a rise in the average and the median age of our societies. Demographic aging has two causes that are completely unrelated to one another: rising life expectancy and declining fertility. The first cause has very positive implications for us. We all belong to the generation with the longest life expectancy ever recorded in human history. The end of this evolution is not yet in sight. In many countries life expectancy continues to increase statistically by two to three months per year. Now that infant and child mortality is very low, the gains in life expectancy are concentrated in the age group 60+. This is why growing life expectancy is leading to increasing numbers of older people, and this development will continue for some time into the future.

Demographic aging also has a second cause, mainly evident in Europe and East Asia. We are not only the generation with – on average – the longest life span. Many parts of the world also experience the lowest number of children per family. In Europe, Japan, China, and a few other rich parts of the world, fertility is already below two children per family. Fewer children automatically increase the share of the older generation.

Demographic and biological aging are two unrelated processes. Demographic aging is a transition from a youthful to a graying society. Such a shift may or may not take place. In contrast, each individual is inevitably subject to biological aging. We grow old as members of a "youthful" society, but also as

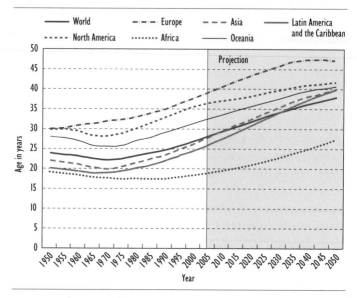

Figure 21 Median age in macro regions of the world, 1950–2050
Source: UN Population Division

members of a "graying society." The dominant age structure
does, however, influence individual opportunities and chances in
life. To give an example: in a graying society, young people face
less competition on the labor market but might have to bear a
larger fiscal burden.

More than 120 million children were born in 1965, at the peak
of the post-war baby boom. Today, they are middle-aged. A considerable number of them will still be alive in the 2040s. During
their lifetimes, the fundamental shift from youthful to rapidly
aging societies is taking place in many parts of the world. They
are the first generation fully affected by this transition.

Average age is rising globally

Demographic aging is a global phenomenon: life expectancy is rising not only in rich countries, but also in the majority of poor countries. The regions in Africa most affected by HIV/AIDS are the only exception.

In the mid-20th century, half of all people worldwide were younger than twenty-four years. The average age then dropped somewhat further. In 1970, half of humankind was younger than twenty-two years. The turning point was reached in the following years. Since then, world population has been aging and will continue to do so throughout the 21st century.

In 2008, the dividing line between the younger and the older half of the global population already was at age twenty-eight. In the coming decades, the aging process will continue to gain momentum. In 2050, the global average age will be thirty-eight years.

Of all world regions, Europe has the oldest population. Here, the aging process already started in the mid-20th century. Today, the average age in the European Union is forty years. In 2050, Western and Central European countries will still have the oldest populations worldwide – alongside Japan. In the European Union average age will rise to approximately forty-eight years. As immigrants tend to be younger, more than half of all EU citizens will be over fifty.

The USA is also affected by demographic aging. Today (2009), 50% of all US residents are below age 36. Until 2050, this average age will rise to 40 years. In Europe and North America, the aging process will decelerate during the second half of the 21st century once the baby boom generation has passed away.

A simple calculation shows how the balances will shift at the global level. Today, for every 100 children and adolescents below age fifteen there are twenty-six persons over age sixty-five. By the mid-21st century, there will be ninety-one older people per one hundred children and adolescents.

For a short period in the early 1970s, more than half of the populations of Asia and South America were below age twenty. Since then, societies in Asia and the Americas have been aging. By 2050, half of the populations of these world regions will most likely be over 40. Compared to the turning point, Asian and American societies are aging the fastest.

Africa has by far the youngest population. Even today, more than half of all Africans are below age twenty. This continent has seen only a slight increase in the average age of the population since the 1990s.

Regional and continental age structure – a time-staggered development

In 1900, the age structure of today's highly developed countries still had the form of a "classic" population pyramid. In 1950, this was no longer the case. At the beginning of the 21st century, the population pyramid looks more like an onion. With a slightly polemical undertone, some commentators also compare it to an urn. In future, the age distribution will increasingly take on the form of a mushroom, indicating that the baby boomers are reaching a higher age. After their death, demographic dynamics in the world's highly developed countries would then give way to a quasi-stationary population resulting in a bell-shape. In European and East Asian societies, however, populations are expected to shrink by 2050. As a consequence, the age distribution will continue to look like a mushroom.

In 1950, the population structure of all low and middle-income countries still looked like a pyramid that continued to

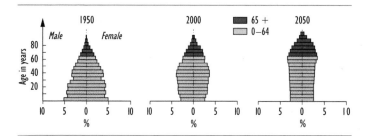

Figure 22 Population pyramids (highly developed countries)
    Source: UN Population Division

widen in the younger age groups. Until today, some see this as an expression of a "healthy" population structure. Yet the narrow tip and the wide base were mainly the result of high mortality among all age groups. Many people already died during their first years of life. The group of zero to five year-olds was therefore much broader than that of the five to ten year olds in the age pyramid of the time. During this period, only a few Asians and Africans reached a higher age.

At the beginning of the 21st century, populations of all low- and middle-income countries combined still had the form of a pyramid. The base, however, was slightly less wide than in 1950. According to the medium variant of UN population projections, the age distribution of these countries will approach a bell shape by the middle of the 21st century.

Finally, we may ask what the age distribution in the poorest and least developed regions of the world looks like. For this, we can use the example of Africa, where most of the poorest countries can be found: we can easily identify the typical pyramid shape. Africa's age distribution in the year 2000 barely varied from that in 1950. The main variant of UN population projections assumes that Africa's population distribution will also move towards a bell form by 2050. This will, however, only take place if Africans further reduce their numbers of children per family.

Childhood and early youth: a modern "invention"

Today, we refer to the ages between birth and fifteen years as childhood and early youth. Childhood is not merely the biological period during which we grow up. In the past 150 years this has emerged as a separate stage in life, distinct from other stages. This is, at least, true for present-day rich countries. This is the phase where playing, learning, acculturation, and school education take place. In rich countries of the Northern hemisphere and in many middle-income countries, children are not expected to secure their own livelihood or to contribute to their family's income. Parents are primarily responsible for this. If they are absent or unable to do so, the welfare state is expected to take care of children and adolescents. Compulsory education, mandatory school attendance, and a ban on child labor reinforce this all. If necessary, police and public administrations try to ensure compliance with these regulations.

Historically speaking, this is a relatively new development which has yet to become universal around the globe. In all pre-modern agrarian societies, children and adolescents had to contribute to their livelihood; for example, by taking care of cattle, helping their parents during harvest seasons, or by taking on tasks in the household. The Industrial Revolution relocated child labor to mining and manufacturing. In poorer countries, both sets of tasks – working as laborers in the agricultural sector and in factories – continues to be a reality for many children today.

Once childhood became accepted as a stage in life distinct from others, relationships between parents and children changed.

As the French historian Philippe Ariès put it pointedly, but with good reason, it was the "invention" of childhood that led to the emergence of modern families. The decrease in infant and child mortality – which has been taking place since the 19th century – also motivated parents to "invest" more time and emotions in the relationships with their children. By the same token, increased life expectancy meant that children on average shared – and continue to share – a much longer life span with their parents.

In 1950, children and adolescents below age fifteen represented more than one quarter (28%) of all people living in highly developed countries. This share continued to rise as a result of the baby boom taking place over the next one and a half decades in the USA and in Europe. Since then, the drop in fertility and birthrates has produced a reverse effect. By 2008, the share of children and adolescents below age fifteen in highly developed countries had fallen to less than 17%. Their number and share will continue to decline somewhat, as in most rich countries of the world the number of births is stagnating or even shrinking.

In 1950, children and adolescents below age fifteen represented 37% – or more than a third – of people living in present-day middle-income countries. Their share then rose to 42% in 1965. This increase was due to high birthrates and falling child mortality. Since then, this share has been declining, reaching 29% in 2007. By 2050, children and adolescents below age fifteen in middle-income countries will make up less than one-fifth of the total population. Despite this, their number will rise from 1.61 billion (2005) to 1.64 billion in 2050, with a peak value that will already be reached in 2020.

To date, in the world's poorest countries children and

adolescents below age fifteen are demographically by far the dominant age group. In 1950, their share was already 41%. In 1975, it reached its peak value of 45% and has since dropped to 41% (2005). There are two reasons for this: continuously high numbers of births recorded in this group of countries and declining infant mortality adding to the size of younger age cohorts. Whether or not this will continue depends on several factors: the desire in the world's poorest societies to have fewer children, better access to family planning, a gradual shift from children as cheap family labor to better-educated children, etc. In any event, a rapid decline in numbers of births is not to be expected, as high numbers of children born in the recent past and lower mortality in younger age groups have a clear outcome. Never before have there been so many potential parents living in the world's poorest countries. The number of children per family may gradually decline in these parts of the world, but the annual number of births will not. As a consequence, the UN forecasts that the absolute number of children and adolescents below age fifteen will increase from 317 million in 2005 to 502 million in 2050. This is an additional 200 million young people in less than half a century, representing a dramatic challenge for the world's poorest regions. Hundreds of thousands of additional medical doctors, nurses, new schools, and teachers will be necessary to merely maintain medical services and education at today's insufficient level. In order to carry out urgently needed improvements, much more effort would be necessary. The next task would then be to create jobs for this continuously growing younger generation.

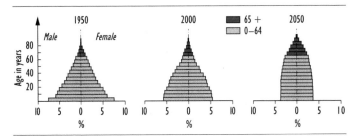

Figure 23 Population pyramids (less developed countries)
Source: UN Population Division

People of working age

In 19th-century Europe and North America, no legal or socially accepted age limits existed that defined the parameters of the beginning and end of a person's working life. This is still the case in many regions of Asia, Africa, and Latin America, with child labor continuing to be a reality. In these world regions, the majority of countries do not have public pension schemes covering the entire economically active population. As a result, some people do not have a chance to retire and receive retirement benefits.

Nonetheless, persons belonging to the age group between fifteen and sixty-five years are considered to be in their main productive years. Naturally, this does not mean that all adolescents and adults between the ages of fifteen and sixty-five are gainfully employed. In this age group, depending on the analyzed country, actual labor force participation is between 60% and 75%. Others continue to go to school, study, take care of their children, are unemployed, or are already in early retirement. A third group occasionally engages in family business – subsistence farming, trade or commercial activities – without being fully involved.

A glimpse at individual biographies shows that boundaries

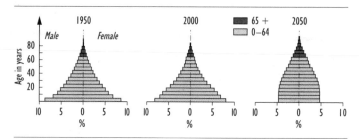

Figure 24 Population pyramids (Africa)
Source: UN Population Division

are blurred. Especially in rich countries, adolescence has long ceased to end at age fifteen as the majority of young people continue their education – although social class plays an important role in determining the age of entry into the labor market. Many young people complete high school or some form of professional or vocational training. University graduates only begin their professional lives in their early to mid-twenties. Subsequently, they also start to have families at a later age – if at all.

A similar development is taking place at the upper end of working lives. Even in poorer countries growing numbers of people are retiring at the end of their professional lives. In rich countries – the USA, Europe, and Japan in particular – this has become the rule. In these parts of the world, the majority of people can rely on secure retirement schemes. The desire to fully enjoy life in the "golden years" then comes into play, motivating a growing number of people in rich societies to opt for early retirement. In Europe today only a minority of economically active people work until they have reached their legal age of retirement.

In 2007, the situation in the European Union was the following: the share of the economically active population was only

8% in the age group sixty-five to sixty-nine, and 27% in the age group sixty to sixty-four. The main reason for this is early retirement. In the USA, labor force participation among the elderly is considerably higher: 15.4% in the age group sixty-five and above, and a considerable 63.7 % in the age group fifty-five to sixty-four.

In Europe, North America, and Japan, the age group fifteen to sixty-five already constituted almost two-thirds (65%) of the population in 1950. In 2005, their share was only slightly larger (68%). From a demographic point of view, this was and is a novelty. In the 20th century – for the first time in history – societies emerged in which the most productive age groups are the demographic majority. Today the largest cohorts within these age groups are the baby boomers of the 1950s and 1960s.

In the developed countries of the Northern hemisphere, the share of people in their main productive years (age fifteen to sixty-five) will become smaller over the coming years: it will most likely shrink to 58% in 2050. The UN population projection also expects a decline in absolute numbers: from 820 million in 2005 to 722 million in 2050.

The working-age population will only decrease in Europe, Russia, and Japan, but not in the USA. If labor force participation rates remain constant, this would also translate into a smaller labor force. This could, of course, have significant consequences for economic output, tax revenues, and social security systems. Whether it will actually happen depends on individual and political decisions as there are two other alternatives. First: people could remain in the labor force for longer periods instead of retiring at an early age. A few countries – including Britain and Germany – have already taken steps in this direction by discussing or actually raising the legal retirement age. Second: Europe and Japan could attract more qualified immigrants in order to fill the gap caused by low fertility. In that sense, foreign immigrants would substitute domestic offspring. Experts call this *replacement migration*.

The share of the working age population in present-day low and middle-income countries grew from 59% in 1950 to 64% in 2005. The UN population projection assumes that this share will remain constant until 2050 (65%). This, however, means a significant rise in absolute numbers. In 2005, 3.4 billion people of working age lived in all low- and middle-income countries. In 2050, this population group will most likely reach 5.1 billion. In China, however – currently the most populous country in the world – the number of people between age fifteen and age sixty-five will shrink from 934 million to 845 million.

After 1950, the proportion of people between age fifteen and age sixty-five in the world's poorest countries declined only marginally because shrinking infant mortality led to a growing number of surviving children. At first, this increased the share of children and adolescents below age fifteen. Since the 1980s, the share of the age group fifteen to sixty-five has begun to increase again. In 2005 its share was 55%. It will rise to 65% in 2050. This increase is far more impressive in absolute numbers. In 1950, only 112 million people of working age lived in the world's poorest countries. By 2005, there were already 418 million people between age fifteen and sixty-five in these countries. In 2050 their number will reach 1.1 billion.

Strong growth in this age group confronts developing countries with considerable challenges. A rapidly growing number of young adults almost automatically means more job seekers. This increases pressure on the local labor markets. If the economy does not offer additional employment opportunities at the same scale, the number of underemployed and discontented individuals will rise. They will then begin to either look for political or religious alternatives or attempt to emigrate. Wealthier countries will be the main destinations. The irregular inflows at the US – Mexico border, the Canary Islands and at Europe's Mediterranean shores give us an idea about the magnitude of such migration flows.

More elderly people

Pre-modern societies held their elderly inhabitants in high esteem. Nonetheless, until recently people above age sixty-five have been a conspicuous minority throughout the history of humankind. This only started to change in the course of the 20th century. At the same time, it was only the introduction of a legal retirement age that created a biographical point in time defining that a person belongs to the category of the aged. Today, legal retirement age is between sixty and sixty-five. This, however, is only relevant for a minority of the world's economically active population. The majority of adults in Asia, Africa, and Latin America are neither covered by public pension plans nor can they afford private retirement schemes. They will therefore most likely be unable to draw a pension. In poorer countries, today, people aged 60–65 either continue to work or become dependent on their own children. It is unlikely that this will change in the near future.

Today, the elderly constitute the fastest growing age group. In 1950, there were only 131 million people age sixty-five and older on our planet: just 5% of the global population. In 2005, this age group had already increased to 475 million people, representing 7% of the world population. A further rise of about one billion older persons can be expected in the coming four decades. In 2050, 1.5 billion people will belong to the age group 65+. As a result of global aging, their share will increase to 16% of the global population. While overall population growth will

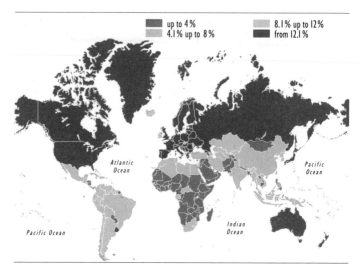

| up to 4 % | 8.1 % up to 12 % |
| 4.1 % up to 8 % | from 12.1 % |

Figure 25 Elderly people (over 65 years) as percentage of the population
Source: UN Population Division

decelerate and come to a standstill over the course of the 21st
century, the growth of the elderly will accelerate.

Increasing numbers of older people can be expected in all
world regions. In absolute numbers, Asia will dominate this
growth, with China leading the way. In relative terms, Europe
and Japan will face the most dramatic demographic aging
process. For it is only in Europe and Japan that the number
of younger native-born adults will decline, while the number
of senior citizens will continue to grow during the next forty
years. In some European countries, the shrinking size of younger
adults is already visible. Many other countries can expect this to
become a reality in the coming decade. This, in turn, will reduce
the number of people of working age. It is most likely that this
will lead to more immigration to Europe.

In 1950, the elderly (65+) in highly developed countries represented just 8% of the total population. In 2005, their share already had risen to 15%. In the mid-21st century, it will reach 26%. Europe, North America, and Japan will therefore be home to significantly more elderly than children and adolescents. Seen from a historical perspective this is a completely new phenomenon.

In low and middle-income countries, the current share of elderly inhabitants is only about 6%. This will, however, change dramatically in the coming decades. According to the main variant of the UN population projection, this share will rise to 15% by 2050. In absolute terms, this growth is even more impressive: in 1950 there were only sixty-seven million elderly living in low- and middle-income countries. In 2005, their size had already reached 291 million. In 2050, there will be 1.1 billion people over age sixty-five living in Asia (without Japan), Africa and Latin America.

In the world's poorest countries, an even more striking increase will take place: in 1950, they were home to seven million elderly; in 2005 their number was twenty-four million. In 2050, some 114 million elderly will live in the world's poorest countries.

From a global perspective, Europe already today looks like an "old continent." By 2050, Europe's population – alongside Japan's – will still have the highest average age of any region. Yet the most dramatic aging process of the 21st century will actually take place in Asia – first in China and later also in India. China today only has just over 100 million elderly citizens. In 2050 at least 330 million Chinese will be over sixty-five. In India, the size of this age group (65+) will grow from sixty million today to 240 million in 2050. In China and India, demographic aging will have significantly more consequences than in Western countries. The majority of Chinese and Indian adults, for example, are not covered by any pension plan or health insurance. And Chinese population policy means that tomorrow's elderly will by no means be able to count on the support of a large number of children.

The very old

The elderly population does not form a uniform group. Today, we distinguish between two groups: first, the "young old," of whom most in Europe are no longer economically active, while in the USA and Japan a considerable share still is at work; and second, the "old old." In any case, the prolongation of our life expectancy leads to a particularly rapid growth among the very old. Usually, persons age 85+ are included in this group. In 1950, barely any people were alive at this age. Globally, only 0.3% of men and 0.5% of women were over eighty-five. That was four per 1000 inhabitants. In 2005, already 0.9% of men and 2.2% of women belonged to this age group. If this development continues, the share of very old people will, more than triple to 5% by 2050. The sociology of aging sees this stage of life as a slow detaching ("desocialization") of humans from their respective social and everyday environments.

Both the nature of aging and its consequences partly depend on a person's gender. Women make up 49.7% of world population. Yet their share among higher age groups is significantly larger: 56% among all elderly people (65+) and 68% among the very old (85+). In highly developed countries, these differences are even more pronounced. In Europe, North America, and Japan, women make up 51.5% of the total population. Among all elderly people (65+), their share is 60% and even reaches 72% among the very old. This is mainly attributable to much greater life expectancy between men and women in rich countries than in low- and middle-income countries.

In highly developed countries, living conditions among the very old often change tremendously. Here, gender also plays an important role. While most men remain in their homes and are taken care of by family members even at a high age, the majority of very old women tend to require professional care. Many more women than men spend their last months or years in institutional care. Most of them are widows. Their partners were usually a few years older, and had died by the time these women were in need of care. Extended family networks with several generations to provide for elderly members hardly exist in industrialized nations.

	1950		2000		2050	
	Number	%	Number	%	Number	%
World	130	5.2	421	6.9	1464	16.1
Europe	54	8.2	107	14.7	180	27.6
North America	14	8.2	39	12.4	93	21.1
Africa	7	3.2	27	3.3	128	6.7
Asia	57	4.1	216	5.9	910	17.5
Latin America	6	3.7	29	5.6	144	18.4
Australia/Pacific	1	7.3	3	9.7	9	19.3

Table 23 Total number and share of elderly people (65+) by world regions, 1950–2050

Values for 2050: UN medium projection variant
Source: UN Population Division (2005)

Active generation vs. young and old

For every age distribution we can ask the following question: how many children and adolescents on the one hand, and elderly on the other, have to be sustained by the working age population? An answer is provided by an index called the dependency ratio. Two factors are relevant for this index. The first factor is the "burden" posed by children, or the ratio of people under fifteen per 100 people between the ages of fifteen and sixty-five. The second factor is the "burden" posed by the aged. This is the ratio of people over age sixty-five per 100 persons between the ages of fifteen and sixty-five. The total burden combines both "non-active" age groups (0–14 and 65+) compared to the size of the working age – and potentially active – population.

An analysis of the demographic dependency ratio shows the following: in the 1970s, 100 members of the active generation had to provide for seventy-five children and elderly persons worldwide. Today, this ratio is fifty-five children and elderly per 100 people of working age. The rise of the demographic dependency ratio until the 1970s and its subsequent fall are exclusively due to rising and declining "burdens" of children. In highly developed countries, there were forty-three children (0–14) per 100 people of working age in 1960 and about twenty-five children per 100 in 2005. In low and middle-income countries, this ratio declined from seventy-seven children per 100 people of working age in 1965 to forty-seven children per 100 in 2005. There, the ratio will most likely continue to decline and reach thirty-two children per 100 people of working age in 2050. If managed well, countries can reap a so-called "demographic dividend" during this period of declining "burdens" caused by children by making investments in educational and other infrastructure.

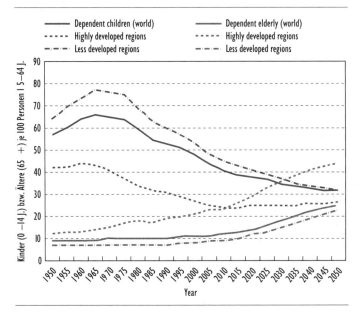

Figure 26 Dependency ratios, 1950–2050
Children (0–14 years) and elderly people (65+) per 100 persons of working age (15–64)
Source: UN Population Division

In contrast, the "burden" of the elderly at the global level has been relatively small to date. In 2005, there were only eleven people above age sixty-five per 100 persons of working age. In the coming forty years, though, this ratio will increase to twenty-four elderly per 100 persons of working age. In other words: the burden will more than double.

In highly developed countries, the old age dependency ratio already reached twenty-four elderly per 100 persons of working age in 2005. By 2050, this ratio will most likely rise to forty-three elderly persons per 100 persons of working age. In low and middle-income economies, this ratio will increase from nine per 100 in 2005 to twenty-three per 100 in 2050.

From an economic point of view, this index only gives us a hint of actual burdens and shared responsibilities. In many poorer countries, children either do not attend school at all or leave school long before their fifteenth birthdays. At that age, many of them already contribute to their families' livelihood and income. In contrast, in rich countries, many adolescents and young adults are enrolled in education beyond age twenty and have not yet begun to earn their own money. The age of sixty-five as a boundary between economically active and non-active life is equally ambivalent. In Europe, most people withdraw from active life before reaching the legal retirement age. In other parts of the world, many continue to work beyond age sixty-five.

10 Too Many People?

The global population is currently growing at a pace of approximately seventy-eight million people per year. Roughly 95% of this worldwide increase takes place in low and middle-income countries. Populations of the poorest countries of Africa, Asia, and Oceania are growing the fastest. This begs the question: What are the living conditions and future opportunities of children born in these countries today? They are the young generation of tomorrow and the future workforce of the world regions most in need of development. At the same time, we may ask ourselves about the living conditions of currently 6.8 billion inhabitants on our planet. During the next four decades, global population will most likely increase to nine billion and peak at ten billion at the end of the 21st century.

From today's perspective, four areas closely connected to population growth can be identified within a larger framework of challenges facing humanity in the 21st century. These are:

- extreme poverty, underdevelopment, and underemployment
- a growing number of international migrants
- global aging
- the creation of humane living conditions that can be reconciled with sustainable development.

Population and development

Famine, malnutrition, and a lack of drinking water are generally not the immediate consequences of large numbers of inhabitants or growing populations. They can also not be explained by a worldwide lack of food. Since the 1970s, the global economy has produced more cereals and other food on an annual basis than people in the world have consumed. Developed parts of the world – mainly in Europe, North America, and Japan – have a highly productive and usually highly subsidized agricultural sector. The subsidized surpluses produced are one of the obstacles for a further liberalization of international trade (as negotiated by WTO in the so-called Doha round).

Famine, malnutrition, and a lack of drinking water have completely different causes. Simon Kuznets, the 1971 Nobel laureate in Economics, rightly posed the question of why population growth would have to impede economic growth. Automatically equating a growing population figure with economic problems stems from a point of view propagated two centuries ago by Thomas R. Malthus and his followers. In reality, a fatal relationship – as postulated by Malthus – does not exist. Amartya Sen, the 1998 Nobel laureate in Economics, proved this using the example of India. He was able to demonstrate that social disparities and badly functioning public institutions and infrastructure in this country are primarily responsible for destitution and underdevelopment. In this sense, governance problems and a lack of political will have to be held accountable for turning population growth into a real development problem.

A series of scientific studies have shown that population growth is not generally the cause of poverty and underdevelopment. But rapid population growth exacerbates the search for solutions, and overtaxes existing infrastructure capacities and the ability of labor markets to absorb a growing workforce. As a result, an increasing number of people in rapidly growing societies have no possibility of attending school or accessing medical care in the event of an illness or during pregnancy.

There may well be some sort of a demographic poverty trap in the least developed countries. These countries most urgently need investment in infrastructure, industrial and agricultural production. However, if half of the population is younger than eighteen years, a considerable share of scarce resources should go towards the educational system and to basic health services. Otherwise, many young people will grow up with diseases, and without basic education. Throughout their adult lives, they will suffer from a lack of skills and diminished economic opportunities. However, public resources allocated cannot be spent on material infrastructure.

Rapid population growth in less developed countries may also stand in the way of economic development because such growth mainly leads to more children and adolescents. Only after a drop in fertility can the share of children and adolescents in the population start to decline, allowing for a rise in the share of young adults of working age. At this point, the "demographic dividend" can start to play a role. Only then can developing countries profit from their age structure. This presupposes, however, that the potential of these young adults at their most productive age can be realized, allowing for a positive correlation between population growth and development opportunities.

"Development is the best contraceptive." Participants agreed on this wording at the 1974 UN Population Conference in Bucharest. It is by no means wrong, but requires detailed elaboration. Rising prosperity and sinking mortality have actually led to falling numbers of children in the world's wealthier countries. Yet additional efforts in the area of family planning and reproductive health are necessary in poorer countries. These global efforts are meeting with success. The best evidence for this is the declining numbers of children in low- and middle-income countries over the past thirty years.

The most important contributor to this global decline in fertility was the increased ability of more people to make conscious decisions about their offspring. Today, we understand and cherish the prerogative to make such decisions as a fundamental human right. A further prerequisite is the knowledge that fewer but better educated children are also economically advantageous. This means that having a larger number of children is no longer a self-evident goal in life that we owe to our god, our family clan, or the nation as a whole. Instead, what counts are individual ambitions and plans. In the end, sexual education, access to family planning, counseling and methods of contraception become crucial.

The right to determine the number of children a person wishes to produce is by no means reality throughout the world. Women and men have a more limited access to family planning in poorer countries especially. This particularly applies to sub-Saharan Africa, and a number of South and West Asian societies.

Empowerment of women

Crucial to economic and social development, as well as to population development, is the status of women in society. In traditional settings, they usually have fewer chances than men. In this context, improving women's rights is just as important as providing access to education and the labor market. Self-determination and empowerment depend on both equal rights and equal opportunities.

Without realizing this crucial role that the status of women plays, the fundamental targets of population, family, and health policies cannot be achieved. These include reducing the number of unplanned pregnancies, decreasing child mortality and the improvement of living standards by strengthening women's participation in the labor force and increasing their earning capacities.

Poverty and hunger

Still today, many people in Asia, Africa, Latin America, and some parts of Eastern Europe cannot satisfy their basic daily needs. Almost half of humanity lives in poverty. Approximately one billion people have to live on less than one dollar a day, as measured in purchasing power parities. Despite overall population growth, the group living in extreme poverty has become smaller over the last two decades. Another two billion people live on something between one and two dollars a day. In the world's poorest countries, this is reality for a large majority of inhabitants. In middle-income countries with higher economic output per capita, generally half the population lives in poverty. In Eastern Europe, this is the case for a considerable minority.

At the top of the global income pyramid is a considerable and constantly growing concentration of wealth. The fortune of the three wealthiest individuals in the world corresponds to the combined annual GDPs of all fifty-one poorest countries. The share of these fifty-one countries in world trade makes up a mere 0.4%. The most affluent 20% of the global population earn about one hundred times as much as the poorest 20%. And the most affluent 20% consume 85% of all goods that are produced for private consumption.

In many cases, poverty means that people do not have permanent and sufficient access to food and drinking water. An estimated 800 million people constantly suffer from hunger; a further 400 million periodically do not have enough to eat. An estimated 1.1 billion cannot access clean drinking water throughout the year. And 2.6 billion live in municipalities that lack sewage systems and do not provide any wastewater removal or treatment.

This has serious implications for those affected. Malnutrition can lead to development disorders in children and adolescents. Hunger weakens people, reduces their productivity and intellectual capacities, and makes them more susceptible to infectious diseases. A lack of clean drinking water and sanitation increases the danger that gastrointestinal diseases will spread. Especially children living in developing countries and emerging economies continue to die of such diseases. Today, in the early 21st century, about nine million people starve to death annually – among them five million children. A further two million annually die of intestinal diseases contracted by drinking contaminated water. An even larger number of children are weakened by a lack of proper nutrition and die of diseases that would otherwise not have taken a deadly course.

There are very different reasons for hunger and destitution. The reasons are usually most evident when the causes have a political background. Time and again, people affected by chaos, civil wars, and other violent conflicts find themselves cut off from provisions and lack the possibility to provide for themselves. In the meantime, the suffering of civilian populations has become one of the "weapons" used by warring factions to put additional pressure on their opponents. Some warring factions even hold their own population hostage or profit from distributing humanitarian aid coming from the outside. Two recent examples for this are the conflict in the West Sudanese region of Darfur and the situation in North Korea.

Natural catastrophes, floods, and long-lasting droughts have similar consequences. Yet, international humanitarian aid and disaster relief are usually easier to provide in these circumstances than in the case of war.

Hunger and poverty are also the result of economic and social marginalization. The poorest 20% of the global population is unable to produce either enough food to sustain themselves or other goods and services to sell or trade for food supplies. This can be due to extremely unequal distribution of land or local prices for agricultural products that offer no incentive to produce surpluses.

State-controlled ceilings for market prices or state-administered prices for staple food exist in several countries. Such measures are intended to ease the burden of purchasing basic foods for the urban underclasses. Urban dwellers can more easily be mobilized and are therefore politically more "danger-ous" for governments than impoverished rural populations. At the end of the day, though, fixed price limits reduce the amount of food available on the market. In some cases, "famine relief" provided by wealthier countries and international organizations has similar negative effects – especially when agro-industrially produced surpluses from Europe and North America are dis-tributed for free or at dumping prices in developing countries. In doing so, local farmers lose their local markets – and, at the same time, any incentive to produce food above and beyond the needs of the family.

In some areas, the most fertile land is earmarked for plan-tations that produce cash crops, animal feed, and luxury arti-cles – like flowers – for export to wealthier countries, while the local populations are left malnourished. Increasing local biofuel production does not feed local populations, regardless of whether ethanol is exported or used as an additive to locally consumed gasoline. The same applies to water used for agricultural irrigation, industrial production, or to generate energy. All of these activities can lead to a lack of drinking water.

In a series of countries, urbanization, depletion of natural resources, or climate change are all contributing to the loss of fertile soils. These lands are being used for real estate and infrastructure development or sacrificed to dam projects, or they become lost to soil erosion, desertification, and salinization.

Finally, poverty can also simply be related to the fact that people have no financial means or access to credit with which to purchase seeds and production equipment. This leaves them unable to produce food, goods, or services – a lost opportunity when a demand for them exists.

Underdevelopment, lacking educational opportunities, underemployment

Poverty and underdevelopment often go hand in hand with a lack of education and literacy. The number of illiterate people is declining, but their proportion is still notably high in the least developed countries. Currently, 770 million adults globally – 13% of all men and 23% of all women – are illiterate. Females still have less access to educational opportunities than males. Countries characterized by the lowest income per capita – and very often the highest birth rates – usually have the greatest differences in educational opportunities for men and women. Girls are attending schools in smaller numbers than boys; and they attend them for shorter periods of time. In such a context, it is clear that high fertility goes hand in hand with low access to education for women. The future evolution of the number of children per family is therefore very closely related to available or absent educational opportunities for women.

An estimated 120 million children and adolescents of school age do not receive any kind of education. They therefore do not learn to read or write or solve basic mathematical problems. It is evident that the majority of these children and adolescents can only take on unskilled and low-pay jobs – if they are lucky enough to find work at all. The majority of people lacking formal education live in sub-Saharan Africa – where fertility is still very high and labor market opportunities are particularly low.

Highly problematic in this respect is the rapid growth of the labor force potential in least developed countries. Their economies often lack the necessary absorbtive capacity, inevitably leading to rising unemployment. Third World societies with a large share of agricultural producers and low savings definitely have problems providing enough employment opportunities when rapid socio-economic transformation takes place. Total populations, and with them labor force potential, are growing. People leave the agricultural sector. Women who were either active in the agricultural sector or in the household more frequently try to find paid work at home or abroad. Millions of these women now work as nannies, caregivers, or other domestic labor, or in unskilled positions in North America, Europe, the Gulf states and other high-income countries and territories such as Hong Kong and Singapore.

In less developed countries between 1980 and 2000, the number of people working or seeking employment grew by 2% per year. This growth continues at an annual rate of +1.6%. How do these people secure their livelihoods? In the majority of less developed countries, economic growth has not been able to keep pace with the growing number of those seeking employment. Globally, 185 million adolescents and adults are unemployed. Almost half of them are between fifteen and twenty-five years of age. A further 400 million people are underemployed.

Global aging

The 20th century was the period with the highest growth ever in world population history. Never before on our planet had there been a quadrupling of the population in such a short time. And never again will such a growth take place.

In the 21st century, humanity will be confronted with unprecedented demographic aging. The number of people above the age of sixty-five will grow from its current level of 500 million to 1.5 billion. Today, Europe, Japan, and North America enjoy the highest life expectancy. And these world regions will also have the oldest populations in the mid-21st century.

At the moment, the age group 65+ makes up about a sixth of all people living in rich countries. A quarter of them are over eighty. In Europe, average age will rise from thirty-eight currently to forty-eight years in 2050. By then, more than half of all "native" EU citizens will be over fifty years old when taking the lower average age of foreign immigrants into account. In North America, aging will be less accentuated. In the USA, the average age will only rise from presently thrity-six years to forty years in 2050.

At the same time, in Europe and Japan the native-born work force will at best stagnate or even decline. This could have consequences for economic development and productivity. Aging negatively affects human capital formation. This at least applies to knowledge that is generated and passed on by schools and universities. In Europe and Japan, smaller cohorts of adolescents and young adults leaving the educational system will mean fewer people entering the labor market with fresh knowledge. There are also indications that demographic aging leads to less innovation. At the same time, the number of elderly people leaving the labor market will inevitably grow as baby boomers reach retirement age. In Europe and Japan this will most likely lead to a lack of native-born labor and skills. Immigration will have to make up for part of this gap.

A declining workforce ultimately leads to fewer taxpayers. The result might be higher public debt per capita.

Effects on the social security system

Demographic aging has significant effects on our social security systems. Public pension systems clearly face a challenge. In pay-as-you-go systems, the economically active generation paying contributions will have to support growing numbers of retirees. In China, in the absence of a public pension system, economically active adults will have to individually support a growing number of elderly family members.

A rapidly growing number of elderly persons, and of very old people in particular, also creates an enormous challenge to the healthcare system. Demographic aging almost automatically leads to higher healthcare expenditures, since the incidence of many ailments increases with age – even if tomorrow's elderly will most likely be healthier than those of today. In particular, the curbing of cancer and cardiovascular diseases leads to a new situation. People are not only becoming older but also suffering from chronic diseases – such as Alzheimer's, Parkinson's, and diabetes – and chronic organ degeneration for a longer period of time. This will inevitably necessitate more home care as well as more institutional care.

In rich countries, low numbers of children, fewer marriages, higher divorce rates, and higher labor force participation of women have led to a transformation of family structures, reducing solidarity within family networks that until now have provided care for free. Long-term professional home care must now fulfill this role, at an increased cost for the frail and chronically ill.

Demographic aging will present highly developed countries with considerable problems. Yet the problems posed by population aging will soon affect emerging economies, and eventually many developing countries outside Africa as well.

By 2050, there will be 570 million elderly Chinese and Indians, exceeding the number of elderly in all rich countries of the Northern hemisphere. No old-age insurance exists for these people. It is currently unclear when and how pension schemes could be introduced for the majority of old people in developing countries and emerging economies. Old age poverty can already be observed in these countries today. It will increase with demographic change as younger people in developing countries today are having fewer children. This means that tomorrow's aged will be confronted with less familial support than today's older generation.

A paramount dilemma of the 21st century

Both from a demographic and a socio-economic point of view, a central dilemma exists that is far from being solved. For almost every person, development implies an improvement in living standards. In the rich countries of today, this has been and continues to be tied to the market economy, social protection, an efficient production of industrial goods and services, and the individualization of lifestyles. Declining fertility came about not only because of worries about future opportunities of children but also about one's own pursuit of happiness. Today, this happiness is no longer measured in terms of the number and "quality" of children, but in terms of career and consumption opportunities, larger living space, cars, travel opportunities, secondary residences, etc. This lifestyle results in significantly higher energy and resource consumption, as well as high levels of pollution, carbon emissions, sewage, and solid waste. The ecological costs of our modern Western lifestyles are high. By the same token, this lifestyle has led to zero population growth and sustainable containment of population size without state interventions. Global costs occur, for example, in the form of global warming, and we contribute substantially to this through our emissions. For many people, new arid regions and the rise of sea levels caused by this warming will spell the loss of their habitats. Great additional waves of migration will be the consequence.

This leads to the central question concerning the choice of an adequate development model: how can the entirely legitimate desire for all persons to participate in universal prosperity be fulfilled? The dilemma lies in the most seemingly plausible answer at first glance: Above and beyond ensuring one's daily survival, people associate development with the attainment of a Western style of living. In developing countries and emerging economies, the living standards of the elite and the growing middle classes serve as a universal model. Yet the Western development and prosperity model is so costly in resource consumption that making it a reality for all citizens of our world is currently almost unimaginable. How can, for example, the desire of a future 1.5 billion Chinese – and soon just as many Indians – to have one to two cars per family, generous living and transportation space, energy consumption at Western levels, and individual mobility, be fulfilled? The lifestyle currently enjoyed by the rich North cannot be applied generally. This is particularly true of the level of consumption and emissions that is currently still the almost unquestioned norm in North America, Japan, and Western Europe. In global terms, a comparably high consumption of energy and resources by all 6.8 and soon more than nine billion people will not be possible. This would overstretch the limits of our ecosystem, not only negatively affecting our quality of life, but also the livelihoods of millions of people. We do not even have the necessary resources to fulfill more modest desires: if all people would claim the amount of meat consumed per capita in the highly developed world, we would have to quadruple the size of the already fairly extensive animal farming industry.

Without a change in lifestyles and resource consumption of the rich North, a life of dignity for everyone is hardly imaginable!

There have always been two main lines of thinking among those who have reflected on population and development: we may label them the population optimists and the population pessimists. Optimists assume that all of the problems outlined above are solvable. For them, population growth in modern times is the best proof of a positive relationship between demographic and economic expansion. In contrast, pessimists assume that a growing number of people create the potential for catastrophes. They stress the threats of general impoverishment, famine, and a general destabilization of society at large. We do not wish to subscribe to either of these "schools of thought" here. As our book shows, population, development, and human evolution are closely linked to one another. But there is no linear relationship between the number of people in a region and the living standards of people in that region. This does, however, leave the dilemma mentioned above unsolved. Our efforts to develop the

Topics for the 21st Century — The Millennium Development Goals

The Millennium Development Goals point to a way of changing the situation. In 2000, the heads of states of 189 countries came together at a summit meeting at the UN headquarters in New York. There, they adopted the Millennium Declaration addressing the global challenges of the 21st century. It identifies four major fields of action within national and international policy:

- peace, security, and disarmament
- development and poverty eradication
- protection of a common environment
- human rights, democracy, and good governance

Eight development goals later emanated from the Declaration. The **Millennium Development Goals** are to be realized by 2015. These goals contain concrete targets that allow their attainment to be measured above and beyond political rhetoric. These eight goals include:

Goal 1: Eradicate extreme poverty and hunger
Goal 2: Achieve universal primary education
Goal 3: Promote gender equality and empower women
Goal 4: Reduce child mortality
Goal 5: Improve maternal health
Goal 6: Combat HIV/AIDS, malaria and other diseases
Goal 7: Ensure environmental sustainability
Goal 8: Develop a global partnership for development

world are geared towards a living standard that – from an ecological perspective – cannot be generalized.

All of these goals are, to some extent, related to population
and development as well as to current demographic problems
and challenges. They also touch upon issues related to trade and
finance, good governance, debt policies, job creation, and patent
protection for medication and technologies relevant to development cooperation.

The UN monitors and documents the achievement of the Millennium Goals. In 2005, 150 heads of state came together at the
Millennium+5 Summit to take stock of progress made on the
goals. The promotion of "reproductive health" was added as an
additional goal.

Selected Online Resources and Web Links

The *UN Population Division* website informs about relevant
figures and indicators for almost all countries and territories
of the world. This includes: births, deaths, natural growth,
population size, age structure, urbanization, contraceptive
use, number of international migrants. It also gives the latest
demographic forecasts (World Population Prospects).
http://esa.un.org/unpp/
http://www.un.org/esa/population/unpop.htm (UN, New York)
The *EUROSTAT* website offers relevant and very detailed
information for all twenty-seven EU member states as well as
for many other European countries: http://www.ec.europa.
eu/eurostat
The website of the US Census Bureau gives detailed
information for the USA and selected figures and indicators
for all countries of the world.
http://www.census.gov (US Census Bureau, Washington DC)
The following websites also contain relevant information:
http://www.prb.org (Population Reference Bureau, Washington
DC)
http://www.worldbank.org/ (World Bank, Washington DC)
http://www.oecd.org/ (OECD, Paris)
http://portal.unesco.org/ (UNESCO, Paris)
http://www.ilo.org/ (International Labor Organization,
Geneva)

http://www.who.int/ (World Health Organization, Geneva)
http://www.fao.org/ (World Food Organization, Rome)

Glossary

Age Pyramid: See *Population Pyramid*

Age Structure: The age structure of a population provides information about the quantitative relationship of different age groups to the total population. It is the result of prior demographically relevant events such as births, deaths, immigration, and emigration. Information about a society's age structure is vital in order to describe current population dynamics and to forecast future developments. See also *Population Pyramid*.

Age-Specific Rate: Any rate attained for a specific age group. An age-specific rate indicates the frequency of demographic events or features, not for the total population but for a specific age group (for example, the death rate among women in age group 75–80).

Anti-Natalist Policy: The policy of a government, society, or social group to slow population growth by attempting to limit the number of children per woman.

Average Age: The arithmetic average of the age of all people within a given population. See also Mean Age.

Baby Boom: A rapidly rising fertility rate leading to a considerable increase in the absolute number of births experienced in several countries following World War II. It first occurred in the USA, Canada, Australia, and New Zealand (1947–1961). With a certain time lag, European

countries also experienced a rise in fertility and in the
number of births. The post-war baby boom had its roots in
the economic and social upturn following the end of World
War II.

Birth Control: Practices applied by individuals and couples
that permit sexual intercourse with reduced likelihood of
conception and birth. The term birth control is often used
synonymously with contraception, fertility control, and
family planning. In a broader sense it also includes abortion.

Cause-Specific Death Rate: The number of deaths attributable
to a specific cause per 100,000 population in a given year.

Carrying Capacity: The largest possible population with
permanent residence in a given ecosystem when taking all
aspects of sustainability into consideration. Limitations
include factors such as food production, carbon emissions,
and waste disposal capacities.

Census, also *Population Count*: A statistical compilation
(head count, survey) of the total population of a country
at a certain point in time. Depending on the structure of
the survey, it supplies comprehensive data on the number,
age, sex, place of birth, citizenship, professional structure,
education, and social composition of the population, as well
as the forms of cohabitation in private households.

Cohort: A group of persons with a common temporal
characteristic, most commonly the year of birth. For
example, all persons born in the same year constitute a birth
or age cohort. However, other temporal commonalities can
be taken as a basis for defining a cohort, such as the year
of marriage, the year of entry into the labor market, or the
year of retirement. These are correspondingly referred to as
marriage, labor market entry, or retirement cohorts.

Cohort Analysis: Observation of a cohort's demographic behavior through life or through a longer period of time; for example, an analysis of fertility of people born between 1960 and 1965 through their entire childbearing years. Rates derived from such cohort analyses are cohort measures. See also *Period Analysis*.

Completed Fertility: The actual number of children born to women at the end of their childbearing years. This number of children can only be determined once the fertile life phase of a female birth cohort has been completed.

Contraceptive prevalence: Percentage of individuals or couples currently using a particular contraceptive method.

Crude Birth Rate: The number of live births in a particular territory per 1000 inhabitants in a given year. Age structure effects become very evident in crude birth rates. See also *Total Fertility Rate (TFR)*.

Crude Death Rate, Crude Mortality Rate: The number of deaths per year and per 1000 persons within a population.

DALY: The abbreviation for *Disease-Adjusted Life Years*. DALY describes not only mortality, but also the impairment of a normal, symptom-free life caused by illness. The number of lost years of life through premature death (see: *Lost Years of Life*) is combined with the loss of life span through disability or disease (in particular, chronic disease). Illnesses and disability years are calculated on a percentage basis as "lost years of life" depending on the degree of impairment.

Demographic Aging: Demographic aging occurs when fertility declines while life expectancy remains constant or improves at a higher age. Furthermore, emigration of younger people adds to demographic aging. As a result, the share of elderly people increases while the share of children, adolescents, and young adults decreases. This is reflected in a rise in average age and median age of the population.

Demographic Momentum, Population Momentum: The tendency of populations to maintain population growth or decline even after the replacement level has been attained. A population whose fertility has decreased to or even below replacement level can continue to grow for several decades, as high fertility rates in the past led to high numbers of people in younger age groups who have now entered fertile age (for example: China). A negative momentum can also be surmised: if Germany were to suddenly reach the replacement level for fertility by 2015 and were able to maintain it for the next 100 years, the population would still continue to decline for a further seventy years (in the absence of immigration) because of the small size of the future parent generation.

Demographic Transition: Refers to the historic process of transition from high birth and death rates to low birth and death rates. The decline of mortality usually precedes the decline in fertility, thus resulting in rapid population growth during the transition period.

Demography: Also called Population Studies, unites elements of sociology, geography, medicine, economics and historiography. It studies human populations by analyzing size, composition, distributions, density, growth, and other population characteristics as well as their variations, causes, and effects.

Dependency Ratio: The ratio of the economically dependent part of the population to the productive part; arbitrarily defined as the ratio of the elderly (age sixty-five and older) plus the young (below age fifteen) to the working age population (ages 15–64). The *total dependency ratio* describes the ratio between economically dependent age groups (persons who are not yet or are no longer of working age) to the working age population. In industrialized countries, longer educational periods and early retirement mean that the productive age is rather assumed to be between twenty and sixty years of age. In less developed countries, the productive age is closer to the range of fifteen to sixty-five years. Children and adolescents as well as and senior citizens can also separately be compared to the productive age group. This is then called *youth dependency ratio* and *old age dependency ratio*. In 2007 in the European Union, there were approximately 100 persons of working age per fifty children and senior citizens (with senior citizens dominating the dependent age groups). In the same year in Brazil, there were 100 persons of working age per fifty-one children and senior citizens (with children dominating the dependent age groups).

Doubling Time: The number of years required for the population of a particular region, country, or continent to double its present size, given the current rate of population growth.

Emigration: The departure from a specific geographic unit (country, region, municipality) in order to assume permanent or long-term residence in another geographic unit.

Epidemiological Transition: A change in the structure of main causes of death in a given historical context. While parasitic and infectious diseases prevailed in pre-industrial societies, nutrition, improved hygiene, and living conditions as well as medical advancements contributed to overcoming such illnesses. The main causes of death in highly developed countries are cardiovascular disease (stroke, heart attack) and cancer. In the future, chronic and degenerative diseases will play an increasingly significant role. Many developing countries have yet to complete the epidemiological transition from infectious to cardiovascular diseases and cancer as the main causes of death.

Epidemiology: An academic discipline that is concerned with the distribution of diseases among a population and their causes. While its original focus was on the study of the distribution and control of infectious diseases, a shift, especially in industrialized countries, has taken place towards the causation (etiology) of cardiovascular diseases, cancer, and chronic diseases.

Family: Usually two or more persons living together and related by birth, marriage, or adoption. Families may consist of siblings or other relatives as well as married couples and any children they have.

Family Planning: Deliberate measures taken by individuals and couples, such as modern or natural methods of contraception, in order to influence the number of children and the spacing of their births. Family planning not only includes contraception in order to prevent pregnancies but also deliberate measures to become pregnant. See also *Anti-Natalist Policy, Pro-Natalist Policy*.

Fertility, Fecundity: In a biological sense, fertility is the potential ability to reproduce and to have children (also called fecundity). In demography the term *fertility* only refers to the actual number of children per woman realized by a couple, a specific group (age group, social group), or an entire population. Demographers measure fertility by calculating general and age-specific fertility rates as well as the *Total Fertility Rate*.

Gross Reproduction Rate (GRR): The average number of daughters who would be born alive to a group of women over their lifetime if their age-specific fertility rates of a given year would remain constant. See also *Net Reproduction Rate*; and *Total Fertility Rate*.

Growth Rate, General: A measure for changes in a population over time. It refers to changes in population size between two points in time, measured as a percentage of population size at the beginning of the observed period. When a population declines (because of an excess of deaths over births or net migration loss), the growth rate can take on a negative value.

Growth Rate, Natural, also *Natural Population Growth*: Natural population growth rate is a measure for the natural *population movement*. It refers to the changes in a population between two points in time, measured as a percentage of the population size at the beginning of the period of observation, by only taking births and deaths into account; immigration and emigration are not included in this rate.

Household: A private household is either (a) a unit of persons (multi-person household) living together and sharing household functions (for example, generating income, cooking); or (b) a person living alone (single household). A household can include family members and/or individuals unrelated by family ties (for example, servants living in a family household, students or migrant workers sharing a flat). In statistical records, families with several domiciles are often documented as multiple households. In addition, several forms of communal and institutional (non-private) households exist, such as boarding schools, orphanages, convents, military barracks, residential homes for senior citizens, residential homes for refugees and asylum seekers, and prisons.

Immigration: Immigration refers to the movement of a person coming from a different territorial unit (municipality, district, province, or state), or from a foreign country in order to establish a permanent or semi-permanent place of residence. A UN definition suggests that a person should be considered an international migrant if he or she intends to stay for at least a year. Some countries, however, start to count people as migrants after a minimal stay of three months.

Infant Mortality, Infant Mortality Rate: The annual number of infants who die before completing their first year of life per 1000 live births in a given calendar year.

Internal Migration: Migratory movements that take place within a particular geographic or political unit. This term usually refers to migration within a state in contrast to international migration. Important internal migration processes include rural-urban migration, suburbanization, and migration for educational purposes.

Life Expectancy: The average age until which a person is expected to live, assuming that current age-specific mortality rates would remain constant. Life expectancy is either calculated for newborns (life expectancy at birth) or for certain age groups (remaining life expectancy at age X) based on *Life tables* that give an organized, complete picture of a population's mortality.

Life Table: Life tables numerically express mortality and the life expectancy of a standardized population (usually 100,000 males and females born at the same time) at any given age. Mortality rates are assumed to remain constant for all age groups at levels of the period for which the table

is established. The parameters gained from cross-section
analyses are recorded as longitudinal parameters. Life tables
allow for the calculation of various indicators such as: life
expectancy at birth, remaining life expectancy at a certain
age, the probability that a person of age X will die within
the next year, as well as the probability of reaching a certain
age.

Maternal Mortality, Maternal Mortality Rate: The
annual number of deaths among women in connection
with pregnancy and childbirth per 100,000 live births.
Maternal mortality involves the death of every woman
during pregnancy or within forty-two days after birth
or termination of a pregnancy if the cause of death is
connected to this pregnancy.

Mean Age: The mathematical average of the age of all people
within a given population. See also Average Age.

Median Age: The age of life in which, statistically speaking, a
population can be divided into two equal groups: 50% of
the population are younger, and 50% are older than this
calculated value.

Megacity, also Very Large City: A city with a population
over ten million inhabitants. As the boundaries between a
megacity and its surroundings are often intricate and the
administrative urban boundaries do not necessarily coincide
with settlement borders, population geography often speaks
of urban agglomerations.

Metropolitan area, also Large City: A city with a population
over 100,000 inhabitants.

Migrant: In contrast to a refugee or displaced person, the term
"migrant" generally refers to a person who has decided to
move more or less voluntarily, at least not under political
pressure. If a person moves to another country, he or she

becomes an international migrant. If the person holds a residence title of the receiving country he or she is a legal migrant; otherwise he or she becomes an irregular/illegal migrant.

Migration: Spatial mobility or the movement of people over a certain minimal distance and for a specific minimum period of time in order to establish a new permanent or temporary domicile. Internal migration or mobility takes place within a specific unit of observation (municipality, county, province, state, country). International migration takes place between two different countries.

Migration Balance, Net Migration: The difference between the number of immigrants and emigrants recorded for a spatial unit within a specific period of time (usually within a calendar year). If immigration and emigration are not recorded separately, net migration is calculated as a residual of population change between two different points in time after accounting for births and deaths.

Morbidity: Frequency and distribution of illnesses, injuries, and disabilities within a population.

Mortality: Deaths per age group and year; see *Life Table*.

Natural Population Growth: Occurs when a population has a surplus of births over deaths. See *Growth Rate, Natural*.

Net Reproduction Rate: A key measure for the demographic reproduction of a population. The net reproduction rate indicates how many daughters on average a group of women would finally have if age-specific fertility and mortality at a given time would remain constant. In contrast to the crude reproduction rate, the net reproduction rate takes into account that some women die before they have concluded their childbearing years. At a net reproduction rate of 1, any population reaches replacement level. In other words: a generation of (potential) mothers is quantitatively replaced entirely by a generation of daughters.

Period Analysis: Observation of a population at a specific period of time. Such an analysis in effect takes a "snapshot" of a population in a relatively short time period – for example, one year. Most rates are derived from period data and therefore are period rates. See also *Cohort Analysis*.

Population: The total number of people with permanent or semi-permanent residence within a certain territory. Populations can, however, also refer to groups of persons united by other common characteristics.

Population Density: The number of inhabitants per territorial unit (municipality, county, province, state, country, continent). Usually population density is calculated as number of inhabitants. Generally, the whole territorial unit is taken as a basis. Selected areas may be excluded (for example, lakes and large rivers, high mountains, deserts) to allow for particular calculations such as the "physiological population density" of a country, which only takes settlements and areas with arable land (permanently settled areas) into consideration.

Population Distribution: Patterns of dispersal of a population in a given space according to its absolute numbers or places of settlement. While population density relates to the average number of people per square kilometer or square mile indicating their "burden" or "weight," population distribution is centered on the concept of distance. In addition to a more or less even population distribution in a given area (dispersion), there are different forms of population concentration. This leads to an agglomeration of people in a particular place (centralized concentration) or in multiple places (decentralized concentration) within a particular area. The other extreme would be an evenly distributed population (total dispersion).

Population Explosion describes a very rapidly growing population. Today, the term is only used in the context of strong population growth in some developing countries. Historically, Europe and North America have also experienced periods of rapid population growth.

Population Growth, Population Decline: Changes in population size in a specific time interval as a result of births and deaths as well as immigration and emigration. See *Population Movement*.

Population Movement: The demographic events (births and deaths, immigration and emigration) within a population over a specific time interval. A distinction is made between natural and spatial population movement. While natural population movement only takes births and deaths into account, spatial population movement comprises immigration and emigration (see also *Migration*). Mathematically, population movement is the sum of the balance between births and deaths and net migration.

Population Momentum: See *Demographic Momentum*.

Population Policy: All political measures taken to influence the size, growth, and spatial distribution of a population. A distinction is made between pro-natalist and anti-natalist population policies with regard to the political measures designed to influence fertility.

Population Policy, Anti-Natalist: Government measures to slow population growth by restricting fertility and subsequently the numbers of births. Many low and middle-income countries that have experienced (or even encouraged) rapid population growth in the past now pursue anti-natalist policies. In the early 21st century, approximately 60%

of all low- and middle-income countries implemented political programs designed to reduce fertility. In essence, such programs advise people on effective contraceptive methods, distribute contraceptives for free, or offer them at a subsidized price. Some countries have introduced fiscal or material incentives to restrict births. Other governments, such as the Indian (1970s) or the Chinese (1980s), have also attempted to reduce the numbers of births by carrying out forced sterilization and abortions. Chinese anti-natalist policies continue to involve repressive measures.

Population Projections: Demographic methods forecasting future size, age, and sex structure, household structure, population distribution, etc., are based on assumptions concerning future trends in fertility, mortality, and migration. Projections are usually calculated by using the cohort-component method, in which calculations are made for overlapping birth cohorts. Most population projections include scenarios for higher and lower fertility. Some are calculated with and without migration.

Population Pyramid, also Age and Gender Pyramid: A graphic means of depicting the age and gender structure of a population. Using a standardized graph, age groups are illustrated and stacked on one another giving their absolute or relative size. It is organized in the form of back-to-back bars for men (left side) and women (right side) radiating from the standardized graph's central axis. By convention, the younger ages are at the bottom and the older ones at the top. Traditional societies with high mortality result in a pyramid-shaped graph from which the original name "population pyramid" derived. Declining fertility and increasing life expectancy can cause the pyramid shape to disappear. The population pyramid always reflects a snapshot of the age and gender structure at a given moment in time.

Population Register: A government data collection system in which the demographic and socio-economic characteristics of all residents or part of the population are continuously recorded. All Scandinavian countries, Austria, and Israel are among the countries that maintain universal registers for demographic purposes – recording major events (birth, marriage, international migration, internal mobility, death) that happen to each individual. Such a register makes up-to-date information on the whole population readily available. Other countries, like Canada, Great Britain, and the United States, have established partial registers, based on social security and voter registration.

Population Stock: Size and composition of population based on age, gender, marital status, and other indicators (for example, nationality, employment status, ethnicity, place of birth) with reference to a particular date; see *Age Structure, Sex Ratio, Population Movement*.

Population Structure: The proportion and distribution of population groups with specific characteristics within a population. In demography, the most frequently used characteristics are age and gender (see *Age Structure, Sex Ratio*). Other possible characteristics include socio-economic status, educational background, income, etc.

Probability of Survival: The proportion of a certain group of persons (for example, those of the same age, gender, or state of health) who are alive both at the beginning of the observation period and at the end of the same period; see *Life Table*.

Pro-Natalist Policy: Government measures aimed at raising fertility and the numbers of births in order to stimulate population growth or prevent (reduce) population decline. This is mainly carried out by means of family policy, including legal provisions as well as fiscal and financial incentives or material benefits for parents and children (for example, maternity leave, birth allowance, child allowance, free crèches and pre-schools, free schooling). Occasionally, governments have also used repressive measures to increase the numbers of births, such as by prohibiting contraceptives or abortions (for example, Romania in the 1970s and 1980s). The long-term effectiveness of fiscal and financial measures to encourage births is limited. Measures aimed at improving the compatibility between female employment and child-rearing have shown a more lasting impact.

Refugee: According to the Geneva Convention, a refugee is a person based outside his/her country of citizenship because of a justified fear of persecution on the grounds of his/her ethnic group, religion, ethnicity, membership within a certain social group, or political beliefs, and who cannot or, based on these fears, does not wish to exercise the right to protection offered by this country. Many countries have asylum laws that define or specify refugee status.

Replacement Level: The average number of children per couple or per women in a population necessary to secure the replacement of the entire parent population and to ensure that the population size remains stable without immigration. To achieve this level in developed societies with low child mortality, an average of 2.1 children per woman is necessary.

Reproductive Age: For the purpose of demographic calculations, the reproductive age of a woman is generally defined as the period between fifteen and forty-nine years of age.

Reproductive Health: A state of complete physical, mental, and social well-being (and not merely the absence of disease or infirmity) in all matters relating to reproduction. According to the Program of Action launched at the UN International Conference on Population and Development (ICPD 1994), reproductive health means that people are entitled to a satisfying and safe sex life and that they have the capability to reproduce and the freedom to decide if, when, and how often to do so.

Resident Population: All inhabitants who – regardless of their nationality – are permanent residents of a specific territorial unit (municipality, county, province, state, country).

Sex Ratio: The ratio of males per 100 females in a given population. The sex ratio is either calculated as the proportion of men to women (for example 48:52) or is indicated as the number of males per 100 females. At birth, the sex ratio is not quite balanced. Normally, more boys are born than girls, with the long-term statistical average of 105 to 106 male births to 100 female births. Modern prenatal diagnostics can lead to selective abortions in countries with a traditionally strong preference for sons, further increasing the number of surplus boys among newborns.

TFR (Total Fertility Rate): Indicates the average number of children a woman will have over the course of her life if the prevailing age-specific fertility rates (period fertility) of the observed population at a given time are assumed to be constant. It is a synthetic indicator summing up all age-specific fertility rates; to distinguish from *Completed Fertility*.

Urban: Countries differ in the way they classify populations as 'urban' or 'rural.' Typically, a community or settlement with a minimum of 2000 inhabitants is considered urban.

A listing of country definitions is published annually in the
United Nations Demographic Yearbook.

Urbanization: The growth of an urban (city) population
as a proportion of the total population. In principle,
urbanization can take place in three ways: through
population growth in cities, through the emergence of new
cities in previously non-urbanized regions, and through
the administrative incorporation of previously non-urban
territories into existing cities. The degree of urbanization
refers to the urban population's share of the total
population of a country or region.

For more information, see the glossaries published by the French
Demographic Research Institute (INED; http://www.ined.fr/en/
lexicon/; glossary in English); the Population Reference Bureau
(PRB), and the UN Population Division (http://www.un.org/esa/
population/unpop.htm) as well as the *World Population Handbook* by Arthur Haupt and Thomas Kane (see: Bibliography)
The glossary of this book has been compiled from these sources.

Bibliography

Acsádi, Gy., J. Nemeskéri. 1970. *History of Human Life Span and Mortality*. Budapest: Akadémiai Kiadó.

Ambrose, Stanley H. 1998. "Late Pleistocene human population bottlenecks, volcanic winter, and differentiation of modern humans," *Journal of Human Evolution* 34: 623–651.

Ambrose, Stanley H. 2003. "Did the Super-eruption of Toba cause a human population bottleneck? Reply to Gathorne-Hardy and Harcourt-Smith," *Journal of Human Evolution* 45: 231–237.

Bairoch, Paul. 1988. *Cities and Economic Development. From the Dawn of History to the Present*. Translated by Christopher Braider. London: Mansell Publishing.

Belloch, Julius. 1886. *Die Bevölkerung der griechisch-römischen Welt. 1. Theil*. Leipzig: Duncker & Humblot.

Belloch, Julius. 1926. *Bevölkerungsgeschichte Italiens*. Berlin: de Gruyter.

Bevolkingsvraagstukken in Nederland anno 1997. Onder redactie von Nico van Nimwegen / Gipss Beets. 1997. NIDI, report no. 50: Den Haag.

Bocquet-Appel, Jean-Pierre. 2002. "Paleoanthropological Traces of a Neolithic Demographic Transition". *Current Anthropology* 43, 637–650.

Bocquet-Appel, Jean-Pierre. 2008. *La paléodémographie. 99,99 % de l'histoire démographique des hommes ou la démographie de la Préhistoire.* Paris : Éditions Errance.

Boserup, Esther. 1981. *Population and Technological Change. A Study of Long-Term Trends.* Chicago: Univ. of Chicago Press.

Böhning, W. Roger. 1991. "Integration and immigration pressures in Western Europe," *International Labour Review* 130: 431–458.

Brown, Lester R., Hal Kane. 1994. *Full House. Reassessing the Earth's Population Carrying Capacity.* New York, London: W. W. Norton.

Burtless, Gary T., Barry Bosworth. 1998, eds. *Aging Societies. The Global Dimension.* Washington: Brookings Institution Press.

Caldwell, John C. 1982. *Theory of Fertility Decline.* London: Academic Press.

Caldwell, John C. 2004. "Fertility Control in the Classical World: Was there an Ancient Fertility Transition?" *Journal of Population Research* 21: 1–17.

Caldwell, John C., Bruce K. Caldwell. 2003. "Was There a Neolithic Mortality Crisis?" *Journal of Population Research* 20: 153–168.

Cameron, Rondo, Larry Neal. 2003, 4th ed. *A Concise Economic History of the World: From Paleolithic Times to the Present.* Oxford University Press.

Chesnais, J.-C. 1992. *The Demographic Transition. Stages, Patterns, and Economic Implications.* Oxford University Press.

Cipolla, Carlo M., Knut Borchardt, eds. 1983–1987, *Europäische Wirtschaftsgeschichte.* 5 vols. Stuttgart/New York: G. Fischer (UTB).

Cliquet, Robert. 1993. ed., *The future of Europe's population. A scenario approach*. Strasbourg: Council of Europe Press.

Cohen, Joel E. 1995. *How Many People Can the Earth Support?* New York. London: W. W. Norton.

Cohen, Mark N. 1994. "Demographic Expansion: Causes and Consequences," in Tim Ingold, ed., *Companion Encyclopedia of Anthropology*. London. New York: Routledge, 265–296.

Condorcet, Jean-Antoine-Nicolas Caritat, marquis de. 1794. *Esquisse d'un tableau historique des progrès de l'esprit humain*. http://socserv.mcmaster.ca/econ/ugcm/3113/condorcet/cindex1.htm

Corvisier, Jean-Nicolas, Wieslaw Suder. 2000. *La population de l'Antiquité classique*. Paris: PUF.

Daniels, John D. 1992. "The Indian Population of North America in 1492," *William and Mary Quarterly*, 3rd Series, Vol. 49: 298–320.

David, Paul A., Warren C. Sanderson. 1987. "The Emergence of a Two-Child-Norm among American Birth-Controllers," *Population and Development Review* 13: 1–41.

Davis, Kingsley. 1945. "The World Demographic Transition," *Annals of the American Academy of Political and Social Science* 237: 1–11.

Deevey, Edward S. 1960. *The Human Population*. Scientific American 203 (September), 194–204.

Diamond, Jared M. 1997. *Guns, Germs and Steel. A Short History of Everybody for the Last 13,000 Years*. London: Jonathan Cape.

Diop-Maes, Louise M. 1985. "Essai d'évaluation de la population de l'Afrique noir aux XVe et XVIe siècle," *Population* 6, 855–890.

Doblhammer-Reiter, Gabriele. 1997. "Soziale Ungleichheit vor dem Tod. Zum Ausmaß sozioökonomischer Unterschiede der Sterblichkeit in Österreich," *Demographische Informationen* 1995/96: 71–81.

Durand, John D. 1960. "The Population Statistics of China," A.D. 2–1953. *Population Studies* 13: 209–256.

Durand, John D. 1967. The Modern Expansion of World Population. *Proceedings of the American Philosophical Society* 111: 136–159.

Ehmer, Josef. 2004. *Bevölkerungsgeschichte und historische Demographie, 1800–2000*. München: Oldenbourg (Enzyklopädie deutscher Geschichte, vol. 71).

Engelen, Th. L. M., J. H. A. Hillebrand. 1986. "Fertility and Nuptiality in the Netherlands, 1850–1960," *Population Studies* 40, 487–503.

Franklin, Benjamin, 1952. *The Autobiography and Selections from his other Writings*. H. W. Schneider, ed. New York: The Liberal Arts Press.

Federici, Nora, Karen O. Mason, Solvi Sogner, eds. 1993. *Womens' Position and Demographic Change*. Oxford University Press.

Frier, Bruce. 1982. "Roman Life Expectancy: Ulpian's Evidence," *Harvard Studies in Classical Philology* 198: 213–251.

Gathorne-Hardy, F. J., W. E. H. Harcourt-Smith. 2003. "The super-eruption of Toba, did it cause a human bottleneck?" *Journal of Human Evolution* 45: 227–230.

Gemery, Henry A. 2005. "England's Population: A History since the Domesday Survey," (review), *Journal of Interdisciplinary History* 35, Number 4: 635–636.

Gilles, J. R., L. A. Tilly, D. Ledvine. eds. 1992. *The European Experience of Declining Fertility*. Cambridge, Ma.: Blackwell.

Goldsmith, Raymond W. 1987. *Premodern Financial Systems. A Historical Comparative Study*. Cambridge University Press.

Gomme, A. W. 1933. *The Population of Athens in the Fifth and Fourth Centuries* BC. Oxford University Press (Greenwood Press Reprint).

Gottfried, R. S. 1983. *The Black Death. Natural and Human Disaster in Medieval Europe*. New York: The Free Press.

Graunt, John. 1662. *Natural and Political Observations Mentioned in a following Index and Made upon the Bills of Mortality*. (http://www.ac.wwu.edu/~s//tephan/Graunt/)

Hall, Ray, Paul White. 1995. eds. *Europe's population. Towards the next century*. London: UCL Press.

Haub, Carl. 1995. "How Many People Have Ever Lived on Earth?" *Population Today* (February), 4–5.

Haupt, Arthur, Thomas T. Kane. 2007. *World Population Handbook*. 5th edition. Washington, DC: Population Reference Bureau.

Häußermann, Hartmut, Walter Siebel. 1993. eds, *New York. Strukturen einer Metropole*. Frankfurt/M.: Suhrkamp.

Howard, Ebenezer. 1902. *Garden Cities of To-Morrow*. London, Reprinted, edited with a Preface by F. J. Osborn and an Introductory Essay by Lewis Mumford. (London: Faber and Faber [1946]).

Hume, David (1987), *Essays, Moral, Political, and Literary*. Edited and with a Foreword and Glossary by Eugene F. Miller. With an apparatus of variant readings from the 1889 edition by T. H. Green and T. H. Grose. Indianapolis: Liberty Classics (in particular: "On the Populousness of Ancient Nations," 377–464).

Jacobs, Jane. 1961. *The Death and Life of Great American Cities.* New York: Vintage Books.

Jarrige, Jean-François. 1987. "Die frühesten Kulturen in Pakistan und ihre Entwicklung," in Philipp von Tabern, ed, *Vergessene Städte am Indus. Frühe Kulturen in Pakistan vom 8. – 2. Jahrtausend v. Chr.* Ausstellungskatalog. Frankfurt: 50–66.

Jarrige, Jean-Francois, Richard H. Meadow. 1980. The antecedents of civilization in the Indus Valley. *Scientific American* 243, 122–133.

Jensen, An-Magritt, L. Knutsen Torbjørn, Anders Skonhoft. 2003. eds. *Visiting Malthus. The Man, his Time, the Issues.* Oslo: Abstrakt forlag.

Kalter, Frank, Nadia Granato. 2002. "Demographic Change, Educational Expansion, and Structural Assimilation of Immigrants: The Case of Germany," in *European Sociology Review* 18: 199–216.

Keyfitz, Nathan. 1976, *Applied Mathematical Demography.* New York: John Wiley and Sons.

Kiernan, Kathleen. 1986. "Leaving Home: Living Arrangements of Young People in Six West-European Countries," *European Journal of Population* 2: 177–184.

Kirk, D. 1996. "Demographic Transition Theory," *Population Studies* 50: 361–387.

Kraus, Jürgen. 2004. *Die Demographie des Alten Ägypten. Eine Phänomenologie an Hand altägyptischer Quellen.* Diss. Phil.: Göttingen. (http://webdoc.sub.gwdg.de/diss/2004/kraus/kraus.pdf; accessed August 14, 2006)

Kremer, M. 1992. "Population Growth and Technological Change: One Million B.C. to 1990," *Journal of Economics* 108: 681–716.

Lesthaege, Ron. 1983. "A Century of Demographic and Cultural Change in Western Europe: An Exploration of Underlying Dimensions," *Population and Development Review* 9: 411–435.

Lesthaege, Ron, Dominique Meekers. 1986. "Value Changes and the Dimensions of Families in the European Community," *European Journal of Population* 2: 225–268.

Lahr, Martha Mirazón, Robert A. Foley. 1998. "Towards a Theory of Modern Human Origins: Geography, Demography, and Diversity in Recent Human Evolution," *Yearbook of Physical Anthropology* 41: 137–176.

Le Corbusier (1994 [1925]). *Urbanisme*. Paris: Flammarion.

Lee, J., Z. F. Wang. 1999. *One Quarter of Humanity. Malthusian Mythologies and Chinese Realities, 1700–2000*. Cambridge, Ma.: Harvard University Press.

Lee, Richard Borshay. 1979. *The !Kung San. Men, Women and Work in a Foraging Society*. Cambridge: Univ. Press.

Lee, Ronald. 2003. "The Demographic Transition: Three Centuries of Fundamental Change," *Journal of Eonomic Perspectives* 17: 167–190.

Livi-Bacci, Massimo. 1998. *A Concise History of World Population*. Oxford: Blackwell.

Livi-Bacci, Massimo. 1998. "The Depopulation of Hispanic America after the Conquest," *Population and Development Review* 32 (2): 1–34.

Lloyd-Sherlock, Peter, ed. 2004. *Living Longer: Ageing, Development and Social Protection*. London: New York: United Nations Research Institute for Social Development and Zed Books.

Maddison, Angus. 2001, 2003. *The World Economy. A Millennial Perspective*. Vol. 2: *The World Economy: Historical Statistics*. Paris: OECD.

Malanima, Paolo. 2005. "Urbanisation and the Italian Economy during the Last Millennium," *European Review of Economic History* 9: 97–122.

Malley-Borg, Mary. 1989. "The Income-Fertility Relationship: Effect of the Net Price," *Demography* 26: 301–310.

Malthus, Thomas Robert. 1970 [1798]. *An Essay On The Principle Of Population* (1798, 1st edition) with *A Summary View* (1830), and an introduction by Antony Flew. Penguin Classics. Harmondsworth: Penguin.

Marschalik, Peter. 1984. *Bevölkerungsgeschichte Deutschland im 19. und 20. Jahrhundert*. Frankfurt/M.: Suhrkamp.

McEvedy, Collin, Richard Jones, 1978. *Atlas of World Population History*. Harmondsworth: Penguin.

Mols, Roger. 1985. "Die Bevölkerung Europas 1500–1700," in Cipolla, Carlo M., Knut Borchardt, eds., *Europäische Wirtschaftsgeschichte*. Vol. II. Stuttgart/New York: G. Fischer (UTB) 5–49.

Mumford, Lewis. 1961. *The City in History: Its Origins, Its Transformations, and Its Prospects*. Toronto: Harcourt, Brace and World.

Muñoz-Perez, Francisco, 1986. "Changement recent de la fécondité en Europe occidentale et nouveaux traits de la formation des familles," *Population* 41: 447–462.

Münz, Rainer, Wolfgang Seifert, Ralf Ulrich. 1996. *Zuwanderung nach Deutschland. Strukturen, Wirkungen, Perspektiven*. Frankfurt: Campus.

Neurath, Paul. 1991. "Die Frühgeschichte der Demographie vor Malthus," *Jahrbücher für Nationalökonomie und Statistik* 208: 505–524.

Noin, David, Robert, Woods, eds. 1993. *The Changing Population of Europe*. Oxford: Blackwell.

Notestein, Frank W. 1945. "Population – The Long View," in Schultz, Theodore W., ed., *Food for the World*. Chicago: University of Chicago Press, 36–57.

Petraglia, Michael, et al. 2007. "Middle Palaeolithic Assemblages from the Indian Subcontinent Before and After the Toba Super-Eruption," *Science* 317 (July 6, 2007): 114–116.

Potter, Lloyd B. 1991. "Socioeconomic Determinants of Black and White Males' Life Expectancy Differentials, 1980," *Demography* 28: 303–321.

Priester, Tom, 1996. ed. *Bevölkerung und Gesellschaft im Wandel. Bericht zur demographischen Lage der Schweiz*. Bern: Bundesamt für Statistik.

Roussel, Louis, 1987. "Deux décennies de mutations démographiques (1965–1985) dans les pays industrialisés," *Population* 42, 429–448.

Russel, J. C. 1983. "Die Bevölkerung Europas 500–1500," in Cipolla, Carlo M., K. Borchardt, eds, *Europäische Wirtschaftsgeschichte. I: Mittelalter*. Stuttgart: G. Fischer, 13–43.

Sassen, Saskia. 1997. *The Global City: London, New York, Tokyo*. Princeton University Press.

Scheidel, Walter, ed. 2001. *Debating Roman Demography*. Leiden: Brill.

Scheidel, Walter. 2004: "*Demographic and Economic Development in the Ancient Mediterranean World*," *JITE* 160: 743–757.

Sellier, P. 1995. "Paléodémographie et archéologie funéraire: les cimetières de Mehrgarh, Pakistan," *Paléorient* 21 (2): 123–143.

Sen, Amartya. 1993. "The Economics of Life and Death," *Scientific American* 268, May: 40–47.

Schran, Peter. 1978. "China's Demographic Evolution 1850–
    1953 Reconsidered," *China Quarterly* 75: 639–646.

Stannard, David. 1992. *American Holocaust*. Oxford University
    Press.

Sueßmilch, Johann Peter 1761. *Die göttliche Ordnung in
    den Veränderungen des menschlichen Geschlechts aus
    der Geburt, dem Tode und der Fortpflanzung desselben
    erwiesen*. Berlin: Im Verlag des Buchladens der Realschule.

Tang, Jianmin, Carolyn MacLeod. 2006. "Labour force ageing
    and productivity performance in Canada," *Canadian Journal
    of Economics / Revue canadienne d'économie* 39: 582–603.

Teitelbaum, M. S., Winter, J. M., eds. 1986. "Population and
    Resources in Western Intellectual Traditions," Supplement
    to: *Population and Development Review* 14.

Tepperman, L. 1974. Ethnic variations in marriage and fertility:
    Canada, 1871. *Canadian Review of Social Anthropology* 11
    (4): 324–343.

UN Population Division. 2000. *Replacement Migration: Is It a
    Solution to Declining and Ageing Populations?* New York: UN.

UN Population Division. 2003. *Long Range Population
    Projections*. Proceedings of the United Nations. Technical
    Working Group on Long-Range Population Projections.
    New York: UN.

UN Population Division. 2005. *World Contraceptive Use 2005*.
    New York: UN.

UN Population Division. 2006. *World Population Policies 2005*.
    New York: UN.

UN Population Division. 2007. *World Population Prospects.
    The 2006 Revision*. New York: UN.

UNAIDS. 2006. *2006 Report on the global AIDS epidemic*.
    Geneva, Joint United Nations Programme on HIV/AIDS
    (and: AIDS epidemic update. 2007).

UN. 2008. *World Mortality Report 2007*. New York: UN.

van de Kaa, Dirk, 1994. "The second demographic transition revisited: Theories and expectations," in Beets, G. C. N., et al., *Population and Family in the Low Countries 1993. Late Fertility and other Current Issues*. Lisse: Swets & Zeitlinger: 81–126.

Vaupel, James W., et al. 1998. "Biodemographic Trajectories of Longevity," *Science* 280: 855–860.

Von Laue, Theodore H. 1987. *The World Revolution of Westernization. The Twentieth Century in Global Perspective*. Oxford: University Press.

Wade, William D. 1979. "On the Estimation of Prehistoric Population Size," *Canadian Review of Physical Anthropology* 1/1: 29–31.

WHO. 2008. *World Health Report 2007: A safer future: global public health security in the 21st century*. Geneva: World Health Organization.

Wrigley, E. Anthony, Roger S. Schofield, with contributions by Ronald Lee and Jim Oeppen. 1981. *The Population History of England, 1541–1871. A Reconstruction*. London: Edward Arnold (2nd Ed. 1989).

World Bank. 2008. *World Development Indicators*. Washington DC.

Wrigley, E., R. Anthony, S. Davies, J. E. Oeppen, R. S. Schofield 1997. *English Population History from Family Reconstruction, 1580–1837*. Cambridge: University Press.

Zelener, Y. 2003, *Smallpox and the Disintegration of the Roman Economy after 165 AD*. New York: Columbia University PhD Thesis.

Zhao, Zhongwei. 1997. "Long-term mortality patterns in Chinese history: Evidence from a recorded clan population," *Population Studies* 51: 117–127.

World Population 2006

Country or area	Mid-year population (millions) 2006	Mid-year population (millions) 2050	Density (pop/km²) Mid-2005	Percentage urban Mid-2005	Average annual population rate of change (per cent) 2000-2005	Rate of natural increase (percent)	Net migration per 1,000 Pop.	Total fertility (children per woman)	Infant mortality rate a)	Percent of married women 15-49 using contraception: All methods	Modern methods	Life expectancy at birth (years) Total	Males	Females	Percentage of population Mid-2005: Under age 15	60 or older
World	6,555	9,076	48	49	1.2	1.2	0	2.6	52	61	54	67	65	69	28	10
More developed regions a	1,216	1,236	23	75	0.3	0.1	2	1.6	6	68	58	77	73	80	17	20
Less developed regions b	5,339	7,840	63	43	1.4	1.5	-1	2.9	57	59	53	65	64	67	31	8
Least developed countries c	...	1,735.4	37	28	2.4	...	...	5.0	...	...	...	...	...	...	42	5
Africa	924	1,937	30	40	2.2	2.3	-0	5.0	84	28	22	52	51	53	41	5
Eastern Africa	284	679	46	27	2.4	2.4	-0	5.6	81	24	19	47	46	47	44	5
Burundi	7.8	25.8	271	11	3.0	2.7	7	6.8	106	16	10	45	44	45	45	4
Comoros	0.7	1.8	357	36	2.6	2.9	-2	4.9	59	26	19	64	62	66	42	4
Djibouti	0.8	1.5	34	85	2.1	1.9	-5	5.1	100	9	6	53	52	54	41	5

Country or area	Mid-year population (millions) 2006	Mid-year population (millions) 2050	Density (pop/km²) Mid-2005	Percentage urban Mid-2005	Average annual rate of population change (per cent) 2000–2005	Rate of natural increase (percent)	Net migration per 1,000 Pop.	Total fertility (children per woman)	Infant mortality rate (a)	Percent of married women 15–49 using contraception — All methods	Percent of married women 15–49 using contraception — Modern methods	Life expectancy at birth (years) Total	Life expectancy at birth (years) Males	Life expectancy at birth (years) Females Mid-2005	Percentage of population Under age 15	Percentage of population 60 or older Mid-2005
Eritrea	4.6	11.2	37	21	4.3	2.8	9	5.5	61	8	5	55	53	57	45	4
Ethiopia	74.8	170.2	70	16	2.4	2.4	–0	5.9	77	15	14	49	48	50	45	5
Kenya	34.7	83.1	59	42	2.2	2.5	0	5.0	77	39	32	48	49	47	43	4
Madagascar	17.8	43.5	32	27	2.8	2.7	0	5.4	83	27	17	55	53	57	44	5
Malawi	12.8	29.5	109	17	2.3	2.6	–0	6.1	76	33	28	45	44	47	47	5
Mauritius¹	1.3	1.5	610	44	1.0	0.8	0	2.0	14.8	76	42	72	69	76	25	10
Mozambique	19.9	37.6	25	38	2.0	2.0	–0	5.5	108	17	12	42	41	42	44	5
Réunion	0.8	1.1	313	92	1.6	1.4	2	2.5	7	70	...	77	72	80	27	10
Rwanda	9.1	18.2	343	22	2.4	2.7	–0	5.7	86	17	10	47	46	48	43	4
Seychelles	0.1	0.1	177	50	0.9	1.0	–21	...	16	...	...	71	66	76	...	...
Somalia	8.9	21.3	13	36	3.2	2.9	5	6.4	119	8	1	48	46	50	44	4
Uganda	27.7	127	120	12	3.4	3.1	–1	7.1	81	20	19	47	47	47	50	4

Country or area	Mid-year population (millions)		Mid-2005		Average annual rate of population change (per cent)	Rate of natural increase (percent)	Net migration per 1,000 Pop.	Total fertility (children per woman)	Infant mortality rate (a)	Percent of married women 15–49 using contraception		Life expectancy at birth (years)			Percentage of population	
	2006	2050	Density (pop/km²)	Percentage urban						All methods	Modern methods	Total	Males	Females	Under age 15	60 or older
							2000–2005							Mid-2005		
United Republic of Tanzania	37.9	66.8	43	38	2.0	2.5	-2	5.0	68	26	20	45	44	45	43	5
Zambia	11.9	22.8	16	37	1.7	1.9	-2	5.7	92	34	23	37	38	37	46	5
Zimbabwe	13.1	15.8	33	36	0.6	0.7	-1	3.6	61	54	50	37	38	37	40	5
Middle Africa	116	303	17	38	2.6	2.8	-0	6.2	98	26	6	48	47	50	46	5
Angola	15.8	43.5	13	37	2.8	2.6	2	6.8	139	6	5	41	39	42	46	4
Cameroon	17.3	26.9	34	53	1.9	2.3	-0	4.6	74	26	13	51	50	52	41	6
Central African Republic	4.3	6.7	6	44	1.3	1.7	0	5.0	94	28	7	44	43	44	43	6
Chad	10.0	31.5	8	26	3.4	2.8	-3	6.7	101	11	2	44	43	45	47	5
Congo	3.7	13.7	12	54	3.0	2.6	-6	6.3	75	44	13	51	50	52	47	5
Dem. Republic of the Congo	62.7	177	25	33	2.8	3.1	0	6.7	95	31	4	50	49	52	47	4
Equatorial Guinea	0.5	1.1	18	50	2.3	2.3	0	5.9	102	:	:	44	43	44	44	6
Gabon	1.4	2.3	5	85	1.7	2.0	-2	4.0	57	33	12	54	53	55	40	6

Country or area	Mid-year population (millions) 2006	2050	Density (pop/km²) Mid-2005	Percentage urban Mid-2005	Average annual population rate of change (per cent) 2000–2005	Rate of natural increase (percent)	Net migration per 1,000 Pop.	Total fertility (children per woman)	Infant mortality rate (a)	Percent of married women 15–49 using contraception: All methods	Modern methods	Life expectancy at birth (years): Total	Males	Females	Percentage of population: Under age 15 Mid-2005	60 or older
Sao Tome and Principe	0.2	0.3	162	38	2.3	2.5	–3	4.1	80	29	27	63	62	64	39	6
Northern Africa	198	312	22	50	1.7	2.0	–1	3.2	42	49	44	69	67	70	33	7
Algeria	33.5	49.5	14	60	1.5	1.7	–1	2.5	30	57	52	75	74	76	30	6
Egypt	75.4	126	74	42	1.9	2.1	–1	3.3	33	59	57	70	67	72	34	7
Libyan Arab Jamahiriya	5.9	9.6	3	87	2.0	2.4	0	3.0	26	49	26	76	74	78	30	6
Morocco	31.7	46.4	70	59	1.5	1.6	–1	2.8	40	63	55	70	68	72	31	7
Sudan	41.2	66.7	14	41	1.9	2.6	–3	4.4	64	10	7	58	57	59	39	6
Tunisia	10.1	12.9	62	64	1.1	1.1	–1	2.0	21	63	53	73	71	75	26	9
Western Sahara	0.4	0.9	1	94	2.6	2.0	6	3.9	53	…	…	64	62	66	34	6
Southern Africa	54	56	20	55	0.7	0.5	1	2.9	55	54	53	46	44	48	33	7
Botswana	1.8	1.7	3	53	0.1	–0.1	–1	3.2	56	40	39	34	35	33	38	5
Lesotho	1.8	1.6	59	18	0.1	0.3	–4	3.6	91	37	35	36	35	36	39	7

Country or area	Mid-year population (millions) 2006	Mid-year population (millions) 2050	Density (pop/km²) Mid-2005	Percentage urban Mid-2005	Average annual population rate of change (per cent)	Rate of natural increase (percent)	Net migration per 1,000 Pop.	Total fertility (children per woman)	Infant mortality rate (a)	Percent of married women 15–49 using contraception — All methods	Percent of married women 15–49 using contraception — Modern methods	Life expectancy at birth (years) Total	Life expectancy at birth (years) Males	Life expectancy at birth (years) Females	Percentage of population Under age 15 Mid-2005	Percentage of population 60 or older Mid-2005
Namibia	2.1	3.1	2	33	1.4	1.4	–0	4.0	44	44	43	47	47	47	42	5
South Africa	47.3	48.7	39	58	0.8	0.5	1	2.8	54	56	55	47	45	49	33	7
Swaziland	1.1	1.0	59	24	0.2	0.1	–1	4.0	74	28	26	34	33	35	41	5
Western Africa	**271**	**587**	**43**	**44**	**2.4**	**2.6**	**0**	**5.8**	**102**	**14**	**9**	**48**	**47**	**48**	**44**	**5**
Benin	8.7	22.1	75	46	3.2	2.9	2	5.9	102	19	7	54	53	55	44	4
Burkina Faso	13.6	39.1	48	19	3.2	2.5	1	6.7	81	14	9	48	48	49	47	4
Cape Verde	0.5	1.0	126	58	2.4	2.5	–6	3.8	28	53	46	71	68	74	40	6
Côte d'Ivoire	19.7	34.0	56	46	1.6	2.5	4	5.1	104	15	7	51	49	53	42	5
Gambia	1.5	3.1	134	26	2.8	2.7	3	4.7	75	10	9	53	52	55	40	6
Ghana	22.6	40.6	93	46	2.1	2.3	–0	4.4	59	25	19	57	57	58	39	6
Guinea	9.8	23.0	38	36	2.2	2.8	–6	5.9	98	9	6	54	54	54	44	6
Guinea-Bissau	1.4	5.3	44	36	3.0	3.0	–1	7.1	116	8	4	45	44	46	48	5

Country or area	Mid-year population (millions)		Mid-2005		Average annual rate of population change (per cent)	Rate of natural increase (percent)	Net migration per 1,000 Pop.	Total fertility (children per woman)	Infant mortality rate (a)	Percent of married women 15-49 using contraception		Life expectancy at birth (years)			Percentage of population	
	2006	2050	Density (pop/km²)	Percentage urban						All methods	Modern methods	Total	Males	Females	Under age 15	60 or older
					2000-2005							Mid-2005				
Liberia	3.4	10.7	29	48	1.4	2.9	-8	6.8	142	...	...	43	41	44	47	4
Mali	13.9	42.0	11	34	3.0	3.2	-2	6.9	130	8	6	49	48	49	48	4
Mauritania	3.2	7.5	3	64	3.0	2.8	2	5.8	74	8	5	54	53	55	43	5
Niger	14.4	50.2	11	23	3.4	3.4	0	7.9	149	14	4	44	44	44	49	3
Nigeria	135	258	142	48	2.2	2.4	-0	5.8	100	12	8	44	43	44	44	5
Senegal	11.9	23.1	59	51	2.4	2.9	-2	5.0	61	12	10	56	55	58	43	5
Sierra Leone	5.7	13.8	77	40	4.1	2.3	-3	6.5	163	4	4	41	39	42	43	5
Togo	6.3	13.5	108	36	2.7	2.6	0	5.4	90	26	9	55	53	57	43	5
Asia	3,968	5,217	123	40	1.2	1.2	-0	2.5	49	65	59	68	66	70	28	9
Eastern Asia	1,544	1,587	130	45	0.6	0.5	-0	1.7	25	84	82	73	71	75	21	12
China [3]	1,311	1,392	137	41	0.6	0.6	-0	1.7	27	87	86	72	70	74	21	11
China, Hong Kong SAR [4]	7.0	9.2	6,407	100	1.2	0.3	5	0.9	2.4	...	...	81	79	84	14	15

Country or area	Mid-year population (millions) 2006	Mid-year population (millions) 2050	Density (pop/km²) Mid-2005	Percentage urban Mid-2005	Average annual rate of change of population (per cent)	Rate of natural increase (percent)	Net migration per 1,000 Pop.	Total fertility (children per woman)	Infant mortality rate (a)	Percent of married women 15-49 using contraception All methods	Percent of married women 15-49 using contraception Modern methods	Life expectancy at birth (years) Total	Life expectancy Males	Life expectancy Females	Percentage of population Under age 15	Percentage of population 60 or older
China, Macao SAR [1]	0.5	0.5	17 699	99	0.7	0.4	44	0.8	3	...	...	79	77	82	16	11
Dem. People's Rep. of Korea	23.1	24.2	187	62	0.6	0.9	0	2.0	21	69	58	71	68	73	25	11
Japan	128	112	339	66	0.2	0.0	0	1.3	2.8	56	48	82	79	86	14	26
Mongolia	2.6	3.6	2	57	1.2	1.2	0	2.4	21	67	54	66	64	68	30	6
Republic of Korea	48.5	44.6	480	81	0.4	0.4	-1	1.2	5	81	67	77	74	81	19	14
South-Central Asia	1,642	2,495	149	31	1.6	1.7	-1	3.2	64	51	43	63	62	64	33	7
Afghanistan	31.1	97.3	46	24	4.6	2.6	0	7.5	166	10	9	42	41	42	46	4
Bangladesh	147	243	985	25	1.9	1.9	-0	3.2	65	58	47	61	61	62	35	6
Bhutan	0.7	0.8	46	9	2.2	1.3	0	4.4	40	...	31	63	62	64	38	7
India	1,122	1,593	336	29	1.6	1.7	-0	3.1	58	53	46	63	62	63	32	8
Iran	70.3	102	42	68	0.9	1.2	-4	2.1	32	74	56	70	69	72	29	6
Kazakhstan	15.3	13.1	5	56	-0.3	0.8	1	2.0	29	66	53	66	61	72	23	11

Country or area	Mid-year population (millions)		Mid-2005		Average annual population rate of change (per cent)	2000–2005				Percent of married women 15–49 using contraception		Life expectancy at birth (years) Mid-2005			Percentage of population	
	2006	2050	Density (pop/km²)	Percentage urban		Rate of natural increase (percent)	Net migration per 1,000 Pop.	Total fertility (children per woman)	Infant mortality rate (a)	All methods	Modern methods	Total	Males	Females	Under age 15	60 or older
Kyrgyzstan	5.2	6.7	26	34	1.2	1.4	–5	2.7	30	60	49	68	64	72	31	8
Maldives	0.3	0.7	1,105	30	2.5	1.5	0	4.3	15	40	35	70	70	70	41	5
Nepal	26.0	51.2	184	16	2.1	2.2	–1	3.7	64	39	35	62	62	63	39	6
Pakistan	165.8	304.7	198	35	2.0	2.4	–1	4.3	79	28	20	62	61	63	38	6
Sri Lanka	19.9	23.6	316	21	0.9	1.3	–1	2.0	11	70	50	74	71	77	24	11
Tajikistan	7.0	10.4	45	24	1.1	2.2	–0	3.8	89	34	27	64	61	66	39	5
Turkmenistan	5.3	6.8	10	46	1.4	1.6	–0	2.8	74	62	53	62	58	67	32	6
Uzbekistan	26.2	38.7	59	36	1.5	1.6	–2	2.7	58	68	63	67	63	70	33	6
South-Eastern Asia	565	752	124	44	1.4	1.4	–1	2.5	34	60	52	69	66	71	30	8
Brunei	0.4	0.7	65	78	2.3	1.7	2	2.5	9	...	...	75	72	77	30	5
Cambodia	14.1	26.0	78	20	2.0	2.1	–0	4.1	91	24	19	60	57	63	37	6
East Timor	1.0	3.3	64	8	5.4	2.7	1	7.8	88	10	9	56	54	57	41	5

Country or area	Mid-year population (millions) 2006	2050	Density (pop/km²) Mid-2005	Percentage urban Mid-2005	Average annual rate of population change (per cent)	Rate of natural increase (percent)	Net migration per 1,000 Pop.	Total fertility (children per woman) 2000–2005	Infant mortality rate (a) 2000–2005	Percent of married women 15–49 using contraception: All methods	Modern methods	Life expectancy at birth (years) Mid-2005: Total	Males	Females	Percentage of population: Under age 15 Mid-2005	60 or older
Indonesia	226	285	117	48	1.3	1.4	–1	2.4	35	60	57	69	67	72	28	8
Laos	6.1	11.6	25	22	2.3	2.3	–0	4.8	88	32	29	54	53	56	41	5
Malaysia	26.9	38.9	77	65	1.9	1.6	4	2.9	10	55	30	74	72	76	32	7
Myanmar/Burma	51.0	63.7	75	31	1.1	1.1	0	2.5	75	37	33	60	57	63	29	8
Philippines	86.3	127	277	63	1.8	2.1	–2	3.2	27	49	33	70	67	72	35	6
Singapore	4.5	5.2	6333	100	1.5	0.6	20	1.4	2.1	62	55	80	78	82	20	12
Thailand	65.2	74.6	125	32	0.9	0.7	–0	1.9	20	79	79	71	68	75	24	10
Vietnam	84.2	117	254	27	1.4	1.3	–0	2.3	18	77	66	72	70	73	30	7
Western Asia	218	383	44	66	2.1	2.0	2	3.4	42	51	32	69	67	71	34	7
Armenia	3.0	2.5	101	64	–0.4	0.4	–3	1.3	26	53	20	71	67	75	21	15
Azerbaijan	8.5	9.6	97	50	0.6	1.1	0	1.9	9	55	12	72	70	75	26	9
Bahrain	0.7	1.2	1047	90	1.6	1.8	7	2.5	10	65	…	74	73	75	27	4

Country or area	Mid-year population (millions) 2006	2050	Density (pop/km²) Mid-2005	Percentage urban	Average annual rate of population change (per cent) 2000-2005	Rate of natural increase (percent)	Net migration per 1,000 Pop.	Total fertility (children per woman)	Infant mortality rate (a)	Percent of married women 15-49 using contraception All methods	Modern methods	Life expectancy at birth (years) Total	Males	Females Mid-2005	Percentage of population Under age 15	60 or older
Cyprus	1.0	1.2	90	69	1.2	0.4	16	1.6	5	...	...	78	75	80	20	17
Georgia	4.4	3.0	64	51	-1.1	0.1	-9	1.5	25	47	27	72	69	75	19	18
Iraq	29.6	63.7	66	67	2.8	2.6	0	4.8	88	44	25	59	57	60	41	5
Israel	7.2	10.4	304	92	2.0	1.5	2	2.9	4.2	...	...	80	78	82	28	13
Jordan	5.6	10.2	64	79	2.7	2.4	2	3.5	24	56	41	72	71	72	37	5
Kuwait	2.7	5.3	151	96	3.7	1.7	14	2.4	10	52	39	78	77	79	24	3
Lebanon	3.9	4.7	344	88	1.0	1.5	-2	2.3	17	63	40	72	70	74	29	10
Palestinian Territories	3.9	10.1	615	72	3.2	3.3	...	5.6	21	51	37	72	71	74	45	4
Oman	2.6	5.0	8	79	1.0	2.0	12	3.8	10	24	18	74	73	75	34	4
Qatar	0.8	1.3	74	92	5.9	1.6	40	3.0	9	43	32	73	71	76	22	3
Saudi Arabia	24.1	49.5	11	88	2.7	2.7	2	4.1	23	32	29	72	70	74	37	5
Syrian Arab Republic	19.5	35.9	103	50	2.5	2.5	0	3.5	18	47	35	73	71	75	37	5

Country or area	Mid-year population (millions) 2006	2050	Density (pop/km²) Mid-2005	Percentage urban Mid-2005	Average annual population change rate (per cent)	Rate of natural increase (percent)	Net migration per 1,000 Pop.	Total fertility (children per woman) 2000–2005	Infant mortality rate (a)	Percent of married women 15–49 using contraception: All methods	Modern methods	Life expectancy at birth (years): Total	Males	Females Mid-2005	Percentage of population Under age 15	60 or older
Turkey	73.7	101	93	67	1.4	1.3	0	2.5	25	71	43	71	69	74	29	8
United Arab Emirates	4.9	9.1	54	85	6.5	1.3	54	2.5	9	28	24	77	75	80	22	2
Yemen	21.6	59.5	40	26	3.1	3.2	−1	6.2	75	23	13	60	59	62	46	4
Europe	732	653	32	73	0.0	−0.1	2	1.4	7	68	53	75	71	79	16	21
Eastern Europe	296	224	16	68	−0.5	−0.5	0	1.3	10	64	42	69	63	74	15	18
Belarus	9.7	7.0	47	72	−0.6	−0.6	0	1.2	8	50	42	69	63	75	15	19
Bulgaria	7.7	5.1	70	70	−0.7	−0.5	−0	1.2	10.4	41	26	72	69	76	14	22
Czech Republic	10.3	8.5	130	75	−0.1	−0.1	4	1.2	3.4	67	58	76	73	79	15	20
Hungary	10.1	8.3	109	66	−0.3	−0.3	0	1.3	6.1	77	68	73	69	77	16	21
Poland	38.1	31.9	119	62	−0.1	−0	−0	1.3	6.4	49	19	75	71	79	16	17
Moldova	4.0	3.3	124	46	−0.3	−0.2	1	1.2	12	62	43	69	65	72	18	14
Romania	21.6	16.8	91	55	−0.4	−0.2	−1	1.3	16.8	64	30	71	68	75	15	19

Country or area	Mid-year population (millions) 2006	2050	Density (pop/km²) Mid-2005	Percentage urban Mid-2005	Average annual rate of population change (per cent) 2000–2005	Rate of natural increase (percent)	Net migration per 1,000 Pop.	Total fertility (children per woman)	Infant mortality rate (a)	Percent of married women 15–49 using contraception: All methods	Modern methods	Life expectancy at birth (years) Total	Males	Females	Percentage of population Under age 15 Mid-2005	60 or older
Russian Federation	142	112	8	73	-0.5	-0.6	1	1.3	11	67	49	65	59	72	15	17
Slovakia	5.4	4.6	110	58	0.0	0.0	1	1.2	6.8	74	41	74	70	78	17	16
Ukraine	46.8	26.4	77	67	-1.1	-0.8	0	1.1	10	68	38	68	63	74	15	21
Northern Europe	97	106	53	84	0.3	0.2	4	1.7	5	82	76	78	75	81	18	21
Channel Islands	0.2	0.2	766	31	0.4	0.2	...	1.4	3.4	...	...	78	76	80	16	19
Denmark	5.4	5.9	126	86	0.3	0.2	1	1.8	4.4	...	...	78	76	80	19	21
Estonia	1.3	1.1	29	70	-0.6	-0.2	-0	1.4	6	70	56	72	66	78	15	22
Faeroe Islands	47.0	0.1	34	39	0.6			...							...	...
Finland	5.3	5.3	16	61	0.3	0.2	1	1.7	3	79	78	79	75	82	17	21
Iceland	0.3	0.4	3	93	0.9	0.8	5	2.0	2.5	...	...	81	79	83	22	16
Ireland	4.2	5.8	59	60	1.7	0.8	13	1.9	4.7	...	...	78	75	80	20	15
Isle of Man	77.0	0.1	134	52	-0.1			...							...	...

Country or area	Mid-year population (millions)		Density (pop/km²) Mid-2005	Percentage urban Mid-2005	Average annual rate of population change (per cent)	Rate of natural increase (percent)	Net migration per 1,000 Pop.	Total fertility (children per woman)	Infant mortality rate (a)	Percent of married women 15-49 using contraception		Life expectancy at birth (years) Mid-2005			Percentage of population Mid-2005	
	2006	2050								All methods	Modern methods	Total	Males	Females	Under age 15	60 or older
Latvia	2.3	1.7	36	66	-0.6	-0.5	-0	1.3	7	85	60	73	67	77	15	23
Lithuania	3.4	2.6	53	67	-0.4	-0.4	-3	1.3	7	47	30	72	66	78	17	21
Norway	4.7	5.4	12	80	0.5	0.3	4	1.8	3.1	...	...	80	78	83	20	20
Sweden	9.1	10.1	20	83	0.4	0.1	4	1.6	2.4	...	...	81	78	83	17	23
United Kingdom	60.5	67.1	246	89	0.3	0.2	4	1.7	5.1	84	79	78	76	81	18	21
Southern Europe	152	139	113	66	0.4	0.1	5	1.3	5	59	43	79	76	82	15	23
Albania	3.2	3.5	109	45	0.4	0.8	-3	2.3	8	75	8	75	72	79	27	12
Andorra	0.1	0.1	143	91	0.4	0.7	43	...	3.9	...	...	...	...	...	...	...
Bosnia and Herzegovina	3.9	3.2	76	45	0.3	0.1	2	1.3	7	48	16	74	71	77	17	19
Croatia	4.4	3.7	81	60	0.2	-0.2	3	1.3	6.1	...	...	75	71	78	16	22
Gibraltar	0.03	0.03	4 654	100	0.2										...	...
Greece	11.1	10.7	84	61	0.3	0.0	3	1.3	4	...	...	79	77	81	14	23

Country or area	Mid-year population (millions)		Mid-2005		Average annual rate of population change (per cent)	2000-2005					Percent of married women 15-49 using contraception		Life expectancy at birth (years) Mid-2005			Percentage of population Mid-2005	
	2006	2050	Density (pop/km²)	Percentage urban		Rate of natural increase (percent)	Net migration per 1,000 Pop.	Total fertility (children per woman)	Infant mortality rate (a)		All methods	Modern methods	Total	Males	Females	Under age 15	60 or older
Italy	59.0	50.9	193	68	0.1	-0	5	1.3	4.1		60	39	80	78	83	14	26
Malta	0.4	0.4	1,271	92	0.5	0.2	5	1.5	5.9		86	43	79	77	81	18	19
Portugal	10.6	10.7	114	56	0.5	0.1	5	1.5	3.8		...	...	78	75	81	16	22
San Marino*	0.03	0.03	461	89	0.8	0.3	11	...	6.7		...	...	81	78	84	...	...
Serbia and Montenegro	10.1	9.4	103	52	-0.1	0.4	1	1.7	18.0		58	33	72	69	75	18	18
Slovenia	2.0	1.6	97	51	0.0	-0	3	1.2	3.9		71	57	77	74	81	14	20
Spain	45.5	42.5	85	77	1.1	0.2	6	1.3	4.0		56	53	81	77	84	14	21
Macedonia [7]	2.0	1.9	79	60	0.2	0.2	-0	1.5	11.3		...	...	73	71	76	20	15
Western Europe [7]	187	185	168	81	0.2	0.1	2	1.6	4		74	70	79	76	82	16	23
Austria	8.3	8.1	98	66	0.2	0	7	1.4	4.1		67	65	79	76	82	16	23
Belgium	10.5	10.3	341	97	0.2	0.1	3	1.7	4.8		79	75	79	76	82	17	22
France	61.2	63.1	110	77	0.4	0.4	2	1.9	3.6		75	69	80	77	84	18	21

Country or area	Mid-year population (millions) 2006	2050	Density (pop/km²) Mid-2005	Percentage urban Mid-2005	Average annual rate of population change (per cent)	Rate of natural increase (percent)	Net migration per 1,000 Pop.	Total fertility (children per woman) 2000-2005	Infant mortality rate (a)	Percent of married women 15–49 using contraception: All methods	Modern methods	Life expectancy at birth (years): Total	Males	Females	Under age 15	60 or older
Germany	82.4	78.8	232	88	0.1	-0.2	1	1.3	3.9	75	72	79	76	82	14	25
Liechtenstein	0.04	0.04	216	22	1.0	0.5	2	...	2.9	...	...	80	79	82	...	...
Luxembourg	0.5	0.7	180	92	1.3	0.4	3	1.7	3.9	...	...	78	75	81	19	18
Monaco	0.03	0.1	23 660	100	1.1	0.6	8	...	...	...	...	...	...	...	...	...
Netherlands	16.4	17.1	392	67	0.5	0.3	-2	1.7	4.9	79	76	79	77	81	18	19
Switzerland	7.5	7.3	176	68	0.2	0.2	5	1.4	4.3	57	54	81	79	84	16	22
Latin America and the Caribbean	566	783	27	78	1.4	1.5	-1	2.5	26	71	63	72	69	75	30	9
Caribbean	39.0	46.4	167	65	0.9	1.2	-3	2.5	40	61	57	69	67	71	28	11
Antigua and Barbuda	0.1	0.1	184	38	1.3	1.3	-6	...	21	...	...	71	69	74	...	...
Aruba	0.1	0.1	553	45	1.5			...							...	...
Bahamas	0.3	0.5	23	90	1.4	1.0	-2	2.3	12.7	...	...	70	67	73	28	9
Barbados	0.3	0.3	627	53	0.3	0.6	-1	1.5	14.2	...	...	72	70	74	19	13

Country or area	Mid-year population (millions) 2006	2050	Density (pop/km²) Mid-2005	Percentage urban	Average annual population rate of change (per cent)	Rate of natural increase (percent)	Net migration per 1,000 Pop.	Total fertility (children per woman)	Infant mortality rate (a)	Percent of married women 15–49 using contraception All methods	Modern methods	Life expectancy at birth (years) Total	Males	Females	Percentage of population Under age 15	60 or older
British Virgin Islands	22.0	0.03	146	65	1.4			:							:	:
Cayman Islands	0.5	0.5	171	100	2.5			:							:	:
Cuba	11.3	9.7	102	76	0.3	0.4	–3	1.6	5.8	73	72	77	75	79	19	15
Dominica	0.1	0.1	105	73	0.3	0.8	–16	:	22.2	:	:	74	71	77	:	:
Dominican Republic	9.0	12.7	183	60	1.5	1.7	–3	2.7	31	70	66	68	66	69	33	6
Grenada	0.1	0.2	299	42	0.3	1.2	–15	:	17	54	49	71	:	:	:	:
Guadeloupe	0.5	0.5	263	100	0.9	1.0	–1	2.1	7.9	:	:	78	75	82	25	14
Haiti	8.5	13.0	307	39	1.4	2.3	–3	4.0	73	28	22	52	51	54	37	6
Jamaica	2.7	2.6	241	52	0.5	1.3	–7	2.4	24	66	63	71	69	73	31	10
Martinique	0.4	0.4	359	96	0.5	0.7	–1	2.0	6	:	:	79	76	82	21	17
Netherlands Antilles	0.2	0.2	228	70	0.8	0.5	21	2.1	9	:	:	76	72	79	23	14
Puerto Rico	3.9	4.4	446	97	0.6	0.6	–1	1.9	8.6	78	68	77	73	81	22	17

Country or area	Mid-year population (millions) 2006	2050	Density (pop/km²) Mid-2005	Percentage urban	Average annual population rate of change (per cent)	Rate of natural increase (percent)	Net migration per 1,000 Pop.	Total fertility (children per woman) 2000–2005	Infant mortality rate (a)	Percent of married women 15–49 using contraception: All methods	Modern methods	Life expectancy at birth (years) Mid-2005: Total	Males	Females	Percentage of population: Under age 15	60 or older
Saint Kitts and Nevis	0.05	0.1	164	32	1.1	1.0	-6	...	15	...	...	70	68	72	...	...
Saint Lucia	0.2	0.2	298	31	0.8	1.5	2	2.2	15.6	...	...	74	72	77	29	10
Saint Vincent and the Grenadines	0.1	0.1	307	60	0.5	1.1	-8	2.3	18.1	...	...	71	68	74	29	9
Trinidad and Tobago	1.3	1.2	254	76	0.3	0.6	-3	1.6	18.6	...	...	70	67	73	22	11
United States Virgin Islands	0.1	0.1	322	94	0.2			2.2							24	17
Central America	149	210	59	70	1.6	1.9	-3	2.7	24	66	57	74	71	76	33	7
Belize	0.3	0.4	12	49	2.1	2.3	10	3.2	31	56	49	70	67	74	37	6
Costa Rica	4.3	6.4	85	62	1.9	1.3	1	2.3	10	80	72	79	77	81	28	8
El Salvador	7.0	10.8	327	60	1.8	2.0	-1	2.9	25	67	61	70	67	73	34	8
Guatemala	13.0	25.6	116	47	2.4	2.8	-4	4.6	35	43	34	67	63	71	43	6
Honduras	7.4	12.8	64	46	2.3	2.5	-2	3.7	30	62	51	71	67	74	39	6
Mexico	108.3	139.0	55	76	1.3	1.7	-4	2.4	21	68	59	75	73	78	31	8

Country or area	Mid-year population (millions) 2006	2050	Density (pop/km²) Mid-2005	Percentage urban Mid-2005	Average annual population rate of change (per cent)	Rate of natural increase (percent)	Net migration per 1,000 Pop.	Total fertility (children per woman)	Infant mortality rate (a)	Percent of married women 15-49 using contraception: All methods	Modern methods	Life expectancy at birth (years) Total	Males	Females	Under age 15	60 or older
					2000-2005									Mid-2005		
Nicaragua	5.6	9.4	42	58	2.0	2.4	-4	3.3	36	69	66	69	66	70	39	5
Panama	3.3	5.1	43	58	1.8	1.7	0	2.7	19	…	…	75	73	78	30	9
South America	378	527	21	82	1.4	1.4	-1	2.5	25	75	66	72	69	76	29	9
Argentina	39.0	51.4	14	91	1.0	1.1	-1	2.4	16.8	…	…	74	71	78	26	14
Bolivia	9.1	14.9	8	64	2.0	2.2	-2	4.0	54	58	35	64	62	66	38	7
Brazil	187	253	22	84	1.4	1.4	0	2.3	27	76	70	72	68	76	28	9
Chile	16.4	20.7	22	88	1.1	1.0	2	2.0	7.8	…	…	78	75	81	25	12
Colombia	46.8	65.7	40	77	1.6	1.5	-1	2.6	19	78	68	72	69	75	31	8
Ecuador	13.3	19.2	47	63	1.4	2.1	-4	2.8	29	73	59	74	71	77	32	8
French Guiana	0.2	0.4	2	76	2.6	2.7	10	3.4	10	…	…	75	72	79	34	6
Guyana	0.7	0.5	3	38	0.2	1.3	-11	2.3	46	37	36	76	72	80	29	7
Paraguay	6.3	12.1	15	58	2.4	1.7	-1	3.9	29	73	61	71	69	73	38	6

Country or area	Mid-year population (millions) 2006	Mid-year population (millions) 2050	Density (pop/km²) Mid-2005	Percentage urban Mid-2005	Average annual rate of population change (per cent)	Rate of natural increase (percent)	Net migration per 1,000 Pop.	Total fertility (children per woman) 2000–2005	Infant mortality rate [a] 2000–2005	Percent of married women 15–49 using contraception — All methods	Percent of married women 15–49 using contraception — Modern methods	Life expectancy at birth (years) Mid-2005 — Total	Males	Females	Percentage of population Mid-2005 — Under age 15	60 or older
Peru	28.4	42.6	22	75	1.5	1.3	−2	2.9	33	71	47	70	67	72	32	8
Suriname	0.5	0.4	3	77	0.7	1.4	−7	2.6	20	42	41	69	66	73	30	9
Uruguay	3.3	4.0	20	93	0.7	0.5	−3	2.3	15.3	…	…	75	71	79		17
Venezuela	27.0	42.0	29	88	1.8	1.7	0	2.7	17.5	…	…	73	70	76	31	8
Northern America	332	438	15	81	1.0	0.6	4	2.0	7	73	69	78	75	81	20	17
Bermuda	0.06	0.06	1,211	100	0.4	…	…	…	…	…	…	…	…	…	…	18
Canada	32.6	42.8	3	81	1.0	0.3	7	1.5	5.3	75	73	80	77	82	18	18
Greenland	0.06	0.1	0	83	0.3	…	…	…	…	…	…	…	…	…	…	…
United States of America	299	395	31	81	1.0	0.6	3	2.0	6.7	73	68	78	75	80	21	17
Oceania	34	48	4	73	1.3	1.0	3	2.3	27	72	63	75	73	77	25	14
Australia/New Zealand	24.7	32.7	3	92	1.1	1.3	7	1.8	10.0	159	147	160	155	164	20	17
Australia [a]	20.6	27.9	3	93	1.1	0.6	5	1.7	4.9	85	75	81	78	83	20	17

Country or area	Mid-year population (millions) 2006	Mid-year population (millions) 2050	Density (pop/km²) Mid-2005	Percentage urban Mid-2005	Average annual rate of population change (per cent)	Rate of natural increase (percent)	Net migration per 1,000 Pop.	Total fertility (children per woman)	Infant mortality rate (a) 2000–2005	Percent of married women 15–49 using contraception — All methods	Modern methods	Life expectancy at birth (years) Total Mid-2005	Males	Females	Percentage of population Under age 15 Mid-2005	60 or older
New Zealand	4.1	4.8	15	86	1.1	0.7	2	2.0	5.1	74	72	79	77	81	21	17
Melanesia	8.1	13.2	14	20	2.0			3.9		:	:				39	4
Fiji	0.8	0.9	46	53	0.9	1.4	−5	2.9	16	:	:	68	66	71	32	6
New Caledonia	0.2	0.4	13	62	1.9	1.2	7	2.4	6	:	:	74	71	77	28	9
Papua New Guinea	6.0	10.6	13	13	2.1	2.1	0	4.1	64	26	20	55	55	56	40	4
Solomon Islands	0.5	0.9	17	17	2.6	2.6	0	4.3	48	:	:	62	62	63	41	4
Vanuatu	0.2	0.4	17	24	2.0	2.5	:	4.2	27	:	20	67	66	69	40	5
Micronesia	0.1	0.8	179	70	1.9	2.0	−19	3.4	40	:	:	67	67	67	33	7
Guam	0.2	0.3	309	94	1.8	1.6	0	2.9	11.2	:	:	78	75	81	30	9
Kiribati	0.1	0.2	137	50	2.1	2.3	0	:	43	:	:	61	58	64	:	:
Marshall Islands	0.1	0.2	342	67	3.5	3.3	−6	:	29	:	:	70	:	:	:	:
Fed. States of Micronesia	110.0	0.1	157	30	0.6	2.0	−19	4.4	40	:	:	67	67	67	39	5

Country or area	Mid-year population (millions) 2006	Mid-year population (millions) 2050	Density (pop/km²) Mid-2005	Percentage urban Mid-2005	Average annual population rate of change (per cent)	Rate of natural increase (percent)	Net migration per 1,000 Pop.	Total fertility (children per woman)	Infant mortality rate (a)	Percent of married women 15-49 using contraception – All methods	Percent of married women 15-49 using contraception – Modern methods	Life expectancy at birth (years) Total	Males	Females	Percentage of population Under age 15	Percentage of population 60 or older
Northern Mariana Islands	0.08	0.1	174	95	2.9			...							...	...
Palau	0.02	0.02	43	68	0.7	0.7	1	...	18	...	...	71	69	73	...	...
Polynesia	0.7	0.8	78	44	1.2			3.3							34	8
American Samoa	0.07	0.1	326	91	2.3			...							...	...
French Polynesia	0.3	0.4	64	52	1.7	1.3	2	2.4	5.2	...	...	74	72	77	28	8
Samoa	0.2	0.2	65	22	0.8	2.4	-1	4.4	20	...	...	73	72	74	41	7
Tonga	0.1	0.1	157	34	0.4	1.8	-14	3.5	19	...	...	71	70	72	36	9

The figures presented are from the medium variant of the 2004 Revision of the official United Nations population estimates and projections prepared by the United Nations Population Division. www.unpopulation.org

Three dots (...) indicate that data are not available.

An em dash (-) indicates that the amount is nil or very small.

a More developed regions comprise all regions of Europe plus Northern America, Australia/New Zealand and Japan.

b Less developed regions comprise all regions of Africa, Asia (excluding Japan) and Latin America and the Caribbean, as well as Melanesia,

Micronesia and Polynesia.

c The group of least developed countries, as defined by the United Nations General Assembly in 2003, comprises 50 countries: Afghanistan, Angola, Bangladesh, Benin, Bhutan, Burkina Faso, Burundi, Cambodia, Cape Verde, Central African Republic, Chad, Comoros, Democratic Republic of the Congo, Democratic Republic of Timor-Leste, Djibouti, Equatorial Guinea, Eritrea, Ethiopia, Gambia, Guinea, Guinea-Bissau, Haiti, Kiribati, Lao People's Democratic Republic, Lesotho, Liberia, Madagascar, Malawi, Maldives, Mali, Mauritania, Mozambique, Myanmar, Nepal, Niger, Rwanda, Samoa, Sao Tome and Principe, Senegal, Sierra Leone, Solomon Islands, Somalia, Sudan, Togo, Tuvalu, Uganda, United Republic of Tanzania, Vanuatu, Yemen and Zambia.

1 Including Agalega, Rodrigues and Saint Brandon.

2 Including Ascension and Tristan da Cunha.

3 For statistical purposes, the data for China do not include Hong Kong and Macao, Special Administrative Regions (SAR) of China.

4 As of 1 July 1997, Hong Kong became a Special Administrative Region (SAR) of China.

5 As of 20 December 1999, Macao became a Special Administrative Region (SAR) of China.

6 Refers to the Vatican City State.

7 The former Yugoslav Republic of Macedonia.

8 Including Christmas Islands, Cocos (Keeling) Islands and Norfolk Island.

Source: Population Division of the Department of Economic and Social Affairs of the United Nations Secretariat (2005). *World Population Prospects: The 2004 Revision.* New York: United Nations.